LOVING THE TASMANIAN DEVIL

REFLECTIONS ON MARRIAGE AND ASPERGER SYNDROME

MAUREEN McCARTHY BARTLETT

P.O. Box 23173
Shawnee Mission, Kansas 66283-0173
877-277-8254
www.aapcpublishing.net

PUBLISHING

© 2011 AAPC
P.O. Box 23173
Shawnee Mission, Kansas 66283-0173
www.aapcpublishing.net

Publisher's Cataloging-in-Publication

Bartlett, Maureen McCarthy.

Loving the Tasmanian Devil : reflections on marriage and Asperger
syndrome / Maureen McCarthy Bartlett. -- Shawnee Mission, Kan. :
AAPC Publishing, c2011.

p. ; cm.

ISBN: 978-1-934575-81-9
LCCN: 2011904083
Includes bibliographical references.

1. Bartlett, Andy. 2. Asperger's syndrome--Patients--Family
relationships. 3. Autism spectrum disorders--Patients--Family
relationships. 4. People with mental disabilities--Marriage.
5. Interpersonal communication. 6. Asperger's syndrome--Social
aspects. 7. Spouses. I. Title.

RC553.A88 B37 2011
616.85/8832--dc22   1104

This book is designed in Trajan and Minion.

Cover: ©Sher Fick, 2007, "Kerplunk" Sculpture, internal view
Materials: Encaustic (beeswax and damar crystals); fabric; bone and steel
knitting needles; photo transfer; marbles; www.sherfickart.com

Printed in the United States of America.

To my husband, Andrew Tyler Bartlett,
for our twentieth anniversary

As you so accurately pointed out, without you,
this book could never have been written

TABLE OF CONTENTS

INTRODUCTION

T his book began as a series of letters I wrote to my husband, Andy, during the summer of 2008. In March of that year, I had heard of Asperger Syndrome for the first time, and, realizing immediately that the characteristics fit my husband of twenty years, I had spent the intervening months reading anything about Asperger's that I could get my hands on. I was reeling from the amount of information I was suddenly trying to integrate, not to mention the emotions that accompanied this paradigm shift in my understanding of my husband.

I am a teacher, and when school ended that June and my schedule freed up, my brain was fully available for this task. Because I think better in writing, I decided to start every morning by composing a letter to Andy about something new I had learned and what that information had made me realize about him. This exercise had two purposes: one, it allowed me to process what I was learning; and two, it allowed me to "teach" Andy about Asperger Syndrome (AS). After his initial review of the information in the spring and his acknowledgment that yes, it did seem to fit him perfectly, he had returned to other things, namely, farming and fishing. Meanwhile, I was still processing new information and dealing with the tectonic shift that the "diagnosis" was going to make in our lives – well, at least in my life.

The process went like this: I would awaken around 5 AM – already thinking about some newly named characteristic like "the special interest" – and start typing away at my computer. Because I am a readery-writery kind of person, this factoid would coalesce with a bunch of other things I had read or heard, from Steve Martin songs to *The Wind in the Willows*. I would hammer out an essay-as-letter, print it out, and hand it to Andy to read over breakfast after he was done with his morning chores. He would read it, almost always chuckle or laugh out loud at what I had written, grin and give me a kiss, and then go on about his day.

That fall, I also started chatting on a blog posted by one of my favorite writers. I live in very rural Central New York and have found very few women I can truly relate to. None of the other farm wives are voracious readers, and none of the other voracious readers in the area are farm wives. I am an oddball here in Chenango County! So I had become used to being a bit of hermit with no real close friends, just trying to farm, teach, raise my kids, and find friends in novels. However, on this blog I had stumbled upon, I suddenly found my tribe. Scattered from sea to shining sea and from near Canada to near Mexico, here was this group of people who read like me, wrote like me, thought like me ... and who liked me! I started to feel as if my peculiar thoughts were not only understood but cherished by other people.

Emboldened by this sudden and unexpected group of friends, I launched a blog of my own where I shared this odd journey of Asperg-

Introduction

er's discovery I was on. And voila! Another tribe of women popped up, this time from across the world. Women from the United States and from England and Australia chimed in to say that they too were married to a man with Asperger Syndrome, and that they thoroughly agreed with what I was saying. They appreciated my efforts to embrace the idiosyncrasies and to write about the day-to-day challenges they present. Marriage to someone with AS creates an unusual type of life that is hard to discuss with people who have not experienced it.

I started to realize that perhaps I did have a unique outlook on the Asperger's marriage and that maybe I should finally put my writing abilities to some purpose by sharing my thoughts with others. With Andy's permission, I started to seek a publisher and began to revise my letters to him into a series of "conversations" with the people scattered across the planet who might be interested in my ramblings. I also realized that many of the challenges associated with marriage to a man with Asperger Syndrome are not much different than the challenges associated with marriage in general, and that perhaps my thoughts about my specific relationship might bring a chuckle, a realization, or a new appreciation to people in any kind of marriage.

In July of 2009, the ever-gracious John Elder Robison, author of *Look Me in the Eye: My Life with Asperger's* and a committed advocate for AS, agreed to meet me for lunch while I was visiting friends in Central Massachusetts. He had read one of my blog entries (because I had e-mailed him about it) and enjoyed it, and when I sought his advice about possibly getting a book of such stories published, he recommended AAPC Publishing, whom I contacted that fall. The day I received AAPC's letter and contract in the mail, my scream of joy must have been heard throughout the state. My life-long dream of having a book published, delayed for twenty years after college, was finally going to come true.

Over the year that this book has been headed toward print, the American Psychiatric Association has decided that Asperger Syndrome, previously listed as a distinct condition in the fourth edition of the *Diagnostic and Statistical Manual of Mental Disorders* [1](DSM-IV), will be subsumed under the broader category of autism spectrum disorder (ASD) in the fifth edition, expected to be released in 2013.

Like many others touched by Asperger's, I am of two minds about this. If I had not heard about Asperger Syndrome as a distinct condition, I would most likely *not* have identified Andy as a person with an autism spectrum disorder. On the other hand, knowing that AS is a condition on the autism spectrum allows the information about non-Asperger's autism to have relevance even for the higher-functioning folks. For example, the other night we watched *Rainman,* [2] a 1988 movie about a young man, played by Tom Cruise, whose brother, Raymond, played by Dustin Hoffmann, has autism. Andy said he suddenly felt a bizarre but enlightening solidarity with Raymond that he had not felt when he originally saw the movie, to the point that he has now jokingly added to his conversation sprinklers "Uh-oh!" and "I'm a very good driver." Similarly, when I now read anything by Temple Grandin[3] or when I saw the recent movie about her, I had much more empathy for Andy, realizing he was not all that far away on the spectrum. Furthermore, classifying Asperger's as ASD will hopefully make more services available for children who are identified as having AS.

Introduction

Now that I am fully immersed in the world of autism and Asperger's, I so appreciate the work AAPC does in bringing information, hope, ideas, and solutions to all the families out there who face the challenges and embrace the joys that autism brings. For all those readers whose daily lives are touched by Asperger's and for those who want to understand, may my thoughts and ruminations bring some understanding and maybe even a smile. And for all those readers not directly touched by autism, may you see that marriage to an Aspergian is really just one more example of how life on this wild and wonderful planet gives us all opportunities to accept and embrace the diversity of the human experience.

Summer 2010

---

[1] American Psychiatric Association. (2000). *Diagnostic and Statistical Manual of Mental Disorders* (4th ed., text rev.). Washington, DC: Author.

[2] *Rainman.* (1988). Los Angeles, CA: MGM.

[3] More on Temple Grandin to follow. She is a brilliant animal scientist who has high-functioning autism, and who speaks and writes frequently on both animal behavior and autism.

PROLOGUE

When I saw my friend Joanne walking down Main Street the other day, I ran over and gave her an enormous hug. I hadn't seen her in almost a year. She had moved out of the area to take a nursing job at a big university hospital, but she was back in town to attend a special service for her mother, who had died the year before.

Seeing her again, I realized just how much I missed her. During ten years of teaching together, I had been her confidante, and she had been mine. I had supported her through the end of a horrendously damaging relationship, and she in return had sympathized and comforted me at every twist and turn of my strange marriage: my frustrations, my anxiety, but also my joys and happiness.

Her moving had been like having a limb torn off.

By the time we had exchanged updates on kids, jobs, etc., most of the nearby shoppers and pedestrians had either hopped in their cars or left the vicinity. Joanne and I were alone among the falling leaves under an autumn sky.

I looked around to see if anyone was within ear-shot, and then grabbed both her hands and looked her right in the eye. "Joanne. Andy has Asperger Syndrome."

She stared. She gaped. She is a medical person – I had no need to explain. We stood under the bright blue sky for countable seconds, eyes locked.

"NO WAY!" she finally exclaimed.

"Yep. I'm sure. Absolutely sure."

She stepped back, paused, and gave me a long look.

"Well," she said finally, having mentally cross-referenced every marital tale I had ever told her with this new data. "That explains a lot, doesn't it?"

"It explains everything!"

Well, it doesn't explain everything, but it sure explains a lot. My husband and I have been together for twenty-three years, married for most of that. We have three children, a 200-acre farm, multiple vehicles – an entire life. We also have had a long and somewhat convoluted relationship, full of joys and passion but also full of some huge frustrations, many of which were unexplainable to me. Until recently.

In March of 2008 the words "Asperger Syndrome" entered my life, and indeed they did explain an enormous amount of what had been baffling in my relationship with Andy. The quote that told me I had hit the nail right on the head was by the partner of someone with Asperger's who described "the paradox of an apparently kind and gentle man

8

behaving with cold cruelty, and then being distressed and surprised by the result."[1]

This was it in a nutshell. The "kind and gentle man" was whom I loved; the "cold cruelty" is what infuriated me, but the fact that he was "distressed and surprised by the result" was the part that had been consistently baffling. This was a highly intelligent man. Why did he so often seem so oblivious? How could he not understand that what he did was sometimes so hurtful? And how, the next minute, could he be so wonderful?

Finding out about Asperger's changed everything: my understanding of my husband's behaviors, my own responses – both marital and spiritual – my expectations and goals, truly everything. Here's how it happened.

---

[1] Quote is taken from "Partners of People with Asperger's Syndrome: A Guide" on the National Autistic Society website at http://nas.qa.clearpeople.net/en-gb/living-with-autism/parents%20relatives%20and%20carers/partners/partners-of-people-with-asperger-syndrome-a-guide.aspx

CHAPTER 1

AHA! MOMENT – MAKING THE "DIAGNOSIS"

S unday was Andy's day off. Our hired man was covering for him, running our dairy farm in Central New York. I asked my beloved if he wanted to go out for breakfast, and he lit up like a little kid.

"Yeah! That would be great!"

We left Eldest son fast asleep; Middle and Youngest sons were playing a video game. We hopped into our Jeep, Andy driving and me holding a pile of books and papers on my lap, and headed the ten miles into town.

I knew it was better to plunge right in and get him warmed up to the topic as soon as possible. "So. I've been reading a little about something called Asperger Syndrome."

"Yeah. I've noticed."

We looked at the new buds on the trees, the little ridges of dirty snow left here and there in the hedgerows.

"Do you think that's what I've got?" he asked.

"I don't know. Maybe. I'd like to hear what you think about it."

"Hmm."

Often, talking to Andy is like luring a calf back to its pen. You have to pique its curiosity, jiggle some baling twine, do wiggly fingers behind your back – all the while not looking at it directly. I sat quietly and looked out the window. I waited.

"So, what is it, exactly?" Andy asked.

"Well, it's considered a form of autism – very high functioning. Actually, one of the traits is above-average intelligence and sometimes genius in certain areas."

"Hmm."

We drove by the MacIntyre farm.

"Amy MacIntyre is an awesome speech teacher," I said. "She has been so great about letting my student Erin shadow her."

"Oh, yeah?"

I shuffled the pile of papers in my lap. Andy gave them a sideways glance.

He nodded his head sideways at the pile. "Is that information about Ass Burner Syndrome?"

Aha! Moment: Making the "Diagnosis"

I snorted a laugh. "Yep," I said, smiling.

"Did you want to talk about that over breakfast?"

"We could."

We were heading out of the countryside and down the rather steep road known as West Hill into Norwich, the small city where I teach.

"OK," Andy said.

We were down the hill now, going along Main Street.

"Carmen's?" he asked. Our favorite diner.

"Yeah, that's fine."

Andy turned left at the light onto the rather deserted Sunday-morning North Broad Street, which constitutes the six blocks of downtown.

We parked, went into the small diner, sat down, accepted two mugs of coffee.

"So," he said, "tell me more about this Aspen-burger thing," giving me his charming, heart-melting grin.

A few weeks prior, I had been in our sitting room grading some student writing assignments, listening to a weekend news show on the radio with my "underbrain,"[1] when the show's host introduced an interview with Bram Cohen, the computer genius. She started by describing Cohen's brilliance, his writing computer code at age five, his invention of BitTorrent at twenty-six. And then his characteristics as a person with Asperger Syndrome: problems understanding social interactions, difficulty in reading body language and facial expressions, and lack of both empathy and instinctive social skills.

I stopped writing.

The host continued her description. The upside of Asperger's? Cohen's ability to be engrossed in computer code for days and never need social interaction, the ability to see abstractions in his head. The downside: People told him it was strange to talk to him so he had to train himself to look people in the eye.[2]

Suddenly, everything inside my head went silent. The camera zoomed in on my stunned face. My jaw dropped. The little lightbulb zinged on above me.

Andy and I had just passed the twentieth anniversary of meeting each other in the dining hall kitchen at Amherst College where I had been earning my bachelor's degree. At the time, Andy had just graduated from nearby University of Massachusetts Amherst with three bachelor's degrees (biochemistry, agricultural finance, and social theory/economic policy), and was working as a buyer for a produce company that delivered fruit and vegetables to the five colleges in the area while he was starting his own farm. Within a year we were engaged, and as soon as I graduated, we moved to Central New York to start a farm, which had grown to a successful operation. We had been married for over eighteen years, our three boys were all in or moving quickly toward adolescence. I had established a teaching career. We had a swimming pool and a fishing boat.

Aha! Moment: Making the "Diagnosis"

We had also, by dint of isolation and lots of hard work, forged a strong marriage, an incredible friendship, and a healthy sex life. But we had also had many moments when I was not sure I could handle some of Andy's idiosyncrasies. And we both knew they went beyond idiosyncrasies; some of his behavior seemed downright bizarre.

But this? Asperger Syndrome? Those characteristics sounded way too familiar.

The radio host was done with the interview and had moved on to another story. I grabbed my laptop and Googled "Asperger Syndrome." What I found on my first hit: Pedantic speech. Involvement with "special interests" to the point of obsession. Honesty in situations where it is inappropriate. Mechanical movements.

I zoomed to another site, my heart pounding.

How had I not run into this before? How could I have worked in education for so long and not have heard the term Asperger Syndrome? How could I know so much about autism and have sat through at least five student presentations and numerous television programs about pervasive developmental disorders and not have figured out that this was what explained my husband?

For the next week I was obsessed: I web-surfed until my fingers blistered. I scoured the local library. I sent e-mails to anyone I knew who also knew Andy. I took Asperger's self-assessments on his behalf. I got Tony Attwood's book *The Complete Guide to Asperger's Syndrome*,[3] considered the Bible of Asperger's, and sticky-noted about every tenth page, my jaw dropping. This had to be it – the previously unnamable but oh-so-obvious "thing" that wound through our lives. I simply could not believe that so many seemingly disparate traits could be explained by one thing.

It was like when my sister went to hear the results of her allergy skin prick tests. The doctor at one point said to her, "So, you're allergic to honeydew melon?" My sister hesitated because her allergy to honeydew was kind of strange. The doctor saw her hesitation and added, "perhaps only during the month of June?"

This is an example of when a medical degree truly seems worth eight years of schooling. "YES! YES!" she exclaimed. "How did you know that?!"

Apparently, when June grass pollinates, it affects honeydew melon. So eating it then can cause allergies when every other month of the year it doesn't. That day my sister's doctor went from being just a doctor to being the Great and Powerful Oz.

I felt the same when reading Tony Attwood. Over many years of trying to figure out a reason for Andy's unusual behaviors, I had looked at adult attention deficit-hyperactivity disorder (ADHD), but that didn't seem quite right. I had looked at obsessive compulsive disorder, but that didn't seem quite right. I looked at whether Andy was just a huge jerk, but that didn't seem quite right. And then this. This seemed to be so right it was uncanny. How could so many of his "bizarre" traits be explained by one thing?[4]

> Unaware of unwritten social rules of adult recreation? Check.
> Unaware of offending others? Check.
> Needs frequent reassurance that things are OK? Check.

Indifference to normal peer pressure or fashion? Check.

Vocalizes strong disapproval of benign acts? Check.

Has difficulty accepting criticism? Check.

The more I read, the more amazed I was.

Explosive rage? Oh yeah.

Unusually loud? Often.

Misses cues that he is boring others? Mmm hmm.

Avoids eye contact? Now that I think about it, yes.

Encyclopedic knowledge of certain topics? To the point of annoyance.

Trouble following directions? Definitely.

Trouble multitasking? Most definitely.

Exceptional long-term memory? Yep.

Intense negative reaction to change? Yep.

High interest in quality work? Yep.

Self-stimulatory behavior? He calls it "mumming."

Work area arranged just so? Oh yeah.

Trouble in elementary school? I've heard the stories.

Small mole above left shoulder blade? Just kidding.

Really, I was stunned. What little I knew about autism I had linked to "Kanner's autism,"[5] the more "classic" version, assuming it involved significant problems with both communication and normal functioning. I would never have associated it with someone who was able to manage a half-a-million-dollar-a-year agricultural operation.

My obsession continued. I bought the few "Aspie" wife books out there and joined an Aspie spouse forum. I listened to every segment I could find about Asperger Syndrome on NPR. I ignored my job and my children. Asperger's became my own "special interest," and before long I knew, beyond a shadow of a doubt, that this was it. I was 99.9% sure, enough to convict a person of homicide.

Two weeks of this went by, and Andy of course was noticing. One of the chief traits of Asperger Syndrome is inability to NOT notice every single detail. I had decided to go with the oblique approach – I left things lying around the house: books, stories printed off the Internet. Maybe he read them while I was at work. Maybe he ignored it all. I had spent enough years with him, diagnosed or undiagnosed, to know the right way to approach this.

So, over breakfast at Carmen's, I launched in, favoring the scientific angle, which I knew would appeal to Andy's medical mindset. With his dad a retired pathologist and his mom a retired RN, and Andy himself having switched college majors from pre-med to agricultural biochemistry, I knew this was the right way to go.

I said, "From what I've read, which isn't that much, Asperger Syndrome is a neurological difference in certain people. They think Einstein might have had it, either Asperger's or high-functioning autism."

"What kind of neurological difference?"

"They are not completely sure. There's a bunch of different theories out there, but they think it's a difference in the part of the brain called the … I'm not sure how you say it … the amygdala?"

"Oh, right. Near the hippocampus, part of the limbic system."

"Yeah. So it's related to autism." This was repetition on my part, but the first pitch was while he was driving, and I know enough about my husband to restate important information when there are minimal distractions.

"Really!" he said. (I have always loved the way Andy says "Really." Not as a question, but as an exclamation.) "Like Temple Grandin?"

"Well, she actually has high-functioning autism, not Asperger's." (While many lump high-functioning autism and AS together, there is a distinction in that individuals with AS typically don't experience speech delay; but Temple Grandin didn't speak until she was four, and that was only after intense therapy.)

"Wow. That's intense."

The waitress arrived. "Can I take your order, folks?" Andy ordered the western omelet with wheat toast and home fries (as always), and I ordered two eggs over easy with wheat toast and corned beef hash (as always). The waitress left.

I continued. "That's one of the big differences between autism and Asperger's. With Asperger's there is above-normal linguistic ability. They sometimes call it Little Professor Syndrome because children who have it talk like adults."

"Really!"

"Aspergians,[6] as some people call them, are usually incredibly gifted in some area – way above the norm. Like, you know how you try to talk to Brent about how you make farm investment decisions and he just cannot get it? He probably really cannot get it. You have that unbelievable ability to see patterns and relationships and see them all at the same time."

"Then what's the problem side?" (I bit my tongue here to prevent being sarcastic.)

"Well, a neurological system that can get easily overloaded and explode in rage." I gave him a knowing smile and batted my eyelashes coyly.

"Mmmm hmmm," he grinned back.

"And problems with knowing acceptable forms of social interaction – though it's sometimes hard to identify this in adults because many have taught themselves how to do the social things that they see others do. Remember you told me that in tenth grade you actually studied how popular guys interacted with girls, copied that, and then you were a girl magnet?"

"Well, yeah, but don't all teenagers do that? Doesn't every adolescent feel kind of socially awkward?"

"Sure, but us so-called neurotypical people have an *instinctive* ability to pick up on social cues and read facial expressions and use them ourselves. We just do it, almost like a reflex, but those with Asperger's have to cognitively process the steps. One boy with Asperger's said it's like most people use Windows to do the social stuff but he has to use DOS."[7]

"Hmmm."

Aha! Moment: Making the "Diagnosis"

"And also there can be sensory issues, like certain sounds or lights can be almost painful."

"Hmmm. I would say that's true of me."

"You know how you always have to wear your sunglasses whenever you're outside? Even on a cloudy day? I guess that's pretty typical of 'Aspies.'" I gave this term the ironic pronunciation and the double-hooked fingers to put it in quotation marks.

"That's what they call us?" Andy smirked.

"Well, yeah, some call themselves that."

"I don't like that."

"OK, sorry."

"I don't find that funny. Aspies."

"OK. I won't say it."

"It sounds demeaning!"

"OK. SORRY," I said through gritted teeth.

"I have been labeled so many things over the years, I don't really want some humiliating nickname like Aspie!" People at the next table looked our way.

"OK, OK!" I whispered insistently, putting my hand on his. "Sorry."

"So ..." I continued in a soft voice, "us non-gifted NT people have an

21

instinctive ability to read other people's social cues, where those with Asperger's … "

"Could we just call it Tazberger?" Andy said, referring to my sometime nickname for him: the Tasmanian Devil.

I smiled. "Sure. Whatever. Those with Tazberger have to cognitively process social cues and cognitively choose the correct response, which is what makes socializing so exhausting for them."

"Hmm," Andy paused and drank some coffee. "That actually sounds pretty familiar, kind of uncomfortably familiar."

I drank some coffee, too. I decided to pause and let this all sink in a little.

"What's that book?" Andy asked.

"It's by an Australian psychologist named Tony Attwood. He is a guru on As-Tazberger Syndrome."

Andy slid the book over to his own side of the table and started glancing through it. I headed off to the ladies' room to let him digest some of this, on the way back taking my time to glance at the newspaper and read the notices on the bulletin board. When I finally returned to our table, Andy was engrossed in the chapter on sensory overload. As I sat down, he looked up.

"I do experience this," he said pointing to the page. "I couldn't wear a tie when I was a kid. I felt like I was choking. I remember my dad practically wrestling me to the ground to get a tie on me for church, and then I would take it off as soon as we got in the car. And certain noises – are really painful. And the sunglasses thing. I guess that is a common trait with Asperger's." In five minutes he had scanned the whole book and understood the condition in its entirety.

He closed the book and looked me right in the eye. "Thank you," he said. "Thank you for finding this and figuring this out. I know you have put a lot of time into this. That was very loving of you."

So, that's where we began. It all went much better than I had anticipated. Now, a few years later, we bandy about the symptoms like members of the family. For example:

Andy: "Sorry, just my Asperger's kicking in."

Me: "Hey, you, you're tazzing again."

Andy: "Oops, was that pedantic?"

Me: "You're being boring. Please stop talking about Dipsy Divers."[8]

Andy: "Excuse me, I must go pursue my special interest."

Me: "Take a deep breath: I think you're overstimmed."

What I so love about Andy is how willing he was to hear this, study it, and accept it. Eventually, I am sure, he will be able to, if not control, at least manage it. That's the way he is and one of the really wonderful sides of Asperger's.

Don't get me wrong. I confess to many days of anger and hopelessness since I made the "diagnosis." I periodically realize all over again that (1) Andy will always have Asperger's, (2) I will always have to deal with his Asperger's, and (3) it's going to be hard work to learn effective techniques for managing Asperger's now that we know what it is. Sigh. More hard work, after twenty years of struggle and endless labor establishing a farm.

I went to my own counselor during one of these fits of pique, and she just kept saying, "Focus on the positives. Remember all the good sides." In the many many months since the diagnosis, I have spent countless hours not only reading the scientific literature about Asperger Syndrome but also grappling with my personal response to having a husband with this condition. Certainly, the heartaches and frustration Asperger symptoms cause have been enough to make me throw up my hands any number of times and consider escape. Doubly hard has been trying to remain positive through it all.

How do you continue to show love to your espoused when so often he is hurling hurt your way? And what if he can't even help it? What would Gandhi suggest when the rage and rudeness of the opposition are physiologically beyond his control? What would Jesus do? Hard to say – neither was ever married to an Aspie!

Modern American culture would counsel that I get the hell out, look for my own satisfaction, concentrate on my own fulfillment. In fact, I received an e-mail from an ex-wife of an Aspie who recommended I do just that. On many days, only some kind of a literary or spiritual compass can remind me that difficulty is part of the human experience and that a human's highest pursuit is to maintain integrity and compassion even in the most dire circumstances. At least, that's what I typically try to hammer into my English students.

Aha! Moment: Making the "Diagnosis"

If I am honest about it, living with Asperger's has challenged my emotional and spiritual maturity and brought to the surface parts of me that need work. So partly, I think of Asperger's as a gift to me: No other teachers – by which I mean both my husband and Asperger Syndrome itself – could have taught me more about the personal gunk that stands in my way and pointed out the ways in which I need to grow. But partly, I hope, I am also a gift to Andy, that after many years of his feeling misunderstood and abnormal, I can help him know himself and know that he is loved exactly as he was created. Even when it's hard. Even when it hurts.

Part of what has kept me trying is Andy himself – the wonderful sides of him. Another thing that has kept me working at it is our three children. And a third is the gift I was given of a desire to try to be a decent and mature person. And I say "gift" because this desire doesn't seem to come from me. My regular self often wants to be lazy, snarly, egocentric, and alone. But some other thing is pulling me toward forging a better self and a more tolerant world.

And so, as I look back on my life so far with this beloved man with Asperger Syndrome, I find that I always return to the pluses, because they do far outweigh the minuses. I hope that I can always do this in a way that honors Andy and his experiences, that honors me and my experiences, and that provides one more lens through which to see this world's wondrous diversity.

Loving the Tasmanian Devil

[1]   I must credit my friend Judy Busch, former librarian at Norwich High School and Colgate University, and wife of novelist Frederick Busch, both now deceased, for introducing me to the term "underbrain."

[2]   Andrea Seabrook's March 30, 2008, interview with Bram Cohen, called "The Young Genius Behind BitTorrent," may be found on the NPR website at www.npr.org/templates/story/story.php?storyId=89225415.

[3]   Attwood, Tony. (2007). *The Complete Guide to Asperger's Syndrome*. Philadelphia, PA: Jessica Kingsley Publishers.

[4]   This list of traits is taken from the draft version of *The Adult Version of the Australian Scale for Asperger Syndrome* by Garnett and Attwood, 1995, found at the website of Roger N. Meyer at http://www.rogernmeyer.com/adult_acts_and_consequences_adult_version.html.

[5]   Kanner, L. (1943). Autistic disturbances of affective contact. *Nervous Child, 2*, 217-250.

[6]   John Elder Robison coined this term in his memoir *Look Me in the Eye: My Life with Asperger's*. (2008). New York, NY: Three Rivers Press; pages 241-246.

[7]   I have been very lucky to hear Temple Grandin relate this story in person. Dr. Grandin served as the Frank H. T. Rhodes Class of '56 Professor at Cornell University from 2005 through 2010. In that capacity, she visited Cornell for a week each year, teaching classes at the Animal Sciences School and delivering a public lecture, which I attended two years in a row.

[8]   In case you are curious, a Dipsy Diver is a kind of fishing tackle that allows mid-level trolling with spoons.

CHAPTER 2

PRECIOUS COCONUT – APPRECIATING THE ASPERGIAN BRAIN

I n high school I belonged to a youth group called Interfaith. It was a group of kids of different religious denominations who gathered in order to ... I don't know that we actually knew what we gathered to do, except that it meant we got to attend weekend-long retreats and trips and be in very close proximity to our best friends and crushes with minimal supervision. We also escaped from school one afternoon a week and took a bus to the old mansion that served as our city's cultural center for ecumenical religious classes.

Our big activity every Saturday all winter long was making peanut brittle, the fundraiser for our year-end trip to a different big city each year. I remember going to Boston one year and New York City another. (On the NYC trip, my friend and I decided to go into a peep show on a dare. See what I mean about our spurious intentions?)

one weekend retreat we had to do an exercise with a partner, and ended up with one of the parent chaperones. I was less than thrilled about this. I think all teens find the older generation a bit repellent: They have wrinkles, they lack style, and they are clueless. I would much rather have had one of my friend's trendy heads in my lap.

But here I was, paired with this woman whose existence symbolized the horrific aging process – and she was to be my comrade for a rather intimate activity. I had to sit on the floor cross-legged and hold her head in my hands. We were told to hold our partner's head and imagine it was the most precious object in the world, a fragile treasure that held mysteries and secrets beyond our comprehension. To my teenage credit, I did this, despite my distaste. And it worked! As I concentrated and thought, I realized that what I held in my hands was a miracle, a mystery. Behind the facade was an entity I could not really imagine; the outward middle-aged woman was just a fraction of this creation, whose real essence I did not know. I was humbled, realizing that my seventeen-year-old understanding was so limited in the presence of what I held. (Perhaps that was the point of the exercise?)

Since the Asperger's "diagnosis," I feel the same way when I hold Andy's curly head, except that this involves no revulsion on my part. I have always found his head dear, especially now that I realize that what's inside might be quite different from what's inside mine. Andy's head is the dearest and softest of coconuts: hard, round, covered in uncontrollable curls of dirty-blond hair, and holding inside a sweet mystery. Even after twenty years of barely ever being apart, I realize that I only know a fraction of all that he is. And now I find out that a small part of his brain, nestled like a sweet almond in the midst of his gray matter, might be very different from mine, endowing him with senses like an eagle's and thought patterns very dissimilar to my own.

The other day I was telling Andy about Temple Grandin's ability to run mental video clips of cattle equipment designs in her head and see the flaws and necessary improvements.[1]

He looked at me quizzically and said, "Doesn't everybody do that?"

"No. I can't do it."

"I do that all the time," he said, sounding rather distressed. "I can see everything, all at once, in great detail and how it all connects."

"You know, don't you, that that's why the farm has made it. You did that. That way of thinking did that."

"Yeah, but the problem is I can't turn it off. I see everything that way. It's exhausting."

We have a wonderful photo of Andy standing in the decrepit barn when we were looking to buy the farm. He has stopped in the middle of the gutted lower floor, with old wooden stanchions leaning this way and that. He is gazing around entranced.

In a moment of frightening perceptiveness, my mother, who was with us, said to him, "I wish I could see what you're seeing."

Andy actually saw not only what was there, but also what could be there, and all the steps along the way.

We had never talked about our thought processes or shared our own metacognition before. It would be kind of like slicing open your left side and pulling out your intestines and saying, "Here's how mine work. How about yours?"

But since the "diagnosis," we have shared our ways of thinking, and for me it's like meeting someone new. Andy will explain how the schedule for the day's tasks, his mental blueprint for the addition to the barn, or the cost-benefit analysis on the rake purchase flows through his thoughts, and I'll explain how sentences sort, reshape, and balance in mine. He will talk about choosing the right "video" response from his files of social interactions, and I'll say how hearing a word can take me straight through its etymology and back again to its current nuances and connotations.

This all feels tenuous and vulnerable and new. When we first met, we poured out our factual lives pretty quickly, and over time we broke down most emotional barriers as we came to feel safe with each other. But this, this describing of our brain waves, is new territory. Back in college, I would sit and talk books endlessly with my fellow English majors, but since Andy and I moved to rural upstate New York, I have had few opportunities to engage in those kinds of discussion. Even so, garden-variety linguistic intelligence like mine is fairly commonplace. Get any English teacher in the country started, and we'll all go on at length about our annoyance over certain grammatical or word-choice errors.

But what I am hearing Andy describe these days, now that we can name it, is both strange and precious. It is like hearing your newborn baby verbalize his feelings or having a dolphin explain dolphin thought to you. I feel like I am on our first date again, not really sure who this man is but fascinated with finding out. It makes the Andy I have loved for twenty years even more dear, filled with extraordinary hues of light that form a different spectrum than my own.

Ever the English teacher's right-hand man, Shakespeare communicated the fact that the brain is what sets us apart from the rest of creation. Via Hamlet, Shakespeare said,

What a piece of work is man!
>How noble in reason!
>How infinite in faculties!
>In form and moving!
>How express and admirable!
>In action how like an angel!
>In apprehension how like a god![2]

Scientifically speaking, we have reached a point where we know that cognition and consciousness and everything that happens in our brains is what makes us human and marks our distinctive evolutionary advantage. But then there is the Asperger's brain, which is distinct in its own right.

In Madeleine L'Engle's wonderful young-adult novel *A Wrinkle in Time*, Meg Murray's youngest brother, Charles Wallace, is obviously endowed with cerebral gifts beyond those of his family. Seen as "retarded" by the locals, Charles Wallace is in reality uniquely brilliant. To Meg's friend Calvin O'Keefe, Charles Wallace calls himself a "sport … a change in gene resulting in the appearance in the offspring of a character which is not present in the parents but which is poten-tially transmissible to their offspring." In the context of the novel, these traits include the ability to literally read others' thoughts (like Asperger's in reverse) as well as ease with using the tesseract (L'Engle's fictional mode of time/space travel). His brilliant scientist parents are well aware of his unusual gifts and had already realized that he was gifted. He is "Different. New … in essence ..," Mrs. Murray tells Meg.[3]

As a young girl reader of twelve and the youngest in my family, I longed for a sweet, unusual, gifted companion like Charles Wallace, and I seem to have landed myself one in my husband. I loved all of the books in this series, and I especially love Madeleine L'Engle's belief that creation is as awe-inspiring on the molecular level as it is on the galactic level. There is a wonderful set of photographs on the Internet from Florida State University that proceeds from seeing the Milky Way from a distance of 10 million light years away down in equal orders of magnitude to a tall oak tree. Then the photos move by the same order of magnitude from a leaf all the way down to its component protons and neutrons.[4] There are just as many steps down from leaf to molecular as there were down from galactic to leaf, which means that the opportunities to observe creation's grandeur are as vast within us as they are above us.

I am always face to face with the glories of the sky. When I am home on the farm for a full day, I see the sun at its rising and at its setting, and at night, in the absence of artificial light, the stars are brilliant and countless. In the past, I spent far less time contemplating the wonders of human brain cells, I guess because they are not so visible, but I pay more attention now. As Andy and I discuss our patterns of thought –

Aspergian and neurotypical (NT) – I begin to contemplate the intricacies of neurons and electric impulses with the same sense of wonder.

Both scientists and novelists tell us that creation's grandeur is equally displayed from the largest to the smallest order of magnitude. Along with space, the brain is truly another final frontier, and I am fortunate to have such a rare example here at my side in which to discover it. I hope that my boring old NT brain is as interesting to my Aspie co-explorer. It is both majestic adventure and intimate delight to contemplate each other's thought patterns. Here's to the ultimate act of exploration, and to tasting the precious sweet meat of each other's cognition.

[1] To see this dramatized, I recommend the new movie *Temple Grandin*, starring Claire Danes. You can also see information on Temple Grandin's designs at her website http://www.grandin.com/

[2] William Shakespeare. *Hamlet.* Act II, Scene 2.

[3] L'Engle, Madeleine. (1962). *A Wrinkle in Time.* New York, NY: Quality Paperback Book Club; page 44.

[4] These images may be found at *Secret Worlds: The Universe Within* on the Florida State University website at http://micro.magnet.fsu.edu/primer/java/scienceopticsu/powersof10/

CHAPTER 3

MEETING ALMANZO – FALLING IN LOVE WITH AN ASPIE

On February 5, 1988, I saw my future husband for the first time when he walked into the kitchen of Valentine Dining Hall at Amherst College in Massachusetts. He was the delivery guy from Squash, Incorporated,[1] a local produce delivery business that brought fresh fruit and vegetables from the Chelsea Market in Boston to the five colleges and local restaurants in the Five-College Area of the Connecticut River Valley of Central Massachusetts.

I heard a voice first, dusky, singing the James Taylor song "Damn, this traffic jam. How I hate to be late,"[2] and then this guy turned the corner into the workspace where Harriet, Mavis, Rose, and I were working.

I looked up, took him in pushing a dolly of lettuce boxes, and responded in song, "It hurts my motor to go so slow."

He looked at me surprised, smiled, exclaimed, "All right!" and continued past me, ringing out, "Good morning, Harriet! Good morning, Mavis! Good morning, Rose!" with a smiling nod to each in turn.

"Good morning,' Chowda'! Whatta you doin' hea'?" I heard Harriet beam, in her strong Central Mass accent, obviously delighted to see this scruffy man with the vegetables.

I remember so clearly Andy that morning. I remember what he was wearing: faded Levi's, a navy blue L.L. Bean reindeer sweater, an old red bandanna around his neck, a black Australian cowboy hat, and Timberland work boots. I remember how he smelled: like wood smoke and fresh strawberries. I remember how he sounded: His voice was smoky but kind of high – a tenor for sure. I remember his grin and his dirty-blond curls poking out around his ears. I remember the sense of his size: tall, strong, big hands, long legs, capable.

This so-called "Chowder" stopped and leaned both forearms on the handles of his dolly. "Well, J.P. called in sick today, so Marge asked if I'd do the deliveries."

"Good! Good! So, how's it goin'?" Harriet asked. I loved Harriet. She was my mom-away-from-mom, my rough-handed, kitchen-ruling, middle-aged boss with short, graying black hair under her regulation hair net, sharp chin, and thick glasses. Harriet didn't take any crap from the cooks but had taken me under her wing as a babe lost in the woods of the college below grounds that most students never see – or want to see.

My work-study job that semester was to make bag lunches for students whose classes went right through lunchtime. I would arrive in the basement of the dining commons at 7 AM, set my bowls of tuna and egg salad on the counter, lay out forty pieces of bread, and slather the correct number of slices with the correct sandwich spreads – egg or tuna salad – and slap the top pieces on. Then I would baggie them up, put each in a brown bag with a package of cookies, a juice box, a yogurt cup, a plastic spoon, and a bag of chips. I labeled each with the student's name and set it in a box to be picked up at the end of breakfast by the unfortunate few who had to cram eating their sandwiches between classes instead of lounging for a leisurely lunch with their buddies in the Commons.

I took my job seriously. I initiated a check-off form so students could request their personalized combo of sandwich, chips, and cookies. I felt I had to perform well after an embarrassing short-lived effort at trying to cook short-order eggs upstairs in the dining room.

As I worked on my stainless steel counter to one side, Mavis, a small, quiet Caribbean woman, and Rose, a soft-fleshed, white-haired grandma type, would be cutting vegetables for the salad bar and mixing tuna and egg salad in preparation for the lunch hour. Harriet kept us all hopping at a brisk pace and variously yelled at or took orders from the twenty-something big-guy cooks or the ever-so-poised head of Dining Services who floated by periodically.

It was loud in the kitchen and busy. People coming and going and shouting, clouds of steam and huge trays of hot breakfast foods, clanking spoons and pots, men with wrenches fixing pipes, and delivery guys arriving and departing.

But this Chowder person stopped and stood. He rested one foot on top of the other, toes and knee pointed in like a little boy, and leaned on his dolly to chat with Harriet. And she melted like a star-struck fan.

"Well, Harriet, my day always goes better when I get to see you," he said with a grin.

Harriet blushed and gave him a swat. "Ah, you! How's the sheep?"

Sheep? I thought.

"They're fine. I had two lambs born this morning. More on the way."

"Aww. They must be so cute."

Sheep? I thought again.

I hadn't heard mention of an animal in two and a half years of college. BMWs, yes, literary theory, yes, ski trips, yes. But sheep? Every one of my senses was leaning his way.

"Yeah, they're pretty great," he said. "Anywhere specific you'd like this lettuce?"

The two of them went into the walk-in cooler, and I took a quick assessment of my vitals: heart rate fast, breathing shallow, face red.

And so I was swept off my feet by the vegetable delivery man.

Now, I'll admit I was not your standard fare at Amherst College. From a middle-class Western New York Irish family, born with my dad's smarts and gifts with language, I soared through high school at the top of my class, nailed the SAT, and had my pick of colleges.

Amherst was really a bit of an accident. At the time, I was entranced with the Alps for some reason (I confess to the inspiration probably being *Heidi*) and had decided that European Studies was my calling. In my high school guidance office, I typed in "Small. Liberal Arts. European Studies. Selective. Rural. New England." And Amherst was my top hit. I had never heard of it, nor had any of my friends. None of us knew it regularly topped the *U.S. News and World Report* list of top liberal arts schools or that its selectivity was correspondingly intense. I applied and was accepted.

Looking back, I probably got in because I provided some socio-economic and ethnic diversity to the Class of 1989: smart lower-middle-class Irish from way Upstate.

But the most unusual thing about me compared to my Amherst peers was that I was a closet farmgirl. I grew up in a small-city suburb of Buffalo with next-door neighbors only a driveway away. But in my heart I knew I belonged in the country. I had discovered Laura Ingalls Wilder[3] in first grade and knew she was my soul sister. I read every book in the Little House series over and over and then all the non-fiction about Laura that only the true groupies unearth.

I knew every moment of Laura's life: when she slapped her sister Mary over the Indian beads, when the log fell on Ma's ankle, when Laura almost drowned in Plum Creek, Laura arriving first at the Surveyor's House (ah, the Surveyor's House!), and then, of course, meeting Almanzo.

In the beginning of *The Long Winter*, Laura Ingalls gets lost in the Big Slough on her way to town to buy a cutter blade for Pa. She and her little sister Carrie are wandering in the high grass when they hear two brothers stacking hay. It is Almanzo Wilder and his brother Royal, homesteading young men, working out in the sun. I bet they smelled warm and sweet like honest sweat and baking bread. Laura is barely able to look at these two, but they point her through the high grass toward Pa. Laura does note that Almanzo's eyes twinkle down at her.[4]

We learn that Almanzo has arrived in South Dakota at age nineteen (officially swearing he is twenty-one) to stake a claim using money made raising a wheat crop in Minnesota and he has the finest pair of matched Morgans in the area. Despite a potential blizzard, he heroically goes after one of them, Lady, after she runs off with an antelope herd. But it's at the end of *The Long Winter* that Almanzo really shows his stuff: what a stud! With his buddy Cap Garland, he risks his life to bring back wheat for their starving town. He even faces down the storekeeper who wants to overcharge the townspeople for the grain he brought back. It's no wonder Laura falls for him.

While growing up, I would sneak off to the nasty little wooded drainage creek a few blocks from my house and pretend I was on the frontier. My sister and I would have nights when we turned off all the lights and ate with wooden spoons by candlelight. Because of my rural fetish and my being from a GM factory town, I was more than a little out of my social league at Amherst. There, I was hob-nobbing with the daughter of the president of NBC and a grandson of a U.S. Supreme Court justice.

Although I was most definitely in rural New England and loved to go running through the farmland on the outskirts of town, my day-to-day life did not involve any interaction with the country people or their lives. UMass was the place with the Ag school, but I was intellectually far more at home in literary criticism classes at Amherst College.

But this Chowder fellow, he was so different from the Amherst College guys with their expensive and deliberately worn casual clothes, their classy cars and subtle aroma of Polo, their urbane wit and unflappable good spirits. I realized this delivery man was a real live "townie," but a townie was downright traffic-stopping after one too many Amherst guys had flaunted his unassailable right to privilege and prestige in my direction. I was middle-class. I liked a real man.

Three years into Amherst, although I had been involved with a few guys heading toward law school or med school, my secret male ideal was still that 1880s homesteader with the draft horses. And magically, here was this guy, fitting the description. He had a farm. He raised sheep. He smelled like woodsmoke. I was smitten.

Looking back through the lens of Asperger's, I can see that my "smiter" had accumulated a wide repertoire of social skills by this point in his life – age twenty-nine. He was quite the charmer. Oftentimes, people with Asperger Syndrome struggle with social cues and social niceties – they do not come instinctually to them, nor do they seem logical. But this man had them down. I am sure it came from dealing with Italian dockside vegetable brokers and various restaurateurs and farmers in the area, not to mention tough kitchen women like Harriet. By college, Andy had also analyzed and adopted the moves for attracting a female. I saw the charming grin, heard the easy banter, smelled smoke on his sweater, and melted like hot butter.

Harriet, God bless her, realized that I was moonstruck after Andy left, especially since I pumped her for information.

"Who was that guy?"

"Why? You got the hots for him?" she asked.

"Well, he is pretty cute," I responded.

Unbeknownst to me (until Andy told me later), Harriet called Squash Inc. later that day and requested that Chowder make all the Amherst College deliveries – and she told them why! So I suppose Andy was primed when a week later I asked him why his nickname was Chowder.

He paused, looked at the ground, looked back up with a charming smile, and said, "How about I tell you over dinner?" Just like a line from a romantic movie. (Actually, I am sure that is where he got it.) He wrote down his full real name – Andrew Tyler Bartlett – and his phone number, and we set a date for the upcoming Sunday evening at Panda East, the best Chinese restaurant in town.[5]

There, over a dinner I barely tasted, I found out this Chowder farmer dude was a recent biochemistry, social thought/political economy, and ag finance graduate from UMass (formerly pre-med at Earlham College). We talked about everything under the sun and moon – the latter was high and bright by the time he finally dropped me off at my dorm.

And so, off I was swept. We met in Valentine Hall and had our first date on Valentine's Day. He had brought me a red rose, winning for me a challenge I had made with one of my best friends from high school. Over the preceding Christmas break, she and I had pledged that both of us, mutually still distraught over recently failed romances, would receive a red rose from someone new by February 14.

My spring semester that year was a whirlwind of new experiences. On Chowder's rented farm,[6] I watched ewes give birth, tedded hay on a tractor, tended the famed woodstove, rode shotgun in a pick-up truck, hauled round bales from the farm down the road, strung high-tensile fence, ate fresh eggs from chickens I had personally met, trimmed hooves, gave sheep shots, unrolled water line. It was as if someone had plucked me off the Amherst campus and set me down in South Dakota with that dashing young Wilder brother. This was something I had always dreamed of but had relegated to my mental video library of literature-inspired fantasies.

How could I not fall head over heels? And, in true Asperger fashion, once Andy had decided I was the one, he proposed inside of a year. So I was one of the truly rare Amherst seniors who was "engaged." I was completely oblivious to the fact that this made me a bit of a social pariah. Everyone else was applying to grad school or interviewing for high-profile jobs. I was living *Green Acres.*

My last semester Andy and I shared an apartment near the farm, and I drove back and forth to campus in a used car he bought for me. My new friends were other townies much older than me, I had "future in-laws," and Andy and I subjected ourselves to the meeting of the two sets of parents.

Andy and I spent my last summer after college farm shopping, and finally settled on 200 acres in Central New York. Two years almost to the day of meeting each other, we signed the mortgage on a farm in Chenango County, New York.

Of course, the tale of these past twenty years is another story, but I can say that Andy, my Almanzo, is still my main squeeze. After we had purchased the farm, I received *Little House in the Ozarks,*[7] a compilation of

Laura Ingalls Wilder's weekly columns for the *Missouri Ruralist* penned after she and Almanzo had bought Rocky Ridge Farm near Mansfield, Missouri. My mother, who suffered my childhood obsessions, had inscribed this book "For Maureen, on her own Rocky Ridge Farm."

I have not intentionally modeled my life on Laura's, nor did I consciously choose Andy because he seemed like Almanzo. It's more like Andy and I are sort of channeling these two people. I think we both had the impression of having been born into the wrong century, into the wrong setting. I can see us as children: Andy in the suburbs of Hartford, Connecticut, with an MD dad and RN mom, fishing every chance he got, entranced by visiting his great-grandparents' strawberry farm and dairy on the island of Öland in Sweden. Me in Lockport, New York, a GM factory town, riding ten miles on my bike to get into the countryside where I could see horses and cows, and bathing my brain in Little House books.

Perhaps I retreated to Laura's world as a refuge from my loving but dysfunctional family. Perhaps Andy retreated to his daydream of a Swedish farm as a refuge from a social milieu he could not navigate as a child with Asperger's, back when Asperger's wasn't even in the American lexicon. We were children of the 60s longing for the Populist Era, chancing to meet each other in a college kitchen, recognizing in each other our other half, like the two parts of Plato's sphere.[8]

And here we are, nearly a quarter century later. He still makes my heart go thump when I see him in the hot summer sun on a tractor. I still feel fulfilled when I sit by the woodstove braiding onion tops. How wonderful, really, that two quirky souls, who had found their true selves in a world bygone, met each other and rode off into society's agricultural frontier. "Hartford Pathologist's Son Goes Dairy." "GM Accountant's Valedictorian Daughter Milks Cows." Pretty radical, actually.

We turned and looked west, back in time but forward for us into the rural world our grandparents had fought to leave behind. Sometimes I feel like we are childhood best friends, holding hands and grinning in our secret hideout. I did not wonder at the time why this man had been delivered to my feet. I just grabbed him and ran. It now seems so incredibly unlikely, so remarkably serendipitous. Our early romance was a tornado, a tidal wave of compatibility and passion that erased any other plans that I or my parents or my fine college had in mind for me. There was no question in my mind: I had been granted the man I had always longed for. It felt like a gift, a blessing, like exactly what I was supposed to do. It still feels that way, though twenty years of challenges and difficulties have given me a more mature view of the word "gift."

Every once in a while, usually when my college alumni magazine arrives in the mail, I question my decision. My fellow grads and former boyfriends are off teaching at universities, managing mutual funds, practicing corporate law, editing magazines. I am milking cows. At such times I run upstairs to grab my worn copy of *These Happy Golden Years*[9] and reread the final chapter. Laura and Almanzo have just married and driven the beautiful Morgans to their Little Gray Home in the west. They sit on their doorstep and look at the night. The horses are snuffling in the grass, their beloved dog Shep is at their feet, the stars are softly shining. Andy and I do this, too – often, in fact – and the feeling in my heart is the same as theirs: full to overflowing.

Loving the Tasmanian Devil

Squash, Incorporated is still alive and well as of my last visit to the area in the summer of 2009.

If you don't know this song, you can find it on James Taylor's 1977 album *JT* or download it from his website at http://www.jamestaylor.com/music/discography/cd/JT_AlbumDetails.aspx?albumid=274f9c73-6455-4534-be7b-9fd6c8fd8cb4.

I recommend that every person alive read the entire Little House series: *Little House in the Big Woods, Little House on the Prairie, Farmer Boy, On the Banks of Plum Creek, By the Shores of Silver Lake, The Long Winter, Little Town on the Prairie, These Happy Golden Years,* and *The First Four Years.* Available through Harper Row. The junkies can then go on to all the other books by and about Laura.

Wilder, Laura Ingalls. (1940). *The Long Winter.* New York, NY: HarperCollins; page 25.

Alas, Panda East was no longer extant on my last visit to Amherst.

The farm he rented land on was part of the New England Small Farm Institute, still very much active in Belchertown, MA. Their website is www.smallfarm.org.

Wilder, Laura Ingalls. (1996). *Little House in the Ozarks: The Rediscovered Writings* (Stephen H. Hines, Ed.). New York, NY: Galahad Books.

Plato believed that we are all one half of sphere that split in two at our birth. When we find the other half of our birth sphere, there is an attraction.

Wilder, Laura Ingalls. (1943). *These Happy Golden Years.* New York, NY: HarperCollins; page 289.

CHAPTER 4

VLÄDAFEESH –
THE CHILDLIKE
WONDER OF ASPERGER'S

In my last year at Amherst College, I lucked into the most amazing housing situation. The dean of students and his wife had bought a home off-campus but still had one semester left in their college rental house and were looking for some students to sublet it. I had worked for the dean for two semesters, and he asked me if I would like to gather some friends together to live there. Ummmm, yes.

Andy and I were already engaged, though with two semesters of college left, I felt this was kind of an "intentionality" type of engagement rather than a real one (no ring, after all). So Andy was over at our sublet house a lot. I remember one specific day when I was the only one home and he stopped by. We young co-eds had moved the kitchen table into the room with the fireplace and the huge window that overlooked the back yard, and that's where Andy and I were sitting, eating lunch together.

I don't remember why, but Andy launched into a little chant to amuse me. It went like this:

"Vlädafeesh-feesh vee doe foe." Beat. "Vlädafeesh-feesh vee doe." Long beat. "Vlädafeesh-feesh vee doe foe, video foe. Foe."

For some reason this tickled me beyond reason. Perhaps it was the accumulated stress of the semester. Perhaps it was young love. So he chanted it again:

"Vlädafeesh-feesh vee doe foe." Beat. "Vlädafeesh-feesh vee doe." Long beat. "Vlädafeesh-feesh vee doe foe, video foe. Foe."

Andy had this mock concentrated look on his face and had pitched his voice low as if he were some sort of Nordic shaman performing a ritual to bring back the sun. I laughed and laughed.

Then he transitioned into another oddly amusing persona, intoning, "For heaffen's sake, Mrs. Heiffershmorsh" with his lips compressed and looking left and right in an agitated way. I laughed so hard that tears rolled down my cheeks.

I wonder now, as I wondered then, how did he come up with that? The sounds are Scandinavian, not surprising considering Andy's half-Swedish background and growing up around his Mormor (mother's mother). But the rhythm, the facial expression, the very fact that a twenty-nine-year-old man would be performing such ditties, where does that come from?

Maybe my Amherst years had wrung some of the child out of me, or maybe my linguistic tendencies bent me more toward reciting "Whan that aprill, with his shoures soote/The droghte of March hath perced to the roote"[1] in my best Middle English, but I could never have composed, on the spot, the "Vlädafeesh" chant.

Vlädafeesh – The Childlike Wonder of Asperger's

This is one of the earliest memories I have of Andy's wonderful childlike side. Apparently, this is a Bartlett trait, not specifically Asperger's (though it's possible the Asperger genes run in the Bartlett blood) because I have heard tales of Andy's grandmother's similar whimsical sense of humor.

For example, as Andy's dad tells it, one day when she and her husband (my father-in-law's parents) came home from the grocery store, five lemons they had bought rolled out of their bag, unbeknownst to the grandfolks. When they later looked for the lemons and could not find them, they thought they had either left them at the store or misplaced the bag they were in. Weeks later, they found the lemons, which had rolled behind a door in the kitchen, desiccated and rattling like small maracas. Instead of being disposed of, the lemons were given the exalted status of "rogue citrus" and "allowed," for years, to roll around and stay hidden in various places in the house: under the dining room hutch, behind an umbrella in the entrance hall. The lemons remained on the lam until Andy's grandfather died and his grandmother sold the house and moved to a nursing facility.

Apparently, this childlike trait is genetic. When we were up at the Bartlett camp in the Berkshires recently, Andy filled me in about the photos in the loft of the A-frame, which I had always assumed were purchased. In the photos, a small group of stuffed bears and a giraffe are on a boat floating on a lake. I thought these were by the same photographer who created the children's photographically illustrated book *The Lonely Doll*,[2] but no. On the wall between these two photos was the actual papier maché boat from the photo resting on a wooden platform made especially for it. Andy told me that his dad had crafted the boat, staged the voyage, photographed it, and then told Andy and his brother and sister stories about the fanciful expedition.

Loving the Tasmanian Devil

I can visualize this because I know Andy's dad. He can go from the driest, most technical explanation of methillin-resistant staph aureus infections to the most child-like of tale. He just loves the 1931 picture book *Joe Buys Nails*,[3] which is only tangentially about young Joe's time at the hardware store and predominantly about his adventures through the woods en route.

And then there's Andy. Most of the time he is quite technical and precise. Asked by one of our boys what a bruise is, he will respond with, "Well, a contusion against the bone will dissipate blood under the epidermis until the lymphatic fluid dissolves it." All three boys turn their heads to me for the translation. "A bruise is blood that oozed out of a vein when it broke and then got stuck under your skin."

"Well," Andy says, "that's not precisely what happens …"

At this point I hold up my hand and say, "Close enough until they get to med school."

"I'm just trying to be accurate."

But then there are things like Vlädafeesh and Mrs. Heiffershmorsh, and when Andy invites the boys to a foam noodle battle in the pool, he seems to be the one having the most fun. Apparently, the same neurological difference that leads to anxiety and temper tantrums – the immature amygdala – also leads to the other child-like emotions: joy, whimsy, and playfulness.

Einstein, widely suspected of having been on the autism spectrum, attributed his discovery of the theory of relativity to his delayed emotional development. He once said, "The normal adult never bothers his head about space-time problems … I, on the contrary, developed so slowly that I only began to wonder about space and time when I was already grown up. In consequence I probed deeper into the problem than an ordinary child would have done."[4] There is that famous photograph of Einstein sticking out his tongue or the one where he is riding his bicycle with a huge grin. The downside to this was that he sometimes had to be fed, told when to go to sleep, and be protected from exploitive people.

Einstein was also a ditty writer, penning, for example, a little poem about Captain Carefree.[5] This poem reminds me of a song from Andy's childhood that he sometimes sings: "Ahoy! Ahoy! I'm captain of my ship. My name is Captain Salty and I live on the sea." Andy intones this chantey in a bold husky voice, standing feet spread with one fist on his chest, grasping the lapel of his pretend captain's coat and looking to the distant horizon, and he unfailingly makes me laugh.

As Andy is the first to admit, he might have Asperger's, but he is "no Einstein," and luckily for me, that means he is not so childlike that he needs me to feed him or tuck him in at night. Well, at least not often. But he is childlike enough to keep life fresh for me, the boring forty-something NT with her "mature" and aging brain. He does funny little dances in the kitchen, plays Legos with the boys, and sings silly songs. But then he'll turn around – with no apparent transition – and analyze the Iraqi economy, calculate our break-even price on a fifty-cow expansion, or re-wire the electrical service to the house.

Appreciating this polarity in an Aspergian is an acquired taste. The rare combination of childlike whimsy and sophisticated intellectual analysis is like one of those sense experiences that contrasts sweet with bitter or sour with salty or hot with cold. It's like amaretto cheesecake with espresso or sweet and sour chicken. Or listening to the various movements of Vivaldi's "Four Seasons." Such contrasts can be exquisite, like leaping from a sauna out into the snow.

But the emotional rollercoaster ride can be taxing, and like an overwhelmed child, Andy frequently falls into bed exhausted by day's end. And so do I, after being hurled from side-splitting laughter at one of his silly personas to dealing with his explosive rage at some lack of precision or efficiency.

The elderly Einstein had that crazy white hair and that impish grin. I can imagine Andy looking very similar in old age. His hair will eventually turn white, though his childlikeness seems to have extrapolated itself into keeping his hair from graying or falling out. And I know that he will be whimsical and beloved of our someday grandchildren.

It seems to be part of the human experience to return to our child self before death, but the Aspie gets to retain that delight and awe throughout life. Eventually, I'll be developmentally back there with him, but in the meantime, Andy tries valiantly to take me along for the ride. He often has to pull me off my middle-aged lawn chair and back into the sandbox. But truthfully, once you're back there, it is a lot of fun.

[1]   From the Prologue to *The Canterbury Tales*.

[2]   Wright, Dare. (1957). *The Lonely Doll*. New York, NY: Houghton Mifflin.

[3]   Wiese, Kurt. (1931). *Joe Buys Nails*. Eau Claire, WI: E. M. Hale Publishers.

[4]   Neffe, Jurgen. (2005). *Einstein: A Biography* (Shelley Frisch, Trans.). New York, NY: Farrar Straus Giroux; page 27.

[5]   Ibid., page 28.

CHAPTER 5

REINDEER GAMES – ASPERGER'S AND SOCIAL CODES

Scene: A rented house on the Amherst College campus

Maureen, her boyfriend, Chowder, and Maureen's college friends, Sue, Emily, and Ann, are playing Monopoly and drinking beer. Chowder is winning. Chowder rolls the dice, moves his player, and lands on Park Place. He rubs his hands together with a greedy Scrooge McDuck glint in his eye. Ann and Emily exchange puzzled glances from the corners of their eyes. Maureen sends them an apologetic smile. Chowder hands over a pile of money, receives eight hotels, and lines them up on Boardwalk and Park Place. Sue rolls the dice and moves her player, landing on Park Place. She counts up her money, mortgages all her properties, and hands the pile of cash to Chowder, who accepts it smugly. She pushes her chair back defeated and sips her beer. Emily rolls and lands on Boardwalk. She also hands over her last cash, shrugs resignedly, and sips her beer. Ann rolls, lands on Park Place, and hands over her money. Chowder is *ecstatic. Maureen smiles at Chowder, shrugs her shoulders, palms up, and starts to gather the cards and playing pieces, the game obviously over. Chowder frowns and hands her the dice. Maureen puts her hands on her hips and shakes her head. Ann, Emily, and Sue look on, confused and apprehensive. Chowder swears and pushes his chair back in irate frustration. One leg of the chair slips into a hole in the floor, and he tumbles over backward. Everyone bursts out laughing ... except for Chowder.*

A typical evening in the life of a young woman in love with an as yet undiagnosed Aspergian.

One of the Asperger's assessments I took on Andy's behalf contained the criterion "Unaware of unwritten social rules of adult recreation."[1] One such rule is "Don't take *Monopoly* too seriously, especially when meeting your girlfriend's best friends."

Yes, Andy is remarkably good at understanding money, a fact I am most grateful for; and yes, he was intimidated by my Amherst buddies, feeling like a lowly UMasser himself. (One urban legend claims that the five Scooby Doo characters are based on the five colleges – Smith, Mount Holyoke, UMass, Hampshire, and Amherst – of the Connecticut River Valley, with us Amherst students being the suave and sophisticated Fred and the UMass folks the goofy-faced Scooby. I used to remind Andy that it's usually Scooby that solves the case.)

However, social rules of adult recreation preclude acting like a robber baron while getting to know one's girlfriend's best friends, even if said player does have an above-average IQ and feels it is only logical to use it. We all laughed because we felt Andy deserved the fall to the floor. He had violated obvious social mores. Sure, I was embarrassed. Sure, I wish he had neither acted like a jerk nor fallen off his chair. I was confused that night: stuck between adoring this man and feeling that something was very off.

Even so, my friends and I were all thankful for Andy's Aspier traits later that summer when we were house-sitting up in the hills outside of Amherst. The owners, both professors, had left for the summer, leaving us to care for their 200-year-old house, a tennis court, horse barn, and pond. With only a week left before their return, we were all distraught at the amount of work we needed to do – especially because we had spent most of the summer writing sestinas instead of tending to the house and property – and we were flailing about helplessly.

But then Andy just happened to drop by and solved our problems. In four hours, he had finished nailing in the facing for the box stalls, killed the weeds in the tennis court, removed the algae from the pond, reprogrammed the Jacuzzi, and healed the dog from a porcupine attack.

Thinking back on these two events, I am reminded of the scene in *Rudolph the Red-Nosed Reindeer*[2] in which Rudolph demonstrates his flying skills in front of the other young bucks but then is shunned when his black camouflage ball falls off and his red nose glares. The studly and obnoxious Coach Comet widens his eyes in fear but then says to the others, "From now on, gang, we won't let Rudolph join in any reindeer games." He jerks his jock neck to dismiss his posse, and off they go, leaving poor Rudolph alone, but not before raining down a torrent of insults such as "fire snoot" and "neon nose."

But, when push comes to shove and the toys will not get delivered without the helpful radiance of Rudolph's snout, "then how the reindeer loved him!" This Christmas special is truly a celebration of misfits, with Hermie the elven dentist the only one who can disarm the Abominable Snowman, and Yukon Cornelius (obviously up North because of his off-putting social demeanor) the only one who can rehabilitate the Abominable to join society. And Rudolph, God bless him, instead of rubbing everybody's noses in it (forgive the pun), simply says to Santa's request, "It will be an honor, sir." Now that's graciousness!

I have read similar tales in various books on high-functioning autism, especially those by auties themselves, to the effect of "Sure, we have trouble socializing, but whom do you call to create Microsoft, discover the theory of relativity, or design better slaughter chutes?" As Temple Grandin says, "the social people who sat around the campfire talking were probably not the makers of the first stone spear. It is also likely that the most social people did not create the great culture of our civilization, such as literature, art, engineering, music, science, and mathematics."[3]

A much more acerbic comment came from one Aspergian who reviewed the book *Solutions for Adults with Asperger Syndrome: Maximizing the Benefits, Minimizing the Drawbacks to Achieve Success*[4] on Amazon.com. Though the vast majority of reviewers had found this book helpful, one reviewer said, "It's true AS people do have trouble to recognize and understand others' state of mind and feelings when they are different from their own. BUT ... [the author] is either too arrogant or lacks the intelligence (or both?) to realize and know that what she says works both ways. Neurotypical people always have trouble to recognize and understand an AS person's state of mind and feelings … If this review sounds condescending towards the author, then thought needs to be given to how the author sounds when she says such things as 'People with AS have difficulty getting the gist of the situation.' Maybe so in the instances she gives. However, NTs also have difficulty getting the gist of the situation in certain instances that AS people have no trouble with (such as rapidly noticing a long-range pattern that a typical person could never grasp)." Ouch.

I also think of the Matt Damon/Ben Affleck film *Good Will Hunting*, when Professor Lambeau of MIT, reviewing a difficult proof that his genius protégé Will has easily solved, scolds him for not showing up for a job interview. Will says, "Maybe I don't want to spend my life sittin' around and explaining s*?+ to people." He holds up his mathematical proof. "You know how f-in' easy this is to me? This is a joke! I'm sorry you can't do this. I really am." He lights the proof on fire and drops it on the ground. Lambeau, dropping in intellectual pain to put out the flames, finally sits back on his heels and says, "You're right, Will. I can't do that proof and you can."[5]

Perhaps the Amazon reviewer is right that "An NT like [the author] gets her book published because most of the people who are seeking to buy a book to learn about AS are NTs and NTs feel most comfortable reading material that doesn't challenge their way of thinking and/or their egos." Again, big ouch.

One counselor Andy and I talked to suggested that Aspergians are the evolutionary avant garde – having intellectual abilities that will move us ahead as a species. But he also said that evolution runs by fits and starts: The Aspies gained the pattern-recognition thing, but lost the emotional thing. Oops. Try again. Generations from now, perhaps all humans will have extraordinary pattern-recognition ability AND genius interpersonal skills.

In the meantime, those who got the former and lost some of the latter suffer at the hands of the socially adept. Watch any jock high school student and you will see him acting remarkably like those jerky reindeer troglodytes. I remember my own high school experience, and since I am also in and out of our county's high schools in my current job as an English teacher, I suffer in empathy as Eldest, our high-school-aged son, makes his way through his last years of public education. The jocks have it made. They are the socially accepted and media-saturating ideal, even though they could not invent the lightbulb or television. Evolutionarily speaking, the skills needed for football are left over from the days when men were running down the family meat and beating off saber-tooth tigers.

In today's world, many with AS also have a serious struggle finding and keeping a job. Current estimates place the unemployment rate for people with AS at nearly 90%.[6] Because of sensory sensitivity, literal thinking, emotional outbursts, and social difficulties, many with AS are unable to succeed in the modern American workplace. However, in certain sectors of the economy, the Aspies actually have the upper hand. Steve Silberman, a nationally recognized writer about computer technology, states in *Wired* magazine that "It's a familiar joke in the industry that many of the hardcore programmers in IT strongholds like Intel, Adobe, and Silicon Graphics – coming to work early, leaving late, sucking down Big Gulps in their cubicles while they code for hours – are residing somewhere in the Asperger's domain."[7]

So despite the physical attractiveness and social effortlessness of the sports-heads, they are not the ones who can pull down the big bucks, at least in the tech world. In terms of occupations, the ability to run into other heavy objects, knock them down, and get across a line carrying something melon-sized prepares one pretty clearly for blue-collar work. Of course, many of us with husbands on the spectrum can attest to the fact that our spouse with AS can face significant challenges earning money, unless he can be his own boss or fit into one of these high-paying and isolated technology jobs. However, in this particular niche, Silberman says, the evolutionary tide of mate selection may be turning in favor of the Asperger's geek, with many NT females choosing well-paid AS spouses. Silberman continues, "Compensatory unions of opposites also thrive along the continuum, and in the last 10 years, geekitude has become sexy and associated with financial success." [8]

On the other hand, one unfortunate result in the Silicon Valley, Silberman says, is that these genetic traits are seemingly intensified in children, especially if an Aspie marries an Aspie, with an alarming rise in low-functioning autism among the children in this area of that country.

As Andy said the other night, "One in 110 (which is the current prevalence for ASD according to the Centers for Disease Control and Prevention[9]) is probably about all you NTs really need for us to keep society progressing. Besides, one in 110 is probably about all you guys could tolerate!"

If a night of *Monopoly* is any gauge, I think he's right.

Loving the Tasmanian Devil

Taken from the draft version of *The Adult Version of the Australian Scale for Asperger Syndrome* by Garnett and Attwood, 1995, found at the website of Roger N. Meyer at http://www.rogernmeyer.com/adult_acts_and_consequences_adult_version.html.

2   Kizo Nagashima and Larry Roemer, dirs. (1964). *Rudolph, the Red-Nosed Reindeer.* Los Angeles, CA: Rankin/Bass.

3   Grandin, Temple. (2002 October 1). *The World Needs People With Asperger's Syndrome: American Normal.* This review of the book *American Normal* may be found on the Dana Foundation site at http://www.dana.org/news/cerebrum/detail.aspx?id=2312.

4   This book by psychologist Juanita Lovvett is available from Fair Winds Press. Eleven out of twenty-two reviewers on Amazon gave the book five stars. All the reviews may be read at http://www.amazon.com/Solutions-Adults-Aspergers-Syndrome-Maximizing/product-reviews/1592331645.

5   *Good Will Hunting.* (2008). Los Angeles, CA: Miramax.

6   Edmonds, G., & Beardon, D. (Eds.). (2008). Asperger Syndrome & Employment: Adults Speak out About Asperger Syndrome. *Journal of Autism and Developmental Disorders,* 39(9).

7   Silberman, Steve. The Geek Syndrome. *Wired* 9.12. http://www.wired.com/wired/archive/9.12/aspergers_pr.html.

8   Ibid.

9   *Facts About ASDs.* Centers for Disease Control and Prevention. http://www.cdc.gov/ncbddd/autism/facts.html.

CHAPTER 6

OOPS! I MARRIED A LOBSTER – THE DOWN SIDE OF THE DIAGNOSIS

X

I was so tired when I got home from school. I had been working all day with students on their senior projects, finally kicking the last two students out of my classroom at 5 PM, and then driving one home. I hadn't eaten lunch, so I grabbed three pizza crusts and some ice cream, read a little Laurie Colwin,[1] and curled up for a short snooze.

At 6 PM Andy screamed up to me, "MO! Is something wrong with you?!"

"No, I'm just taking a short snooze."

"Well, get up! We need to think about dinner and figure out calves!!"

Argh! I'm tired, I thought angrily, swinging my legs out of bed and pulling on a pair of jeans.

"I just don't get why you would want to take a nap at 6 PM! We're going to bed in two hours. Why don't we just get done what we need to and then go to sleep?!"

Because I am tired NOW. I want to sleep NOW.

It's pointless to say this aloud, especially now that I know where the tirade is coming from, Andy's pea-sized amygdala. No conception of the fact that I worked all day. No conception that anyone but a farmer could be exhausted. No ability to imagine what I am feeling. He simply CANNOT envision why I could be tired, and his need for completion and efficient timing requires that all my work must be done before HE can relax. Argh!!! And furthermore, he sees absolutely no problem with talking to me this way. After all, don't I realize how much better our lives would be if I did just everything the same way he did?

Saturday afternoon two days later, I woke up from a nap (legitimate according to Andy, because it was mid-day *and* we had *both* worked in the garden all morning *and* we were *both* napping). I looked over at Andy's head on the pillow beside me and suddenly felt as if I had accidentally married a lobster, as if a man-sized crustacean was lying in the bed next to me with its juvenile brain stem and little pincers flailing in the air. If I tried to talk to the lobster, it would scuttle slightly and wave its little tentacle eyes and think its primordial lobster thoughts. But actual communication? I don't think so.

When I realize that Andy cannot instinctively understand my experience or not feel bombarded during even the most routine of days, I realize just how different we are; almost like different species. I see in my mind a diagram of comparative nervous systems in my high school biology textbook and the diagrams of the "Asperger brain" from the Internet, and I become nauseous. How can I remain married to a being that is practically another phylum?

But then I imagine Andy's other traits, his childlike wonder, his extraordinary ability to comprehend and synthesize complex systems, and realize how overwhelmed he must be sometimes. And the lobster on the pillow anthropomorphizes and is suddenly standing at its dressing table, like that whimsical engraving from *Alice in Wonderland*. It has a heart-breaking look on its face as it preens and prepares for the Lobster Quadrille.[2]

So sad, the heart of a lobster, as he "Trims his belt and his buttons, and turns out his toes." I see Andy as a child, protecting his shirt tag from excision by the neighborhood bully. I see him in his sixth-grade class photo hunched in the back row, his cavernous eyes so scared and alone. I see him in college, charged with political fervor, striding across campus in his black overcoat and keffiyeh, his long Roger Daltry curls bouncing down his back. I see him at the Szykowski farm, running a tractor for the first time, so glad to be out under the hot Holyoke sun.

And I see that the lobster I have wed is a Lewis Carroll lobster with personality and an Englishman's brain, with sophisticated emotions inside its crustacean body. And I have sympathy for and understanding of the very real emotions of this creature:

> When the sands are all dry, he is gay as a lark,
> And will talk in contemptuous tones of the shark;
> But, when the tide rises and sharks are around,
> His voice has a timid and tremulous sound.[2]

We're all like that, aren't we? We all talk a good game when the things we fear are far away, but when faced with anxiety, our souls become timid and tremulous. Or worse, like Winston in George Orwell's *1984*, we betray our Julia with the rat an inch from our face.[3] The only difference is that lobsters can't hide it as well. When they are afraid, we know they are afraid. They act afraid – that emotion is worn on the sleeve, or the claw, as it were. We non-crustaceans have those fear reflexes as well, the stimulus does cause the response; it's just that we can process it in the frontal lobes, understand that it is not life-threatening, and keep it hidden.

Perhaps the lobsters in our midst simply remind us too clearly and uncomfortably of those core emotions we have learned to hide socially, that we can hide as a reflex, our great big amygdalas allowing us to do the socially advantageous thing and bury those feelings far beneath the surface. The problem is that for us NTs, those neural impulses just go somewhere else, into a headache, into misdirected anger at an annoying goose, into an hour of web-surfing old boyfriends at the end of the day, into resenting the lobster on the pillow next door.

Perhaps we'd all do well to allow a little of the lobster into ourselves, to go somewhere alone and beat a pillow or address the oak tree gnarl that resembles our boss's face and tell it exactly how we feel about it, or confront the obnoxious colleague who deserves to be put in his place. Should we, then, join the Lobster Quadrille?

> See how eagerly the lobsters and the turtles all advance!
> They are waiting on the shingle – will you come and join the dance?
> You can really have no notion how delightful it will be
> When they take us up and throw us, with the lobsters, out to sea![2]

Oops! I Married a Lobster – The Down Side of the Diagnosis

He waits for me, my wistful lobster, there on the shingle. All the turtles and lobsters are eagerly arriving, there, under the moonlight. They smile and chat, the slow and odd, the misunderstood, the savants, the anxious, they are together and accepted here, they know the measures and etiquette of this minuet. Here, they are the norm, and I am in the minority.

I give my analytical eyebrows a knit and linger on the edge of the beach near a rock. I am too controlled to join this group. Besides, I realize as the dance begins that if I join, I will be thrown far to sea and I resist.

> But the snail replied, 'Too far, too far!' and gave a look askance –
> Said he thanked the whiting kindly, but he would not join the dance.
> "What matters it how far we go?" his scaly friend replied.
> "There is another shore, you know, upon the other side.
> The further off from England the nearer is to France –
> Then turn not pale, beloved snail, but come and join the dance. [2]

And it is true that life with an Aspergian has taken me to some far-off shores, many of them exotic and magical. I now see every wild animal in the landscape no matter how small or far. I understand economics and agriculture in their intricate and dazzling patterns. I can mow a ten-acre hayfield and not miss a blade or waste a drop of diesel. I can cry at the birth of a calf or feel the beating heart of a kitten beneath its endearing fur. I can limit my excessive social niceties and write exactly what needs to be written in a letter to my supervisor. I can sit in the woods still enough to have chipmunks run across my foot.

I have tasted meals from Andy's hands that would rival those created by a four-star chef. I have tasted fresh lettuce and ripe strawberries that he has called forth from the earth. I have splashed into a glorious pool from a beautiful deck that was already manifest in his mind months before shovel touched earth. I have smelled fuchsias and lilies and lilacs that have flowered under his touch. I have seen a run-down farm flourish into a profitable Dairy of Distinction. I have felt the tender touch of a man instinctively expert at animal responses. I have read love poems from him that come from a sense of wonder deeper and more pure than I know. I have stripped off some of the endless layers of social veneer that protects me from intense experiences. I have been to the far shore, seen the wonders of France, drifted there under a moonlit sky with a water-wise lobster at my side, my hand safe in his pincer.

> Will you, won't you, will you, won't you, will you join the dance?
> Will you, won't you, will you, won't you, won't you join the dance? [2]

Yes, I think I will. Lead on, my lobster love.

---

[1] Laurie Colwin is one of my favorite escapes because her novels are so urban. I highly recommend *Goodbye Without Leaving* (1991) or *A Big Storm Knocked It Over* (1994). New York, NY: Poseidon Press.

[2] "The Lobster Quadrille" is Chapter Ten of *Alice's Adventures in Wonderland*. The full text may be found on the Project Gutenberg site at http://www.gutenberg.org/etext/11. The Sir John Tenniel illustrations can be found at http://www.gutenberg.org/files/114/114-h/114-h.htm. The Lobster Primping Before a Mirror is number 36.

[3] Orwell, George. (1949). *1984*. New York, NY: Penguin. At one point, the main character, Winston, has a cage containing a rat strapped to his head. The rat will be released to bite his face unless Winston betrays his lover Julia. Although he has sworn he will not, he does when faced with his greatest fear.

CHAPTER 7

MIND VET, TRACTOR LIMBS, GRASS IMPERSONATIONS – UNIQUE TALENTS OF AN ASPERGIAN

When I was organizing our office one day, I ran into an occupational interest assessment Andy had taken on December 5, 1975, which I recognized as being based on John Holland's hexagon of vocational preferences.[1] Andy must have been sixteen, almost seventeen, at the time and was, therefore, at Westledge,[2] an experimental school in Connecticut that his parents finally sent him to in desperation when his public school principal said there was nothing more they could do to accommodate his behavior.

His high scores for specific interests were in the areas of Nature, Medical Science, Writing, Public Speaking, Law/Politics, Medical Service, Art, Agriculture, and Science. Suggested occupations that would be fulfilling for him were farmer, forester, veterinarian, and minister.

Loving the Tasmanian Devil

In reality, after graduating from Westledge, a slightly circuitous route took Andy first to Earlham College's pre-med program and then, realizing that an MD would mean living life indoors, to a year on the road, Jack Keruoac style, and then to UMass Amherst. After six years there, he finally finished college – the same year as his sister, six years his junior – with three bachelor's degrees: in biochemistry; agriculture and finance; and social thought and political economy.

During the same cleanup, I also ran into Andy's proposal to the UMass BDIC program (bachelor's degree with individual concentration, a special program available at UMass Amherst), in which he proposed his own unique major. He wrote, "The student concerned with agriculture's precarious situation needs to possess a firm scientific background and an understanding of the economic tools used to evaluate alternative cropping and livestock management systems. It is my belief that this can best be accomplished through the BDIC program." He posited a course of study with three components: general production, economics, and pest factors, explaining that "The potential for a synthesis of knowledge from many disciplines to provide a constructive framework for real agricultural progress is an encouraging possibility which represents many of my hopes and aspirations."

And here he is, twenty years later, living out his hopes and aspirations, and stunning the locals with his success. I know that Andy's ability to run our farm so well comes not just from his academic background in plant pest control, animal nutrition, or economic theory but from something much different: autism. Autism, in its Asperger's form, has given him at least three unique traits that have led to his farming success.

Mind Vet, Tractor Limbs, Grass Impersonations –
Unique Talents of an Aspergian

Trait One: Mind Vet

Andy can walk into a barn filled with 150 cows and without even turning on the lights know one of them is sick. Even our vet is stunned by this one. Andy will notice symptoms of illness two days before a "normal" farmer would, and he usually knows what the cow's problem is. This is one part academics and five parts neurologically heightened sensations.

Temple Grandin, an internationally known woman with high-functioning autism who found fulfillment in a similar agricultural career path, explains that people with autism have excruciating sensitivities that can lead to dysfunctional over-reaction to many "normal stimuli" but also to a superb sensitivity to things like breathing rates, abnormal smells, unusual feed patterns, and atypical body temperatures.[3]

The psychologist Oliver Sacks tells the story of a neurotypical medical student who had taken lots of amphetamines and then dreamed that he was a dog. When he awoke, his sense of smell had been intensified to the point that he could distinguish among his twenty patients by scent and had an overwhelming desire to sniff surrounding objects.[4] Luckily for Andy, he already has these extreme perceptions and will wake in the middle of the night knowing a cow is in labor or sure a bad storm is about to hit or sensing trouble in the heifer lot.

Prey animals, Grandin says, are very uncomplaining as a defense mechanism against getting killed. Because they don't make noise or act strangely when in pain, in their distress they do not become an easy target for predators.[5] Unfortunately, neither do they become easy targets for humans looking for animal health problems. A sick cow's symptoms are barely recognizable to most people: cold ears, not eating, unusual posture.

The trained or experienced eye can see them; the autistic eye can't NOT see them. Grandin explains, "I think many or even most autistic people experience the world a lot the way animals experience the world: as a swirling mass of tiny details. We're seeing, hearing, and feeling all the things no one else can."[6] For Andy, this leads to frustration and incredulity when one of our employees fails to recognize the signs of a sick cow for three days while we are away and Andy notices it the split second he returns to the barn.

Grandin relates how in one psychological experiment[7] randomly selected subjects are asked to watch a basketball game on a television screen and count the passes one team or the other makes. Mid-way through, a woman in a gorilla costume runs onto the court, stops and beats her chest, and runs off again. A full 50% of the subjects never even see her. "Normal people see only what they expect to see – because they can't consciously experience the raw data – only the schema their brains create out of the raw data."[8]

So Andy's psychic veterinarian skills are a product of long-term occupational interest, academic training, and Aspergian senses.

Trait Two: Tractor Limbs

I watch Andy operate equipment and use tools all the time. I can tell that unlike the crude movements of own my fumbling and frustration, a tool of any size, either in his hand or under his control, is merely an extension of his body. This must be the result of the amazing spatial and mechanical abilities gifted to him from Asperger's. When Andy is dumping feed into the mixer using the front-end loader bucket on the tractor, he tips the silage or corn meal out of the bucket and then gently shakes out the last specks like a cook gently sprinkling salt out of her hand – all of this using hydraulic levers attached to the 800-pound iron bucket. He can spin on a huge tractor as gracefully as a ballerina in a pirouette. When he uses a screwdriver, it is just an extension of his fingers, resulting in dexterity and finesse.

As a corollary, Andy uses his own body in a very tool-like way. Although his hands and fingers are huge (farmers enlarge their finger muscles from use), he can perform the most delicate of tasks with them. He truly would have made a fine surgeon.

I have read in the scientific literature that gross- and fine-motor skills are typically impaired by AS, with deficiency in this area even used as one common diagnostic criterion. Many with AS find that their kinesthetic skills are below normal, causing infinite embarrassment in physical education class and beyond. However, the opposite may also be the case, where an Aspergian's motor skills are actually uncanny. Clay Marzo,[9] for example, attributes his world-class surfing skills to his Asperger's. This is similar to Andy, whose fine- and gross-motor coordination and visual/spatial skills are both above the norm.

Grandin says that when she is working on an animal system design problem, she can see what is there and what could be there and look at it from every possible angle – all in her mind, like a 3-D video game. I can tell that Andy does this too, because he can walk into a farm situation, like getting silage from an awkward angle or moving cows from here to there, and find an elegant solution without even seeming to think.

The only problem this causes him is frustration and incomprehension when others cannot do the same.

Trait Three: Grass Impersonations

Somewhere toward the end of April, we were sitting in the kitchen. Andy had been outside all morning and was in the house for breakfast. Pointing toward the west pasture outside the kitchen window, he said, "Can you feel the grass out there? It's like this." Then he did an impersonation of the grass: mouth pressed tight in anticipation, eyes squinting and looking eagerly into the future, head strained up toward the sun. I knew exactly what he meant.

It's a rare man who can impersonate grass. Aspies are great at impersonations, I suppose because they can analyze their subject in great detail and in his or its constituent parts – eyes, voice, inflection, speech patterns – and then replicate each of them in combination.

I have also heard Andy explain the "desires" of a flowering plant. I will try to replicate it here: "The plant's goal is to reproduce itself. It grows vegetatively to create maximum energy, it senesces – flowers – and then sends all that energy into the seed pod. When the seed is made, the plant is done. The vegetative growth will stop, and what's left is mostly starch. If you want to keep a plant in its vegetative state (like grass crops or basil or lettuce), then you have to keep it from flowering."

The result of such knowledge on our farm? Twice the hay other farmers get from their fields; lettuce and basil all summer long. And from the other plants, the ones allowed to flower and set seed, enormous vegetables and berries.

And flowers. Andy communes with the flowers. He knows that the two hanging baskets outside the back door like to be watered morning and evening every day. He knows he needs to cut the dead-heads off the fuschias to make them re-flower. He can actually hear the flowers whimper in dry weather.

Grandin claims that "Theoretically, we [all] *could* have extreme perceptions the way animals do if we figured out how to use the sensory processing cells in our brains the way animals do."[10] And I know from living with Andy and hearing him vocalize his every passing thought for twenty years that I too have developed some of these skills. I can spot a sick calf or cow pretty quickly. I can sense changes in the weather. Maybe it's because I have seen and done the exact same thing every day for twenty years straight, so any change in the tedium is bound to be noticeable. But I do know I have become more conscious of some of the things that Andy cannot be *un*conscious of.

The composer Aaron Copland, in his book *What to Listen for in Music,* writes that understanding any type of music requires answering two questions: Are you hearing everything that is going on? and Are you really being sensitive to it? "The main difference between [the composer] and the lay listener is that he is better prepared to listen," Copland claims.[11] So too the Aspie farmer: He is hearing everything that is going on and he is sensitive to it.

Career-wise, Andy has probably fallen into the perfect occupation. Grandin says, "I have been lucky, because my understanding of animals and visual thinking led me to a satisfying career in which my autistic traits don't impede my progress."[12] I know how the sensory sensitivity and awareness of detail tires Andy and keeps his anxiety level at a high intensity, but it has also contributed to his great success as a farmer.

Andy's BDIC proposal was primarily made up of an historical and economic analysis of American agriculture in order to justify the need to combine classes from the agriculture department and the economics department. However, Andy also included a section related to the very personal nature of this occupation: "In my farming experience I have come to see that a close relationship between farmers and the land [and animals] is in fact a basic requirement of farming." At the time, 1986, Andy did not realize just how close that relationship was for him. His nerves vibrate to the doings of the grass. His ears turn to the subtlest of signs from the cows. His muscles extend into steel that does his bidding.

Even at age sixteen, Andy was heading this way. His occupational assessment states, "These areas probably will be sources of satisfaction in your life – occupations related to preventing illness and maintaining health – areas dealing with creativity in expressing thoughts – being in the out-of-doors and studying nature." The survey had no idea it was summarizing the preferred occupations for an Aspergian. Are these activities "Sources of satisfaction" for Andy? Yes. Are they, in fact, "Nodes of genius?" Even more so.

Mind Vet, Tractor Limbs, Grass Impersonations –
Unique Talents of an Aspergian

[1] John Holland's 1973 book was called *Making Vocational Choices: A Theory of Careers* and is available through Prentice Hall, Upper Saddle River, NJ. Holland is currently a professor of cognitive science at Michigan State University.

[2] A radio broadcast about the Westledge School in West Simsbury, CT, may be found on the Connecticut Public Broadcasting Network at http://www.cpbn.org/program/colin-mcenroe-show/episode/cms-westledge-school-lives.

[3] Temple Grandin uses this ability to explain animal thought in her book *Animals in Translation: Using the Mysteries of Autism to Decode Animal Behavior.* (2005). New York, NY: Scribner Books.

[4] This account is in the chapter called "The Dog Beneath the Skin" in Oliver Sacks' *The Man Who Mistook His Wife for a Hat and Other Clinical Tales.* (1985). New York, NY: Summit Books; pages 149-153.

[5] Grandin, Temple. (2005). *Animals in Translation.* New York, NY: Scribner; pages 180-181.

[6] Ibid., page 67.

[7] The experiment called The Gorillas in Our Midst was done by Daniel Simons at the University of Illinois. Grandin relates it in *Animals in Translation* on page 24.

[8] Grandin, *Animals in Translation;* page 65.

[9] Heasley, Shaun. (2009, August 7). Asperger's Secret to Pro Surfer's Success. *Disabilityscoop.* http://www.disabilityscoop.com/2009/08/07/surfer/4506/

[10] Grandin, *Animals in Translation;* page 63.

[11] Copland, Aaron. (1957). *What to Listen for in Music.* New York, NY: McGraw-Hill; page viii.

[12] Grandin, Temple. (2006). *Thinking in Pictures.* New York, NY: Vintage Books; page 111.

CHAPTER 8

THE FOGHORN AND THE ROCK – VOCALIZATION AND VOICE MODULATION

One day Brent, our farmer-neighbor-friend up the road, pulled in at our place to borrow something – medicine, equipment, or something. I happened to be out front of the barn and walked over to chat. ("Sump'n diff'ernt" is always welcome at the farm.) I was leaning on Brent's open car window, wiggling my fingers at his two toddlers in their carseats, when a loud noise began way back behind the barn. It sounded like the county-wide emergency management system alarm.

"Oh, listen," Brent said, cocking his ear in an exaggerated way. "The ships are coming in. No wait, it's just Andy." He gave me a huge grin. Brent has known Andy for a long time.

I smirked.

Andy was way back behind the barn yelling to our hired hand about tightening the pressure on the bagger.

That's my husband. The human foghorn.

One of the traits of Asperger Syndrome is an unusual pattern of vocalization: too loud, too soft, too much, too little. Andy's version is most definitely too loud and too much. When Andy yells, he can be heard pretty clearly within a five-mile radius.

Other friends and colleagues have also witnessed this. One famous incident occurred on a hot day when all the cows went out to the pasture, immediately drank their water trough dry, and in the process tipped it over. Although the automatic filler attached to a waterline was filling it with water, the water was pouring onto the ground, and the cows were having a good old time fighting and drinking the growing puddle and knocking the trough about with their big old wet noses.

Andy ran out there with the nearest bludgeon he could find and flailed the cows away while he attempted to get the trough upright and back under the electric fence wire, which was meant to prevent them from tipping it over in the first place. Of course, he kept getting shocked.

"TURN OFF THE FENCE!!!!!!!"

I ran to the equipment shed where the switch for the fence-charger was and turned it off.

"IS IT OFF!???????!!!!!!!!!!!!!!!!!!!!!!!!"

"YES! IT'S OFF !!!!!!!!!!!"

"OFF?!?!?!?!?!!?!?!?!"

"OFF!!!!!!!!!!!!!!!!!!!!!!!!!!!!!!!!!!!"

A pause as he adjusted something. "TURN IT ON!!!!!!!!!!!!!!!!!!!!!!!!!!!!!"

Pause. "IS IT ON?!?!?!!?!?!?!?!?!!?!?!?!?!?!!?!?"

"YES, IT'S ON!!"

"ON?!?!?!?!!?!?!?!?!!?!?!?!!?!?!?"

You get the picture. This continued for a good ten minutes and is one of the reasons we now have FCC-licensed radios.

A friend of ours witnessed this exchange, and even now, fifteen years later, will bring it up.

"Andy? Loud?" he asks rhetorically. Then he bellows, "IS IT OFF?!?!?! MO, IS IT OFF?!?!?!?!?!!?!"

Andy just grimaces.

It truly is something to hear.

As Beverly Vicker says in her article "Social Communication and Language Characteristics Associated With High Functioning, Verbal Children and Adults With Autism Spectrum Disorder," a person with high-functioning autism often has a tendency to "Speak too loudly or too fast unless taught about the needs of his or her communication partner."[1]

Loving the Tasmanian Devil

Many, many times when Andy and I would be talking in the kitchen, even before the diagnosis, I would reach over, put my hand on his arm, and say, "Shhhh, honey, I'm right next to you." He would sigh and get exasperated, having been told since childhood that he was loud.

Loud is most definitely an issue. There is also the issue of unintentional vocalization. I used to refer to this (if only in my mind) as simulcasting. No matter what emotion passes through Andy's mind, it is shared with the rest of us. Loudly.

According to Temple Grandin, this is quite typical of people on the spectrum. She had to train herself to do not this when in the workplace because people thought her odd.[2]

WrongPlanet.com, a wonderful on-line forum for people on the spectrum, once had a discussion on the topic of talking to oneself, and here is what various people had to say:

"I do this, I try to keep it all internal, but sometimes it slips out when I am around people and I may not realize it. I am having this deep internal monologue with myself and it just sometimes comes out loud."

Another person said, "This happens to be one of my biggest 'signs.' I remember back in middle school one kid that was sitting next to me was trying to get a few other kids' to notice me talking to myself 'Hey look at him, [He's] talking to himself. Isn't that weird?' In actuality, I still talk to myself, and a lot of the times get lost in my own train of thoughts. Sometimes I'll end up that way for 30 minutes, and then catch myself, also noticing I was twirling my pen or rapidly moving my fingers."

Yet another: "Same here. When I'm having a very hazy day, I have to repeat stuff to myself out loud in order to keep my focus on it. I also do it when following instructions, and when I have to call someone I repeat the opening sentence out loud a few times [first]."[3]

Andy does this, especially when he is frustrated. He will talk aloud to keep his thoughts straight. He will verbalize his anger – sometimes swearing or screaming – and he will also use a tractor or car engine, revved to squeal the tires, to express his feelings. It probably is healthier than my coping technique of keeping it all inside.

Unfortunately – or perhaps fortunately – I am an Adult Child of an Alcoholic (ACOA), and I have my own marginally functional methods of vocalizing, or rather not vocalizing. In contrast to too loud and too much, I favor too soft and too little. The typical ACOA, according to one website, exhibits "isolation, fear of people, and fear of authority figures" and is "frightened by angry people and personal criticism."[4]

I remember pretty distinctly in adolescence choosing to become the Rock. Because of problems related to my dad's drinking, I decided it made my life easier to just not expect anything good, not need attention or affection, and not express my feelings. I really did take the Simon and Garfunkel song to heart: "I am a rock. I am an island. A rock feels no pain, and an island never cries."[5]

So imagine the scenario when the Rock and the Foghorn are thrown together. The Foghorn bellows; the Rock shuts down. The Foghorn bellows louder to get a response; the Rock associates bellowing with drunkenness and gets mad. The Foghorn gets so loud he shatters glass; the Rock gets a migraine and suffers in silence.

Loving the Tasmanian Devil

Of course, the purpose of a Foghorn is to alert ships to the presence of a Rock. This irony is not lost on me. Andy claims he fends off headaches by blowing off steam (literally, in fact, since that is how foghorns work), and he claims I give myself headaches by repressing my emotions. What he doesn't seem to grasp is that a foghorn situated at one's left elbow can also give a girl a headache. If we all vocalized – at loud pitch – every passing emotion, life would be a cacophonous roar.

Furthermore, if the foghorn sounded all day long, and not just when the fog made navigation dangerous, people would become immune to its warning. The boy who cried wolf was not believed when there was a real emergency. Some days I feel like I'm living in a firehouse during a perpetual five-alarm blaze. The first few years of living on the farm, I was constantly thinking Andy's left leg had just been severed, but now I take my response to any loud scream and immediately decrease it by about 50%.

In an effort to move past annoyance and toward a place of acceptance and appreciation of this foghorn tendency, I stumbled upon this poem by Sarah Hannah:

For the Fog Horn When There Is No Fog [6]

Still sounding in full sun past the jetty,
While low tide waves lap trinkets at your feet,
And you skip across dried trident trails,
Fling weeds, and do not think of worry.
For the horn that blares although you call it stubborn,
In error, out of place. For the ridicule endured,
And the continuance.
You can count out your beloved – crustaceans –
Winking in spray, still breathing in the wake,
Beneath the hooking flights of gulls,
Through the horn's threnody.
Count them now among the moving. They are.
For weathervane and almanac, ephemeris and augur,
Blameless seer versed in bones, entrails, landed shells.
For everything that tries to counsel vigilance:
The surly sullen bell, before the going,
The warning that reiterates across
The water: there might someday be fog
(They will be lost), there might very well
Be fog someday, and you will have nothing
But remembrance, and you will have to learn
To be grateful.

Must I? Must I learn to be grateful for the reminder that life can be dangerous and that the fog might roll in at any moment?

If nothing else, the foghorn is a reminder to me of how very constant the *feeling* of threat is for those on the spectrum. Grandin and Barron emphasize this as one of their final reminders in *Unwritten Rules of Social Relationships*: "Never underestimate the amount of stress individuals with ASD live under constantly ... Adopt this mantra: All behavior is communication – what is the [foghorn] trying to say?"[7]

There have been long stretches of time, sometimes even a year straight, when there were few to no outbursts – when the farm has been smooth-running, money has been available, the workload has been manageable – and I even temporarily forget the times of constant eruptions. However, when the outbursts are frequent and loud, there is no question about what Andy is communicating: I am scared. I am not liking the amount of change. I am worried about money. I am overtired and over-stimulated. I need help.

The problem is that when this happens, I am the only one who is available to take on the role of his helper, comforter, money-minutiae-manager, and sounding board. At these moments, Andy has no emotional reserves for helping me, and I am not about to voice any of my own needs, knowing that if I add even the smallest variable to the mix, I will only make the situation worse.

And so the Rock stays silent and the Foghorn roars. And slowly, over time, the rock is worn away by the constant smashing of the surf while the foghorn continues to be heard. This is the very last bullet in *Unwritten Rules*: "Children and adults manifest their anger/anxiety/stress in two major ways: active outbursts or passive withdrawal. It's not just the explosive and emotionally demonstrative ASD person who needs our help. The silent, socially-avoidant, passive individual [including the NT spouse] deserves it equally so, but is often overlooked."[8]

That latter is me, though I am not on the spectrum. Due to my own self-repression, my needs are often overlooked, except by my mother and sister, who can read my silences even over the telephone. The advice for wives of Aspergians is that we must verbalize our needs, even if we think the message we are sending nonverbally is obvious. To an Aspie, it's not obvious. We must act as our own advocates, even when it is against our typical modus operandi.

Perhaps what would make this unfamiliar and usually restricted act tolerable is rethinking it as the issuance of a vital warning of impending danger – not for my personal safety but for the safety of the family as a whole. If the whole bunch of us are about to smash onto the rock of Mom's emotional deterioration or of the kids' feelings of neglect, or the raging storm of chaos and uncertainty, someone has to sound the alarm. There has to be at least a buoy bell that sounds when the Rock herself is starting to feel like a danger to others.

Andy and I, like all married people, both go through phases of calling out for help. Usually, one of us is in an emotional or mental position of strength to respond to the other. But once in a while, we are both sending out warning signs: I'm scared. I'm hurting. I'm lost. Help me. And if that happens, and if we attempt to turn to each other, it's just a battle of badness. I go into Rock mode and Andy goes into Foghorn mode, and it's a downward spiral. Neither one of us is able to be either helpful or even to speak clearly or civilly.

The key, I think, is that we need to turn not toward each other but toward someone else. I can turn to my spirituality, and I do. But we also need someone, a trained counselor, to lead us out of the fog. At times, we know what we are groping through but can find no way out. At other times, we can't even find the words for the danger and need someone to describe it from up above the eye of the storm.

There is a story that Seven-Habits trainer Stephen Covey shares based on Frank Koch's record of a battleship captain who awakens one night to find what appears to be a ship right in his lane, directing him to move to starboard. When the captain instead advises the oncoming ship to give way, it refuses, merely commanding once again that the captain change course. When the captain warns that he is a battleship and, therefore, demands that the other ship be the one to move, the other ship responds that he is no ship but the lighthouse.[9]

Covey goes on to use this as an analogy to suggest that his Seven Habits represent unchanging principles by which to guide companies, but the story has equivalent relevance to Andy and me. Although Andy sounds and acts like a foghorn or an unmoving lighthouse, he is merely a boat making his way through the fog just like the rest of us. And though I am silent and act as if I have the goods to be the Rock of Ages, I'm also just a sea-faring vessel weaving about in the mist.

We go through periods when neither of us is in a position to steer the other straight, nor are we on the same boat just enjoying the ride. Only an objective, healing, trained voice can put us back on the correct course, upon which we actually do agree. We both want to be heading in the same direction: We want financial stability; happy, healthy children; time to enjoy our own pursuits; and freedom from stress and exhaustion.

There is no embarrassment in seeking help from outside sources. It does take acknowledgment that both of us are feeling lost and in need of guidance, and it does take faith that whoever we see has the ability to understand and help us. I am reminded of a song on the *Peter, Paul, and Mommy, Too*[10] video that we used to watch with the kids. I can actually understand the Spanish, now that I've been forced to learn a little:

> *Somos el barco, somos el mar,*
> *Yo navego en ti, tu navegas en mi*
> *We are the boat, we are the sea, I sail in you, you sail in me*
>
> *So with our hopes we set the sails*
> *And face the winds once more*
> *And with our hearts we chart the waters never sailed before*

Sorting out our relationship and our roles and our ways of communicating in light of the Asperger diagnosis is a brand-new sea for us. We have no map, but hopefully someone does. Sometimes, we are in really rough waters, with the Foghorn blaring and the Rock silently holding fast. But in truth, all five of us are in the same little boat and we tire of the storm.

At such times, I have found, we need to shush up, hold onto each other, and listen for a Voice, whether divine or with an MSW degree, to steer us out.

[1] Vicker, Beverly. (n.d.). Social Communication and Language Characteristics Associated With High Functioning Verbal Children and Adults With Autism Spectrum Disorder. *BBB AUTISM SUPPORT NETWORK. BBB Autism*; printable article #43. http://www.bbbautism.com/pdf/article_43_social_communication_HFA.pdf.

[2] Grandin, Temple. (2006). *Thinking in Pictures: My Life with Autism.* New York, NY: Vintage.

[3] Talking to Yourself out Loud. *Wrong Planet.* http://www.wrongplanet.net/postx85183-0-0.html&sid=f0b42df44c017cc258b70b707081d26d.

[4] From *Adult Children of Alcoholics.* On Psych Page. website. http://www.psychpage.com/learning/library/assess/subabuse2.htm.

[5] Found on *The Essential Simon and Garfunkel.* Sony, 2000.

[6] "For the fog horn when there is no fog." From *Longing Distance by Sarah Hannah.* North Adams, MA: Tupelo Press, 2004; page 61. Reprinted with permission.

[7] Grandin, Temple, & Barron, Sean. (2005). *Unwritten Rules of Social Relationships: Decoding Social Mysteries Through the Unique Perspectives of Autism.* Arlington, TX: Future Horizons, Inc.; page 313.

[8] Ibid., page 376.

[9] Covey, Steven. (1989). *The 7 Habits of Highly Effective People.* New York, NY: Simon & Schuster; pages 32-33.

[10] *Peter, Paul, and Mommy, Too.* Warner Brothers, 1993.

CHAPTER 9

WEDDING –
MARRIAGE VOWS
ASPERGER STYLE

A ndy and I got married at the top of a mountain in the Connecticut Berkshires at the Bartlett family camp, where there is no electricity and no motorized watercraft on the 50-acre lake. It was a small gathering – our immediate families, the minister and his wife, one friend and that friend's guest for each of us, and a bagpiper. Afterwards my new father-in-law and uncle-in-law grilled chicken, and Andy and I floated out onto the lake in an inflatable raft.

For the ceremony itself, we walked up onto the wooden porch of the main cabin of the compound, which only had room for the minister, Andy and me, his brother, and my sister.

We included two readings in the ceremony. One was 1st Corinthians 13, a traditional passage for weddings, and the second a poem called "A Vision" by farmer and essayist Wendell Berry.

Loving the Tasmanian Devil

A Vision[1]

If we will have the wisdom to survive,
to stand like slow-growing trees on a ruined place,
Renewing it, enriching it,
If we will make our seasons welcome here,
Asking not too much of earth or heaven.
Then a long time after we are dead
the lives our lives prepare will live here,
Their houses strongly placed upon the valley sides,
Fields and gardens rich in the windows.
The river will run clear,
as we will never know it,
And over it, birdsong like a canopy.
On the levels of the hills will be green meadows,
Stock bells in noon shade.
On the steeps where greed and ignorance cut down the old forest,
An old forest will stand,
Its rich leaf-fall drifting on its roots.
The veins of forgotten springs will have opened.
Families will be singing in the fields.
In their voices they will hear a music risen out of the ground.
They will take nothing from the ground they will not return,
whatever the grief at parting.
Memory, native to this valley,
will spread over it like a grove,
and memory will grow into legend,
legend into song, song into sacrament.

The abundance of this place,
the songs of its people and its birds,
will be health and wisdom and indwelling light.
This is no paradise or dream.
Its hardship is its possibility.

We chose this poem because we had just purchased our farm in Central New York; it was a "ruined place" indeed. As we stood that last day in June and committed ourselves to each other, we simultaneously committed ourselves to that piece of earth. We pledged to try to have the wisdom to stand like slow-growing trees on that farm and make it thrive, despite all the hardship it would require.

At the time, this seemed like a far bigger challenge than our First Corinthians pledge to each other. We had been together only two years and had gotten engaged a short nine months after first meeting. We were still in the youthful bloom of our relationship, so stunned at the joyous providence of our meeting that we could see no rain clouds on our relationship horizon. Our attraction was so immediate, our interests and values so aligned, our dreams and goals so similar, that it felt like a marriage of soulmates. I could no more *not* commit to this man than cut off an arm.

After our wedding, my father-in-law divulged that he had put a tape recorder under the porch of the cabin to memorialize every word spoken. We accepted this tape with amusement and, unintentionally but quickly, buried it among all the other tapes from our combined college years: The Grateful Dead, *Phantom of the Opera*, Joni Mitchell, Salamander Crossing.

I didn't need to listen to it, however. I knew what we had said. The Wendell Berry poem was framed and hanging in our kitchen. I saw it every day. And it did capture our commitment to the farm, which was both mutual and firm. We would do whatever it took to keep this ship afloat.

During the five years after our wedding, we pretty much did nothing but work, so most of the time we were too exhausted to consider any other options than continuing to hoe the agricultural row we had chosen. My father-in-law had staked his personal financial assets on us, so we were not in a position to fail. In those early years, we did all the physical labor. ALL. In addition, I worked off the farm so that we would have some stable income and health insurance.

I first worked as a reporter for the local newspaper. This had some benefits: I got to know Norwich and its people and businesses very quickly. I was able to case the joint and get paid for it. I got to write, every day, and as fast as I could. Mostly I wrote news stories, but I also wrote some human interest and some editorials (one of the benefits of employment at a really small paper). But the pay was horrendous, and I was completely shocked when they docked my pay for the Friday I took off to travel east for our wedding.

Job number two came from job number one. As a result of covering the Norwich City School District, I was one of the first to hear about its newly created position of public information officer. This would be the same pay as the newspaper for half the hours (and fewer night meetings), and since the superintendent's best friend had gone to Amherst, the college name meant something on my resume; I got the job. I created newsletters, made public service announcements, and wrote articles for the paper. I also got offered a part-time teaching assistant job at the high school in a video production class and there got bitten hard by the teaching bug.

Since the district had a policy of paying for its employees' college classes, I started a master's in secondary English education at night, and inside a year and a half was provisionally certified to teach. I got a teaching post where I had done my student teaching, ending up in one of the best possible careers for the wife of a farmer in rural Central New York.

During this same period of time, the farm grew from 40 sheep to 600. However, we soon realized we could not sell the lambs that we had been promised we could market through a newly formed lamb-growers co-operative and switched over to dairy cows. So before and after my "town job," I was feeding lambs, trimming hooves, raking hay, killing rats, screeding concrete, learning to milk, and fixing fences.

In retrospect, Andy was driven by a combination of Asperger's and fear of disappointing his father. I was driven by the youngest child's thrill at finally feeling useful, and was sustained by the Irish woman's genetic predisposition for extraordinary endurance.

Over time, the hard work paid off on the farm end of things. It took blood, sweat, and tears, literally, from both of us, for many, many years. But things finally started to turn around. I still remember the first day I sat down at my desk and was able to pay all the bills. And then several years later, we were able to dissolve the partnership with Andy's dad and re-sign all the loans in our own names.

Also, the farm started to look beautiful. Fields that had been scrubby and weedy became green and grassy. Buildings that had begun to tilt were righted. Animals that were born as bottom-of-the-barrel "grades" gave birth to increasingly more genetically promising offspring. We mastered every possible metabolic and microbiological cow ailment and rarely lost an animal.

Andy had time to grow flowers and vegetables. I had some time to paint the living room and tear up the ugly old linoleum. There were summer afternoons when we stripped down to our undies and swam in the pond. Gorgeous fall afternoons would find us in the woods under the brilliant maples stacking firewood into the pickup. New fences were straight and strong. Beautiful auburn cattle ambled back to the barn among the Buddhist chime of cowbells. Meadows began to yield abundant barnfuls of nutritious hay.

All this required hard, hard work and sacrifice with no expensive toys, no vacations, no frills, and no time off. But we were young and strong and committed. We did all that Wendell Berry asked us to do, discovering in the process the truth of that last line: The only possibility for making this situation pan out was hardship.

The non-work half of my life was learning how to be a wife to an undiagnosed Aspergian. At the time of our wedding, the second reading, 1st Corinthians 13, seemed like "Yeah, yeah, of course, no problem." I had been raised as a church-goer as had Andy, and we had both heard these words hundreds of times. They were so familiar as to be nearly unhearable: "Love is patient, love is kind and is not jealous; love does not brag and is not arrogant, does not act unbecomingly; it does not seek its own, is not provoked, does not take into account a wrong suffered, does not rejoice in unrighteousness, but rejoices with the truth; bears all things, believes all things, hopes all things, endures all things."[2]

Well, easier said than done. I have never truly doubted my decision to marry Andy, but very early on, I began to realize that Pledge Number Two, to love this man until death did us part, was going to require just as much hard work as to make the farm succeed, especially since some of his behaviors, which had seemed endearing and merely quirky in the early days, began to seem troubling and a little frightening as time went on.

Granted, the stress of starting a farm from scratch was severe, and the pressure of having one of our parents as a financial backer was enough to cause tensions to run high and mannerisms to become strange. Even so, certain of Andy's behaviors began to emerge as really upsetting. Underneath all my running around, manual labor, and completing a master's degree, a part of me was constantly dealing with this troublesome and increasingly distressing "thing" that I could not figure out.

Andy loved me, he needed me, but sometimes he treated me really badly. His reactions to everything were over the top. He would scream at me for the tiniest of offenses and then tell me how much he needed and appreciated me. If something went wrong, he would press the sides of his head like a vise, as if his head was about to blow off. If he got really upset, he would flip over a table, hurl a bucket, or beat something against the ground.

My reaction, child of an alcoholic that I am, was to turn to stone, go somewhere else, and then get really mad. The hay mow became my fuming zone. I would climb in among the bales, sit among the chickens and cats, and steam. When I felt the tirade must be over, I would return to the house. By this point Andy would have calmed down and be looking apologetic. I, however, would be carrying such a grudge that I would not speak for hours, sometimes days. I would clean up his mess in a demonstrative way and then sleep on the couch.

If either set of our parents happened to be visiting, one would think Andy wouldn't behave this way. But he did. He would come slamming in the back door from the barn, stomp through the kitchen in muddy, disgusting boots, swipe a bunch of dishes out of his way, slam some bread into the toaster, tromp into the bathroom, come back out and grab the toast, and then slam back out the door, leaving behind broken or at least fallen dishes, stinky boot prints, an open bread bag, and my stunned parents.

They would give me a look that said, "Do you want to come back to Lockport with us?" but I would just grit my teeth and hug them goodbye.

Even Andy's own mother would say to me, "I don't like the way Andrew talks to you." To which I would reply, "Well, he's under a lot of stress." And she and my father-in-law would pack up their stuff and return to Connecticut.

Most of the time, though, Andy was all I had. The respective parental units were each a four-hour drive in opposite directions. We had just moved to Chenango County, so we had no friends. I had nowhere to go except the hay mow and no one to turn to except Andy. I suppose this was a blessing, since it forced us to rely on each other regardless of our feelings or behaviors.

Exhaustion and non-stop work put a damper on potential couples counseling. It's also very effective birth control. We were both just happy for another person to fall asleep with, someone with whom to watch "Seinfeld" reruns, when we could get the channel to come in.

"When things were good, they were very, very good. But when they were bad, they were horrid," as the saying goes. There was the occasional day of all-out stress-induced marital war, but most of the time we clung to each other like shipwrecked sailors. We had no choice: It was sink or swim together.

It was a good thing that at some point during these years, M. Scott Peck's *The Road Less Traveled*[3] floated by me on the stream of life. I grabbed onto it like a life preserver off *The Titanic.*

Anyone who has read this book will tell you that sentence number one alone will pretty much reorient your world view: "Life is difficult" (which is a restatement of the Buddha's First Noble Truth "Life is suffering"). And you really DO need someone to point this out directly in order to clear up a major misconception propagated in America. For if romantic comedies, *Good Housekeeping*, or a trip through Home Depot is your only source of truth, you definitely get a very different message. There, life is pleasant, clean, and happy, and problems are resolvable in half an hour.

We did not have television or magazine subscriptions in those days, and it's a good thing. Had I been faced every day with happy loving couples, clean floors, and people relaxing by the swimming pool, my mental manipulations toward enduring all this might have been much harder.

While First Corinthians was practically cliché because I had heard it so many times, Peck's definition of love was new to me: "The will to extend oneself for the purpose of nurturing one's own or another's spiritual growth."[4] He says that real love is NOT the "boundary collapse" of romance, when we allow another person in through our barriers and feel blissfully fused with another. It is NOT dependency, of either the wife on the husband or the husband on the wife. It is NOT a feeling, because if so, love would come and go with the vagaries of change.

Peck maintains that real love is so daunting that the passion and ecstasy of early romantic love is practically an evolutionary trick to force us into a commitment we might not rationally make. But what happens when that radiant feeling wears off? What happens when difficulties or unknown disabilities rear their heads? What if we come to hate the person or at least his behaviors? Is that still love?

According to Peck's definition, the answer is yes, if beyond the afterglow, the honeymoon, and the good times, when the sheep dung hits the fan, you still have the "will to extend [your] self for the purpose of nurturing [your] own or an another's spiritual growth."[5] If you decide to do this, it ain't always pretty, and it sure ain't easy!

From his experience of many years of counseling, Peck outlines what real love involves. First: Attention. Caring about the person and his concerns. For the wife of an Aspergian, this is especially tough. One of the commonly mentioned Asperger symptoms is the tendency of the Aspergian to go on and on past the point of others' tolerance about his special interest topic. How many fishing lures can I want to know about? A common thought passing through my head during one of Andy's angling addresses is "Does this man never shut up?" The complementary Aspie trait is the person's seeming disinterest in other people's concerns. See the paradox? The wife of an Aspergian must be attentive to her husband's endless discussion of his interests but not expect him to be interested in hers.

One trick I have had to learn is what the Bartlett family (ironically enough) calls "undivided." A long-standing tradition for the Bartletts is that each person unwraps his Christmas present enjoying the undivided attention of everyone else. I try to do this with conversations, at least for the first five minutes. I get the basics of drift fishing or Chinooks versus steelheads, and then I let my mind go where it pleases. After all, I only have so much mind to go around. I am usually able, upon quizzing, to answer the fundamental questions correctly and so demonstrate loving attention. And I must admit that when Andy is attentive to my own babblings (which by my nature are rare occurrences), he has a phenomenal memory for minute details.

Love, Peck says, also involves Discipline. I guess this is where I get reciprocation for my extraordinarily onerous burden on the attention requirement. An Aspergian is nothing if not disciplined. Andy and I recently had a disagreement about this one. I had driven out of Norwich and the ten miles home knowing I should have gotten fuel in the truck, but I didn't. (Actually, I weighed Andy's *possible* screaming over the low fuel light against *definite* screaming over my being late and opted to avoid the nearer occasion of scream. I had also built in an intended next-day early-morning gas mission that would prevent even the second scream.)

However, Andy found this out the next morning, and he blew his top. Why? Because for him the true definition of love is disciplined care for another even when you don't want to do what that takes. Andy will go out into the freezing cold in the dark and pour diesel into the house tank to make sure we are warm all night. He would never drive away from the possibility of buying fuel on less than a quarter tank. He feels I have practically punched him in the gut if I fail to take care of something on behalf of the family.

So I guess I accept Andy's lack of Attention and Andy accepts my lack of Discipline.

The other pair of lessons where we have negotiated a trade-off are what Peck calls the Risk of Independence and the Risk of Commitment. Because of the Aspergian's inherent anxiety and difficulty spontaneously performing called-for decision-making and multi-tasking skills, Andy is very dependent on me. For many years, it was hard for me to go away for more than a day because Andy could get really flustered in my absence. He feared he would have to respond to something unexpected and would not be able to handle it. In contrast, I learned to NOT depend on him for anything I might need done quickly or spontaneously. I learned to deal with most problems on my own. Independence, for me, alleviated the stress of my asking for Andy's impromptu help and getting berated.

However, on commitment, Andy's got me beat. That man has had his shoulder to the grindstone for twenty years straight and never shirked. NEVER. His commitment to the farm seems like mania at times, but the underlying reason is his commitment to me, and to our kids. This is rare and appreciated. I am the queen of up-and-down – hormones, dilettantism – I'm up, I'm down, I'm round-and-round. But Andy is dependably solid as a rock when he has committed to something.

The biggest lesson I had to learn from M. Scott Peck is what he calls the Risk of Confrontation. I was raised to *not* confront. If anything, I was raised to avoid confrontation at all costs. Better to work around the problem than risk hard feelings with a conflict. Furthermore, Andy is big. Andy is loud. Andy is extraordinarily articulate. In a verbal argument, he will win every time. Besides which, Andy is seven years older than I am. For many, many years, I accepted whatever he said and whatever he planned. What did I know? Nothing about farming. Nothing about finance. Nothing about relationships. I accepted Andy's lead in all things. If we got in a dispute, I either figured I was wrong or endured my resentment by stomping in the hay mow.

That was until I started to realize that Andy wasn't always right. Sometimes he was dead wrong. For example, one year he bought a new forage chopper without talking to me first. I got home from work and there it was, sitting in the driveway. I have always done the accounting and checkbook balancing, so I knew we could not afford this purchase. So I took him on, all five feet and two inches of me to his six-feet plus. At the end, he called the dealership, and someone came and took the chopper away. Later Andy thanked me and told me I had been right.

This was a precedent, and I have since become increasingly confident about taking him on when I know he is in the wrong. Often I must endure some slammed doors, peeling tires, and Andy disappearing for half an hour. But we've gotten better at fighting and at fighting fair.

Back to First Corinthians. Paul says love is patient and kind; it is not jealous; it does not brag and is not arrogant nor acts unbecomingly; does not seek its own, is not provoked, does not take into account a wrong suffered, does not rejoice in unrighteousness; bears all things, believes all things, hopes all things, endures all things.

In contrast, the typical Aspergian is often impatient and unintentionally unkind, jealous, bragadocious and arrogant and rude, seemingly self-absorbed and easily provoked, carries a grudge, and has difficulty bearing things, believing things, hoping things and enduring things. So what does one do? What does a wife do when her husband is physiologically incapable of living out a vow he has made?

Well, I made the vow, too. And as any good kindergarten teacher will tell her students, "Don't worry about what *Andy* is doing, just worry about what *you* are doing."

And Jesus said the same thing. "Why do you look at the speck of sawdust in your brother's eye and pay no attention to the plank in your own eye?" Now, let's be fair. The Aspie has the plank and the NT has the speck when it comes to negative behaviors. This is biological fact. BUT I can roll with the idea of dealing with my own specks and leaving Andy to deal with his own specks and planks.

And it has been those very planks that have shown me my own woody flecks. It was Andy's excessive and almost involuntary confrontation that showed me my fear of confrontation and my need to overcome it. Andy's maniacal discipline acts as a foil for my own tendency toward disorder, which I need to work on. Andy's passion for discussing his interests ad infinitum contrasts with my customary muteness and makes me question it.

If nothing else, an Aspergian marriage is like devotion boot camp. You know why the spiritual greats had to survive extended time in the desert? It makes you tough. It prepares you to withstand all hardships. It strengthens your spiritual muscles. It trains you for the Olympics of life. Having survived twenty years already, I am the Olympic athlete of wives. I am the slow-growing tree of wifedom, and when I become a mighty oak some day, I will shelter the little seedlings in my shade. Its hardship is its possibility.

[1]   Berry, Wendell. (1998). A Vision. From *The Selected Poems of Wendell Berry*. Berkeley, CA: Counterpoint; page 102. Reprinted with permission.

[2]   First Corinthians 13: 4-7. *The Holy Bible. New American Standard Version.* (1997). La Habra, CA: The Lockman Foundation.

[3]   Peck, M. Scott. (1988). *The Road Less Traveled.* Austin, TX: Touchstone.

[4]   Ibid., page 81.

[5]   Ibid.

CHAPTER 10

ASPERGER AIKIDO – LOSS OF HOPE AND MOVING BEYOND IT

When my sister and I lived in Japan for a year back in the 80s, she attended aikido class once a week, and I would tag along. Aikido is a Japanese style of martial arts that focuses less on attack moves and relies on redirecting the energy of the attacker as a way to defend oneself.

At the weekly sessions, I watched the *sensei* (master teacher) teach students in full-length skirt-like hakama pants to block and counter each other and throw themselves or their opponent to the floor to either attack or prevent attack. I never partook in this back then, but in a sense I do now – and not by choice. Let me present an example.

I awake slowly in the morning, stretch, float downstairs, pour a cup of coffee, read a little – get my soul on straight. And then I hear the back door slam and Andy's boots stomping across the mudroom floor. I brace myself.

Loving the Tasmanian Devil

I am having one of those days when Tazberger Syndrome is really ticking me off. To make it worse, now that I know about AS, everything I used to hurl at Andy as an accusation returns back to me as a clinical description from Dr. Asperger in his white coat or one of his modern-day successors.

"You overreact to everything!!!!!" I scream or think very loudly.

"That's right. People with Asperger's have extreme reactions to perceived threats," calmly responds the tiny Dr. Asperger on my right shoulder.

"You go from nothing immediately into the red zone!!!!!!"

"That's right. Aspergians go from no emotion to the most extreme emotion with no stops in between."

"You're spinning so fast you don't even hear me!!!!!!"

"That's right. Those with Asperger's feel so bombarded with sensation that they can be incapable of hearing or seeing anything around them."

"It's like you have no concept of the fact that I had a tough day too, and that I might be feeling something!!!!!!!"

"That's right. Aspergians have very limited ability to create a theory of mind for someone else – that is, walking in somebody else's shoes."

And so, in one of my days of rage, everything I once accused Andy of as an offense is now countered through redirecting the force of my attack and neutralizing it. I end up in a heap in the corner, hurled down onto the floor after another session of Asperger aikido.

So who's to blame for my bumps and bruises? Me! My anger. Not to blame really, but it's futile. What use is my antagonism except to have it turned back on me? However, these accusations verbalize the traits that bother me, that make me feel sorry for myself, that make me wish at times I was not married to an Aspie. So, I research Aikido to see why I am losing and how I can win.

I find that the one being attacked, the *nage*, blends with the attack and controls its energy. This is why I keep losing. My attack energy is controlled and used against me. I attempt a complaint about behavior and then remember that the behavior is a symptom of the syndrome. The *uke*, that's me, the attacker, must "become calm and flexible in the disadvantageous, off-balance positions in which *nage* places them."[1]

Hmmm. Disadvantageous and off-balance. That's my position to a T. Disadvantageous because it is now difficult to complain. It's like the wife of someone with multiple sclerosis screaming, "You never walk right any more!!!!" Off-balance, because now I don't know how to handle these issues: Do I ignore? Do I retrain? Do I leave? Do I get mad?

I'm like Muley Graves and his son in the film version of *The Grapes of Wrath*,[2] told they must leave their sharecropper's homestead by The Man from the bank.

> MULEY: You mean get off my own land?
> THE MAN: Now don't go to blaming me. It ain't my fault.
> SON: Whose fault is it, then?
> THE MAN: You know who owns the land – the Shawnee
>   Land and Cattle Company.
> MULEY: Who's the Shawnee Land and Cattle Comp'ny?
> THE MAN: It ain't nobody. It's a company.

SON: They got a pres'dent, ain't they? They got somebody that knows what a shotgun's for, ain't they?

THE MAN: Son, it ain't his fault, because the bank tells him what to do.

SON: (angrily) All right. Where's the bank?

THE MAN: Tulsa. But what's the use of picking on him? He ain't anything but the manager, and he's half crazy hisself, trying to keep up with his orders from the east!

MULEY: (bewildered) Then who do we shoot?

Here's my version.

MAUREEN: You mean Andy's always going to be like this?

DR. ASPERGER: Now don't go to blaming him. It ain't his fault.

MAUREEN: Whose fault is it, then?

DR. ASPERGER: You know what Asperger's is, it's a difference in the amygdala.

MAUREEN: Can't you fix a difference in the amygdala?

DR. ASPERGER: There ain't nothing to fix. It's a difference.

MAUREEN: He's got frontal lobes, ain't he? He got brains enough to know what a shotgun's for, ain't he?

DR. ASPERGER: It ain't his fault; his genetics made him that way.

MAUREEN: (angrily) All right. Where's his genetics?

DR. ASPERGER: Coded into his DNA. But what's the use of picking on Andy? He ain't anything but the behaviors, and he's half crazy hisself, trying to keep up with his orders from the amygdala!

MAUREEN: (bewildered) Then who do I shoot?

That's me some days, brandishing my loaded shotgun, looking for a target, and it's elusive. Asperger's is not something you can see, much less cure. And it's certainly not Andy's fault. He's just the bank manager in Tulsa, keeping up with orders from Amygdala Central out East. So, no help here using analogies from the West, Wild or not. Gotta look East, son, for dealing with this opponent.

Ah, those cunning Buddhists. Aikido, as a form of martial arts, is primarily defensive, its goal to "control aggression without inflicting injury," in other words "the Art of Peace." Argh. Another life lesson. Another cross to bear. Is this what I am to learn from Asperger's as my opponent? The Art of Peace? When all I want is to rant and scream that I am tired of the dramas and the lack of empathy and the spinning? I suppose so.

So what can the *uke* do? According to Wikipedia (cited begrudgingly through the gritted teeth of the English teacher), *uke* will sometimes apply reversal techniques to regain balance and pin or throw *nage*.[3] Ah, yes, the old reversal technique. Moms are good at that. Let's play that scene again:

"People with Asperger's have extreme reactions to perceived threats."

"Wow, honey. You really handled that well. You didn't overreact to that ketchup bottle falling over and not spilling."

"Aspergians go from no emotion to the most extreme emotion with no stops in between."

"Good job, honey. You came out of the red zone so quickly! Only five minutes! Next time maybe it will only take you four."

"Those with Asperger's feel so bombarded with sensation that they can be literally incapable of hearing or seeing anything around them."

"Sweetie, good job going into the office and closing the door. That's a great way to decrease sensory overload until you're ready to join the family again."

"Aspergians have limited ability to create a theory of mind for someone else."

"How nice of you to call and find out how my day is going. You remembered that I had a meeting with my boss this morning."

Actually, Andy does remember things like that. He remembers everything, and he does care about me and note my emotions, such as when I feel tense about things. It just takes longer and requires more effort because those data are competing with every other problem in the universe: the cow with hypocalcemia, the supply of corn silage, the meeting of the Federal Reserve, the political situation in Chile, the principal-interest balance on the chopper, our feed-to-milk ratio and profitability benchmarks, the water temperature in Lake Ontario, when to call the carpenter to build the deck, the oil level in my Jeep, the makeup of the Senate Ag Committee, when to order grain, whether Hank remembered to close the manure spreader door, etc., etc., etc.

And Andy did call the other day to ask me how a meeting went. He had written it on his list: "11:45 – Call Mo. 12 Vet check." That was sweet. He was abrupt, but that was his form of love. In the midst of his swirling bombardment of inputs, my face whirled by and caught his eye. He prioritized me on his daily list and looked at his watch twenty-two times to stop exactly at 11:45 and call.

"The meeting was fine. He just wanted my input on something."

"Good. OK. I've gotta go, the vet's here."

"OK. Love ya."

"Yep. Bye."

All righty then. I pick myself up off the floor, brush off my hakama, and bow.

"*Domo arigato, Asperger Sensei.* Thank you, Master."

[1] Homma, Gaku. (1990). *Aikido for Life*. Berkeley, CA: North Atlantic Books; pages 20-30.

[2] *The Grapes of Wrath.* (1940). 20th Century Fox, directed by John Fox. You can read the whole screenplay at http://www.dailyscript.com/scripts/grapes_of_wrath.html.

[3] "Aikido." Wikipedia. http://en.wikipedia.org/wiki/Aikido.

CHAPTER 11

NOT YOUR NEUROTYPICAL GUY – ASPERGIAN BLINDNESS TO GENDER STEREOTYPES

I have a confession to make: I have tracked down every single one of my old boyfriends or potential boyfriends on the Internet: current job, address, and, where possible, photograph. I am hoping this is something most women do and not just another symptom of my neurosis. It's probably more a symptom of PMS. Grrrrrrr ... Look what I passed up. Look at the life I could have had: Wife of a cardiac surgeon. Wife of a securities lawyer. Wife of an English professor. Wife of a chemical engineer.

But I will say this: They have almost all lost their hair. Andy has not.

When I think back to each of these guys, now men, I remember that in most cases I was the one who broke off the relationship or never pursued it or let it fizzle. I had at least a shot at life with each of them if I had wanted it badly enough. But when I met Andy, it was so obvious he was the one I wanted. Even back then, I knew about his more "unusual" traits, even if I didn't have a name or reason for them. But he was the one I wanted. He was the one I chose. After we met, all those other choices faded from my view. There was never a time when I balanced Andy against any of these others for comparison's sake or kept any of them on the back burner, just in case. Andy was instantaneous and exclusive.

Looking back now at those prior boyfriends in contrast with my actual espoused, I can understand my choice. Not that I had a ton of boyfriends, but several of these relationships were intense enough that the person in question might have been a serious contender for my hand. And they were all very nice young men: interesting, sweet. I never dated a jerk and then threw him on the heap.

If anything, I have a desire to call up some of these guys and apologize for my cluelessness. I didn't hit physiological puberty until age eighteen and so was a complete neophyte at love throughout college. My body was leading the charge most of the time, with the brain and any sense of proper behavior in a romantic relationship lagging behind. By the time I met Andy, I was twenty-two and somewhat over the intense, hormone-driven years that most girls have well out of the way by sixteen. Body and mind were working in tandem by that point.

When I think back to these dear young men and consider why none of them seemed worth the quest, and why Andy did, I realize that I was not really interested in the "typical" guy. I guess I wasn't even interested in the "neurotypical" guy. Several of the Aspie wife books analyze the reasons why a woman will fall in love with an Aspergian, and I tend to agree with the analysis.

Maxine Aston points out that many women in this situation are attracted to the fact that most Aspie males are gentle, somewhat naïve and boyish, and have a more developed female side than most typical males. Our AS partners have no problem with cooking or growing flowers. "They do not feel obligated to fulfill and display masculine roles, but are much more likely to do what pleases them, rather than what society states they are supposed to do … Many women interpret this as meaning that they are sure enough of their masculinity to be in touch with their feminine side as well."[1]

Too true. One exemplar event I can share was before my time, but I know that the purple cotton skirt I wore while pregnant was once Andy's. I heard that he attended a college party wearing it, and most of the women said he looked great. This was during the same period of time that Andy was the lone male student in a class on feminism. I can envision Andy wearing a kilt, especially since he is half Scottish. In fact, I would be quite interested in seeing this. There is something about the thought of a studly guy with big muscles and the strongest looking arms I have ever seen wearing a skirt. Like Mel Gibson in *Brave Heart*. Confidence.

I have always found myself put off by the really "typical" males and their interests. Sports. Blondes. Competition. Swagger. It all seems so predictable, so scripted. As if they cannot help but like these things. As if they are but metazoans, responding by stimulus-response to a passing woman or ESPN. They can't not.

It kind of repulses me when the frontal lobes shut down and the cerebellum takes over. I feel that way about a lot of societal behaviors. Like that scene in *To Kill a Mockingbird* when Scout faces down the mob of men that has arrived outside Tom Robinson's cell ready to lynch him. They are armed and agitated and ready for action until Scout greets Mr. Cunningham by name.[2] As the men turn back into individuals instead of a mob, they shame-facedly creep away. Where did their brains go during that time? Were they not – during that time – homo sapiens, "thinking man"? Did brain turn off and spinal cord take over?

I also see this when most guys are watching sports. They can't not react. What is that? It almost makes me sick, like seeing de-evolution happening right in front of me. They regress from being full cognates back into some kind of Neanderthals with limited brain function. But Andy is not like that. Yeah, he'll watch the random sports event, and we have turned the Super Bowl into a family party in the name of cultural literacy. But he doesn't follow any sports team. He doesn't play any kind of organized sport. He has no discomfort wearing a skirt, and, God bless him, he thinks Keira Knightley – as well as many other Hollywood "beauties" – is ugly.

He will look at her in her separate elements and say, "She is not at all beautiful. In fact, she is quite strange-looking. She looks like an anorexia warning poster." This comes from the Aspergian trait of seeing all the details instead of the whole, and in addition being impervious and immune to society's coding.

This coding-blindness is a trait of Andy's I truly love. Having suffered through an eating disorder in high school, I just want to jump up and hug Andy over his ability to look at women's bodies so objectively. He'll see a model on the cover of a women's magazine, frown, and say, "She is truly odd-looking." This is the benefit of Aspergians having difficulty "gestalting" a set of images into the package society prescribes. Ha! Corporate psychology thwarted!

Andy also had some bad experiences in college with "beautiful women" who used their looks as social weaponry. Thus, his aversion to blondes. This is good news for me. Being short, Irish and, therefore, stocky, with mouse-colored hair, I am not by any means society's beauty ideal. But Andy saw through that. I have fairly nice eyes, and I suppose I am what Aston describes as "strong, independent, and nurturing,"[3] the Aspergian male's ideal mate.

But I am also a social rebel, shunning my female birth-right to become a high-maintenance trophy wife (which, in my case, would have required living at the gym, plastic surgery on every part of my body, and full-time, live-in beauticians) in favor of becoming an English geek who has no problem being covered with manure. Andy and I saw in each other a mutual distaste for society's lifestyle and attractiveness norms.

This is why I am sometimes amazed that Andy is good-looking. I did not set out to marry a handsome man. I admit to being attracted to his physical appearance, but it was quickly overshadowed by his, shall we say, unique personality and sometimes odd behaviors. So sometimes I'll see other women ogling him in the grocery store and turn with surprise to notice the figure he cuts. Over six feet tall, dirty-blond hair still all there, long strong limbs from working on the farm, a square jaw and deep-set eyes, a wicked tan (though it stops at the shirtsleeves, ladies), and, when I force him into them, Levi's and an outdoorsy plaid shirt that makes him look like a buff lumberjack who could carry off his girlie with one hand.

At such times, I'll step over and grab his arm or give him a wifely and possessive smile. Back off, girls. This one's mine. English Major: 1. Blonde Bombshell: 0.

Oh sure, once in a while I find myself screaming silently, "Can't you just pretend to be a normal guy?" but most of the time I am quite content with my Yin-Yang Man. Maxine Aston says that "Your partner can offer you a special kind of security that, in these days of high rates of divorce and separation, is very hard to find. He will probably stick by you for all your life."[4] And I know that this is true. Once Andy had made up his mind to choose me, that was it. And I know that he chose me for the very things I feel most make me me. The genetic gifts I feel best about are my fairly high intelligence (from my dad), my passion for words (also from dad), my ability to withstand hardship for long periods of time (the unfortunate but time-honored characteristic of most Irish), my wit when it's up and running, and my underground rebelliousness. It's as if Andy sees past my physical me and sees my essence, and that's what he loves.

As a woman in the 21st century, it still can come as surprise to me to be treated this way, even by my spouse. If the tabloids at the grocery checkout are any kind of reflection of society's feminine ideal, I'm apparently not even of the correct species. I'm not blonde. I'm not thin. I'm not tan. I'm not beautiful. Even the local farmers in the area – the supposed salt of the earth – have been known to take up with a hottie and give the long-suffering and physically depleted farmwife the boot. Even they wouldn't give me a second look. And forget finding any welcoming arms among the ultra-hip soccer moms and dads.

It truly is a blessing to be married to someone who sees through all that, who can turn off society's encoded responses and say, "That woman looks just like a b%*@h in high heels," and instead adore the plain but well-intentioned woman that I hope I am. Yeah, Andy's not your typical guy. He's not even your neurotypical guy. He follows the road less traveled, wearing a skirt and blind to the blondes, and that – for me – has made all the difference.[5]

[1] Aston, Maxine. (2002). *The Other Half of Asperger Syndrome: A Guide to an Intimate Relationship with a Partner who has Asperger Syndrome.* Overland Park, KS: AAPC Publishing; page 29.

[2] Lee, Harper. (1988). *To Kill a Mockingbird.* New York, NY: HarperPerennial.

[3] Aston, *The Other Half of Asperger Syndrome*, page 29.

[4] Ibid., page 77.

[5] Robert Frost. (1990). *The Road Not Taken. Great American Poetry.* New York, NY: Gallery Books; page 575.

CHAPTER 12

THE MUTUAL-SUFFERING POLICY –
EMPATHY AND
THE LACK THEREOF

Over the years, I have looked several times at the printed copy of our wedding vows. I have looked through the partnership agreement for the farm. I even looked through our copy of *The Joy of Sex*[1] and I can't find it. But it seems that somewhere, some time, I must have signed a Mutual-Suffering Policy, promising that whenever Andy was suffering something – hard work, a long day, frustration – I would suffer equally. If my own realms of teaching, family of origin, or physiology offered no equivalent suffering at the time, then I should join in Andy's. I do not remember signing this agreement, but I am nevertheless held to its strictures.

Let me give you an example. It was mid-April and little baby Eldest was a month old. Just prior to his birth, I had finished my student teaching and was newly certified to teach. I was watching the newspaper to apply for my first teaching job to start in September; in fact, I had been told of a job posting with a big smile by the principal at the school where I had student taught. I knew I would have a job come fall, but I was home at the time on unpaid maternity leave. Also, I was still recovering from a Cesarean section. My parents and Andy's parents had already been to see Eldest, their first grandchild, and after staying a week or so while I got back on my feet, had dispersed to their own homes, four hours' drive away.

It was about a week before Easter, and I was in the kitchen coloring eggs with a Paz kit on the kitchen table. Little Eldest was in his windup swing next to me. He was watching and I was talking to him and I believe we were listening to my personalized music mix called "Eldest's Dance Tunes" on the stereo. It was cold and snowy out, winter's last hurrah before pulling out for good.

All of a sudden the back door opened and then slammed shut. Andy stomped through the mudroom and up the two stairs and slammed through the back door into the kitchen.

Then he stopped and glared. "What are YOU doing!?!?!' he thundered.

"Eldest and I are dying Easter eggs," I replied meekly.

"Easter eggs?!?!?" he screamed incredulously.

And in one quick movement, Andy had tipped over the kitchen table, sending Paz-laden vinegar, white and colored eggs, and anything else that had been on the table crashing to the floor and skittering to the far edges of the room. Eldest started crying.

"You Sit up Here in This Warm House While I Am Down Working My ASS off in the Freezing Cold Barn? Coloring Easter Eggs?!?!?!"

"What would you like me to be doing?" I ventured quietly, taking Eldest out of his swing and trying to shush his screams of terror.

"I Don't Know! You Can't F-ing Help Me! Between Your F-ing Surgery and the Baby, I Don't Know How I Am Supposed to Keep up With the Work Around Here!"

Andy kicked a chair out of his way and stormed back out the door and toward the barn. Little Eldest calmed down, and I prayed that this memory would just be filed with "Loud Noises" along with the vacuum cleaner and the smoke alarm.

I look back on all this now and think, "Oh. Yeah. Asperger's." But back then, I broke down in tears. I was twenty-seven years old, far from my family, with a newborn baby, a farm, and a husband who flipped over tables.

I had no choice. I loved this little warm, soft baby Scootie like nothing I had ever loved, and I knew that if push ever came to shove, it would be me and the kid, long gone. But I also knew that I had made a commitment to the farm and to this man. I was not about to give up and go running home. And running home wasn't even possible since we didn't have a vehicle that could make the four-hour drive to our closest relatives.

Also, what was so consistently baffling about these scenes was that a mere hour later, Andy would come creeping hang-dog back into the house, pick up whatever was left on the floor, and put his head on my lap. Then he would pick up little Eldest and hold him gently in the rocking chair until they both fell asleep.

Whatever that sudden hurricane of emotion had been, it was completely gone. A true butt-hole, a man who sincerely resented the baby and me for my "life of leisure," would feel that way straight on through. For example, I heard of a woman who got pregnant against her husband's wishes, and he hung signs around the house saying "Dump It" for all nine months. Now THAT's a butt-hole!

Andy was not that, and he was always apologetic after one of these scenes.

"I'm sorry, Mo."

Silence from me.

"Will you forgive me?"

"I guess so. Wouldn't it be easier to just *not* act that way and save yourself the hour of apologies?"

"Why don't you go nurse Eldest, and I'll get dinner ready."

"OK."

Nursing also meant reading, which was always a welcome escape. I would position Eldest to the left, let him attach, put my book in my left hand, and use my right to turn pages. I read all of *David Copperfield* this way after Middle was born.

With Eldest, I read the end chapters of *What to Expect When You're Expecting*, which fills you in on all the bizarre things that happen post-partum: the week of bleeding no one warns you about, the incredible pain of engorgement, moving your bowels again after much anaesthesia and the wonders of prune juice, hair loss, that weird poodgy skin that remains on your stomach, the difficulties of walking after having layers of skin and muscle and uterus cut open, getting the staples taken out, mastitis (which I only knew in its bovine form), chapping (the nipple variety), the slowly shrinking uterus.

I had also read every page of months One through Nine. (Oh, the strangeness – bleeding gums? Gorgeous hair? Who'd have guessed?) And my parents had sent me a video of *The Miracle of Birth*. I was very in the know.

Andy, on the other hand, was not. Granted, he grew up in a medical family, he was a biochemistry major, he knew this process in dairy cows inside and out (very much the same, right down to length of gestation). So he probably didn't need to brush up. Perhaps he also felt that there was nothing he could do: It was *my* body after all. It would have been like reading the service manual for a Toyota when you owned a Ford. What would be the purpose? It would just be an inefficient use of his time.

I had initially gone to Planned Parenthood after my first skipped period because I didn't have enough money to buy a pregnancy test. Also, I was terrified. I felt weird physically. We hadn't exactly planned this – although we both had agreed to that night's game of Russian Roulette. So alone in Norwich, in the absence of sister or mother or friend or husband (busy

at home on the farm), I stopped at Planned Parenthood so at least someone could hold my hand. The flaming pink cross was pretty clear-cut. I
thanked the woman, who was very kind, accepted a pile of pamphlets,
and drove home stunned.

Andy knew about my appointment, so he immediately came out the
front door when he heard me pull in. It was a hot July afternoon so the
car windows were down.

With a look of trepidation he said, "So … what's up?"

"It's up," I replied. I did not even turn off the car, much less get out. I
had to leave immediately anyway to get to a night class for my master's.

Andy stood looking concerned and apprehensive, but then slowly a
grin began to spread over his face.

"We're going to have a baby," he said.

I'm going to have a baby, I thought, and I already feel awful.

"I've got to get going," I said.

"OK. I'll have dinner ready when you get back."

"OK. Bye." And I pulled out.

My first tri-mester was rough. I was exhausted. I puked every morning – one time in the car. I remember finishing the evening milking and
then curling up in an empty cow stall on the hay and falling asleep. Right
through my ninth month, I milked into stainless steel bucket milkers and
poured each forty-pound one into the dumping station, from which the

milk ran through a long hose through the barn into the bulk tank. We have photos of me in my ratty old purple sweater looking just large, lugging around huge stainless steel milk cans. I even sat down on the floor in the cows' maternity pen, boots against the cow's hind end, and pulled out a calf the week before I went into labor myself.

Now, let me admit that we had no choice through all this. We HAD a dairy farm. We WERE alone with no hired help. I WAS capable of doing chores – plenty of women worldwide pause in the fields, give birth, tie the baby around them, and go back to harvesting. So I felt rather heroic, rather pioneer, rather Germanic hippie. It felt good to live down my Youngest Child status and show the world what I was capable of: She teaches, She milks, She gets a master's degree, She cleans the house. I got a bit of a can-do buzz off the whole experience.

But there were times when I felt very lonely. To give a comparison, our current hired hand recently dislocated his shoulder, and his wife AND daughter went with him to every single physical therapy appointment afterwards. When I was pregnant, I went to every single pre-natal visit alone. After all, would the Toyota owner expect the Ford owner to accompany her on tune-ups or service calls on the Toyota? Why?

But, to be fair, Andy was running the farm alone, and it was a twelve-mile drive from the farm to the obstetrician. If he would have accompanied me, he would have had to take a shower and wash his hair, and for what? For a fifteen-minute weigh-in, uterine measurement, "How are you feeling?" and quick heartbeat listen. When the continued survival of the farm was on the line? No, I don't think so.

I do think this is part of an Aspergian philosophy of life. Andy was keeping the farm going to provide for Little Scootie. The two hours of shower, clothes change, drive to town, holding of hand, drive back, clothes change, and return to barn could have spelled disaster in the form of financial ruin. And to what end? There was nothing he could practically accomplish by being with me.

So we each did our duty. I was hormonal. I was alone. I was scared. I felt awful. I was suffering. However, I am also a stoic, and tried to keep this all under wraps. I also knew Andy's tendency to overreact. Here's what a scene might have looked like, starting with me:

"I don't feel good."

"What do you mean!?! What's wrong!?!? Are you in labor!?!?"

"No, no. I just feel crummy."

"So … what? Do you need to stop milking?!?! I can't milk right now! I need to finish feeding and then fix that water line!!! I won't be in the house until midnight!!!! I have to get up at 4 AM!!!! Could you at least make dinner!?!?! I need to eat, you know!!! I've been working all day in the freezing cold!!!"

Read this all as Fear, Fear, Fear, Aspergian Fear. Fear for my condition, fear he would not be able to complete all the work, fear the farm would fail.

At the time, I read such a scene as the pulling out of the Mutual-Suffering Policy: HE was suffering; in fact, he was suffering more than I was, and my suffering was in no way comparable to his. And now that I understand the emotional and sense-perception relay system of the Aspergian brain, I have to admit that, perhaps his suffering was worse. I was scared, yes. But he was terrified. Terrified of his father, of the enormity of the farm endeavor, of upcoming fatherhood, of keeping the house warm, of the strange thing his wife had become. We're talking TERROR, and I was experiencing mere discomfort.

"No! Never mind. Really, I'm fine. I'm fine. Go back to feeding. I'll finish the milking."

I learned it was better to avoid these scenes by staying mum. At the time, I just figured that he knew better than I (he was seven years older and the Ag major, after all), so I just assumed I was being weak and I bucked up and continued on.

I don't know how Andy managed my first labor. When I stood up from a nap and amniotic fluid gushed out of me all over the floor, he immediately drove me to the hospital, where they told me yes, you're underway. Go home, get some sleep, and come back in eight hours. So we did. We returned home, called the grandparents, Andy did chores, we ate some dinner. I slept with my stopwatch nearby and timed the contractions.

When they were four minutes apart, I picked up my bag, smiled beatifically, and said it was time to go. At the hospital, the nurse looked at my smiling face, realized from my smiles that I was still a long way off, kindly did not tell me this, and asked if I preferred to stay at the hospital.

"Yes, I think I'd better," I said with a calmly concerned look. "I must be getting close if the contractions are four minutes apart."

The nurse patted my hand, deftly hid her look of "Oh, honey, you don't even know what's coming," and handed me a gown.

Andy went back home since his excited family had arrived by now, and his mom the RN volunteered to stay with me. And then the real pain began. I had a nine-pound baby in my five-foot-two self, and he was not very anxious to come out. When active labor finally did begin, I could hardly believe it. How was it possible for this much pain to be normal? You want to talk suffering? I was in labor for a total of thirty-six hours, and my cervix did not want to dilate. In fact, Andy milked the herd THREE TIMES during my labor, at twelve-hour intervals. I knew Andy was coming and going, but his mom was the one who held me through the contractions, which were getting so painful that I could not help but moan in agony. So much for Frontier Woman.

My midwife had me try everything under the sun: standing in the shower, walking around, taking a warm bath. We started a pitocin drip to induce dilation, and did that make the pain worse! I was practically delirious after twenty-four hours of this. And when the beta strep infection was detected, the obstetrician arrived, all smiles and started suiting up. They wheeled me off, with Andy holding my hand. The horrendous pressure of that epidural entering my spine (think Winston at the Ministry of Love in *1984*) was the best thing that happened because all the pain stopped.

Andy was a trooper and the best possible person in the OR. When they finally rolled me off to surgery, he was so excited. He scrubbed up and donned his blue surgical garb and mask. It was Return of Pre-Med Man. He chatted pharmaceuticals with the anesthesiologist and internal organs with the obstetrician. He held my hand and smiled and peeked back and forth from my ashen face to what was happening on the other side of the curtain they had erected to prevent me from watching the horror of a scalpel slicing me open and a slimy, bloody baby being pushed out the breach.

I heard little Eldest scream, saw Andy's child-like and exuberant grin of pure delight, said hello to my little (well, rather big) red, slimy lovely baby, and zonked out into la-la land when they hit me with a general anesthetic to put me all back together.

My father-in-law, the ace photographer, got pictures of everything I missed: Andy giving Eldest a bath, Andy with a huge grin holding Eldest in his little cap, my wonderful midwife smiling at his side, my mother-in-law with tears in her eyes, my fabulous sister-in-law who had made the journey to hold her first nephew, and then finally me, groggy and numb, with little Eldest greedily attached to my udder.

I was in the hospital for almost a week. I did not believe them when they told me that getting up and walking was a good idea. I also had to wait until my vital organs started performing their regular duties again. Actually, being in the hospital was fabulous: clean sheets, meals brought to me, nurses taking the baby so I could nap, forty-seven channels on the TV, reading whenever I chose, someone washing the floor. I would have loved to stay but insurance companies won't let you play hotel at the hospital.

Home we went, through walls of snow, and within six weeks I was in the barn again, just a little, but enough to think I might have ripped myself open after I lifted a bucket of milk replacer and felt A Very Bad Feeling in my lower abdomen. Luckily, I had merely awakened a muscle that had not been used in a while.

Pregnancies two and three were both nail-biters. Middle, in utero, went through three obstetricians due to a series of licensure issues and loss of delivery privileges. I was not assigned the final obstetrician until two days after my due date, but she was a peach. C-section number two went off without a hitch, the obvious route when Ms. Cervix decided to once again stall the proceedings.

Pregnancy three was NOT planned, and happened at a very bad time. We kept it a secret for months, fearing stern scoldings from our parents. Around that time, Eldest and Middle were four and two, respectively, and were into everything, getting hurt at every possible moment. That summer I was at the emergency room four times: One time I walked in with Eldest in an arm cast, Middle with roseola, and me about to pop. The nurse looked from one of us to the other and said, "Which one of you are we seeing today?"

Andy *was* with me through an awful alpha-fetal-protein debacle. I was seeing yet another obstetrician, and I KNEW he had my due date wrong. Because I was over thirty, we had decided to do the alpha fetal protein test, which came back indicating the possibility of Down's Syndrome. We (all four and a half of us) went on the one-hour journey to the big specialty hospital where a high-definition ultrasound proved that *my* calculated due date was right and that there was *no* Down's. We all stopped for ice cream on the way home to celebrate!

Youngest's C-section was by appointment. The doctor did not feel comfortable with me trying for a vaginal birth, since my labor pattern had been consistently non-cooperative. I drove myself to the hospital. Andy was finishing chores and promised to be there for the surgery. My mom was home with the two boys. I pulled into the parking lot in the morning dark and waddled into the lobby and up to my room. Now it's one thing to have a catheter inserted and IVs poked in when you are already in serious labor pain (you don't really notice or feel much of anything in comparison to the contractions). It's quite another to have this done when you are actually feeling quite fine. It was awful.

Andy showed up and off we went – we had the doctor tie up the works while he was in there. When little Youngest was placed in my arms, and I knew he would be my last child, all doubts and fears about the pregnancy disappeared. I did not let him out of my sight or arm's reach. No bassinette for this one. No wheeling him off so I could get some sleep. He was in the bed with me every minute!

And C-section recovery does get easier with practice. I got up right away and started walking, and I healed fast, fast, fast.

I am not a complainer by nature, and even if I had been, I had already positioned myself toward the Silent-Sufferer end of the spectrum to balance out Andy's tendency to vocalize every passing pain and worry. Add to this the Aspie tendency to not be able to imagine another's feelings, and it is no surprise that I did not find much husbandly sympathy for my pregnancy and delivery travails.

In some recently published research, British neuroscientist Simon Baron-Cohen and others actually measured the physiological responses of Aspergians and NTs when observing another's pain. Their research stemmed from the neurotypical phenomenon that "observing [another's] emotions or bodily sensations results in brain activations largely overlapping those occurring during the direct experience of the same feelings."[2] In other words, when NTs see somebody in pain, their brain triggers mirror responses in their own bodies.

In this study, sixteen men with AS and twenty NT controls were shown four videos: a static electricity shock to a right hand, a needle going into a right hand, a cotton swab gently brushing a right hand, and a needle going into a tomato. During this, a device measured "cortico-spinal responses" in the watchers' right hands. While the NT participants showed obvious mirror reactions to the three human video clips, the AS participants showed no response. The conclusion? "Finding no embodiment of others' pain provides neurophysiologic evidence for reduced empathic resonance in people with Asperger Syndrome and further indicates that their empathic difficulties involve not only cognitive dimensions but also a reduction in the basic sensorimotor resonance with others."[3]

In other words, persons with AS have no bodily reaction to another's pain because their nerves just do not do that. It is not merely a cognitive difference; it's also neural. This means a person with AS must personally experience the same pain before he or she can have an empathic response to another's.

A few years ago, Andy had to have a hernia repaired (farming requires much use of the abdominal muscles). This was a one-day, in-and-out lathroscopic surgery, and I was with him from registration to discharge. When he was finally allowed to get up and try to walk, he grimaced in pain and said to the nurse, "Wow! Is this what it feels like after a Cesarean?"

The nurse gave a smirk (ah, nurses) and just said, "Um... no. Take what you are feeling and multiply it by about twenty."

"Oh," Andy said, truly shocked. Then he looked at me and smiled apologetically. "Wow," he said. "I'm sorry you went through that." The empathy was nice, even fifteen years after the fact.

[1]   Comfort, Alex. (1992). *The New Joy of Sex.* New York, NY: Pocket.

[2]   Minio-Paluello, Ilaria, Baron-Cohen, Simon, Avenanti, Alessio, Walsh, Vincent, & Aglioti, Salvatore M. (2009, January). Absence of embodied empathy during pain observation in Asperger Syndrome. *Biological Psychiatry, 65*(1), 55.

[3]   Ibid., page 61.

CHAPTER 13

SAINT MO – FINDING HELP IN SPIRITUALITY

Some Catholics believe in a concept called the "victim soul," a person specially chosen by God to suffer, who accepts this suffering to make up for the sins of others and to elicit compassion from a world sorely in need of practicing it. About three years ago, I offered myself as a victim soul. Maybe I had suffered through an extreme day of adolescent testoster-slosh or the predictable sibling rivalries and their attendant squabbles and fights or the necessary but annoying need of pre-pubescents to talk back and disobey. Whatever it was, I was feeling as if I needed to take the bull by the horns and present my kids with a situation where compassion was called upon. Kind of force them into maturing morally. Getting them onto MTV's show "Exiled" was out, so this was my back-up plan.[1]

So, I offered myself, in desperation considering how my developing cancer, MS, or whatever would help my family to develop compassion.

Thinking like an adolescent myself at that moment, I envisioned every-one grief-stricken at the news, the boys falling over themselves to hug me, rubbing my bald head. I did not propose this lightly. I had watched my father die of lung cancer, so my offer was not flippant, ignorant of the ravages of a terrible illness. I was just hoping that since I was the family rock and the place to which everyone ran for comfort and love, my suffering might be the tragedy to bring the family together. In addition, although Andy's mom and dad have always called me Saint Mo for put-ting up with their son, I knew I needed something more miraculous to seal my canonization.

I should have known to be careful of what I pray for, especially from a God who fashioned the platypus. It was a mere two days after that prayer (I checked this in my journal to be sure) that I heard the As-perger's segment on NPR. *Andy* became the one with the diagnosis. With a loving but wry smile, the Great Finger pointed at the plank in my own eye.[2] Well, there, Ms. Maureen, how compassionate are *you*?

Instead of the image of everyone gathered around my bed – Andy and the three boys bringing me breakfast and telling me how much they appreciated all that I have done for them – suddenly I am the one serving, I am the one remembering that another suffers instead of me. And in truth, when I look at myself in relationship to Asperger's, I must describe my attitude toward Andy's "idiosyncrasies," now identi-fied as "symptoms," as one of annoyance rather than compassion.

It is hard to be compassionate toward someone with a syndrome the main symptom of which appears to be rudeness. South Vietnamese monk Thich Nhat Hanh, who had to learn to accept both North Vietnamese and American soldiers during the Vietnam War, says that the first step toward compassion is understanding.[3] If we can know *why* our brother acts as he does, we can understand him and have empathy.

So, how does one develop compassion in a situation like this? Unintentional "rudeness" in its various guises is one of the noticeable traits of an Aspergian, and is therefore most likely linked to the amygdala's immaturity. Neurologically speaking, for an Aspergian there is no instinctive understanding of tone of voice as a method of communication. I have found this goes both ways. Andy cannot necessarily pick up on others' tones of voice, nor can he understand how his own tones of voice flavor a statement.

Aspies also have trouble with volume modulation, talking too loudly or too softly, often due to problems with sensory integration, in Andy's case too loudly. A further factor is the Aspergian's need to have things orderly and efficient or, in other situations, to limit the amount of sensory input. Add to that a sense of extreme logic, and we have all the ingredients for being unintentionally offensive.

A simple statement, "Would you please turn down the radio?" can sound (1) frantic if Andy is experiencing sensory overload, (2) accidentally angry if his voice modulates too loudly, (3) demeaning if his tone accidentally indicates there are other things I should be doing, and (4) impatient if he is needing quiet to get something done.

If I am ever to attain sainthood, I guess I am going to have to learn to consciously *undo* what Andy has consciously had to learn *to do*. The amount of effort it takes me to unwrap all the emotional layers that I "hear" in his statements is the same amount of effort it takes Andy to add on all the emotional layers to what I say. That realization makes me feel compassion.

Since the diagnosis, every time I think Andy is being rude, I try to peel off his tone of voice, take into account sensory input from the environment, adjust his volume to normal using my mental audio-mixing board, and unthink that he wants me to do something else. I can feel the amount of energy this takes and realize it takes Andy the same amount to read into *my* statements everything I am indicating through my eyes, my body language, my tone, and my context.

One nice thing about Catholicism is the wide array of saints one can call on for inspiration or help. The nave at St. Paul's, our "Irish" Catholic church in Norwich, is quite plain and unadorned compared to the nave of St. Bartholomew's, the "Italian" Catholic church in town. To the uninitiated, the pictures there can be baffling. There is St. Ambrose in his long red robe holding a bee hive. There are three little nude children in a brine bucket behind St. Nicholas, St. Francis of Assisi is petting a deer, St. Christopher is holding a little child on his shoulder while knee-deep in a rushing river. The saints are like family for a Catholic, older uncles and aunts who can offer advice and help and will intercede in a pinch to help you out.

There are books and websites that index the various saints and the special protection they have assumed based on their life stories, especially their persecutions and deaths.[4] Thus, the bizarre paintings of Saint Lawrence holding what looks to be a grill grate, because he had been burned to death on a brazier, crying out mid-torture, "I am already roasted on one side and, if thou wouldst have me well cooked, it is time to turn me on the other." Logically, he is the patron saint of chefs and butchers. Or there is St. Lucy holding her gouged-out eyeballs on a plate, patron saint of the blind. I am a big fan of St. Brigid, Irish of course, known for her great generosity in ladling out her father's milk to the poor. For this reason, she is known as the patron saint of dairy workers and is sometimes depicted standing next to a butter churn.

Is there a patron saint of Asperger Syndrome? Indeed there is; well, a patron saint of neurological issues: Saint Dymphna. Another Irish pagan-turned-Catholic, she at fourteen fled the advances of her grief-crazed father who, after his wife's death, developed a case of pathological incestuousness and chased his daughter down. When she refused him, he decapitated her, thus the pictures of glowing brains on the websites of her followers. For this reason, she is the patron saint of neurological issues, mental illnesses, mental health professionals, runaways, incest victims, and of all things, happy families. This is typical of the saints' patronage – they seek to advance the converse of whatever caused their persecution.

So I can offer up a prayer to Saint Dymphna, calling her to help Andy grapple with his neurological differences, especially at times when the sensory input and whirl of detail overwhelm him: "Lord, our God, you graciously chose St. Dymphna as patroness of those afflicted with mental and neurological illnesses or challenges. She is thus an inspiration and a symbol of charity to the thousands who ask her intercession. Please grant, Lord, through the prayers of this pure youthful martyr, relief and consolation to all suffering such trials, and especially those for whom we pray: [my husband Andrew]. We beg You, Lord, to hear the prayers of St. Dymphna on our behalf. Grant all those for whom we pray patience in their sufferings and resignation to Your divine will. Please fill them with hope, and grant them the relief they so much desire." Perhaps Andy and I both need to carry St. Dymphna medals for protection.

But back to me and my plight. When I am frustrated by a Tasmanian day, I can turn to Dymphna on Andy's behalf, but there is also my own behalf. Where do I get the patience to be compassionate and understanding and use this marital challenge as a way to strengthen my own character?

I find myself turning to the Buddhists and their much more developed protocols for mind and thought management. I usually find Buddhist texts too prescriptive and sequential for my random-concrete style: the four noble truths, the eight-fold path, breathing exercises. I am too nebulous in spirit to channel my soul into such rigid confines. However, I did pull out Santideva's *Guide to the Bodhisattva's Way of Life* and found some verses that offered gems of insight such as this one: "If fishermen, outcasts, farmers, and others, whose minds are fixed merely on their own livelihoods, withstand the adversities of cold and heat, then why do I not endure for the sake of the well being of the world?"[5]

I think of Andy unfailingly rising at 3:30 AM every day, prioritizing his lists, doing the hard things, spreading manure in negative temperatures and blizzards, baling hay in the blistering summer sun. I have had to do these things too, but not nearly to the same extent as he does. If I compare his exertions to the effort it takes me to unpack and disregard Andy's seeming rudeness, mine is negligible. Besides which, Santideva also says, "Mental afflictions [mine in this case] do not exist in sense objects, or in sense faculties, or in the space between, and not anywhere else. Then where do they exist and agitate the whole world? This is an illusion only. Liberate your fearing heart and cultivate perseverance for the sake of wisdom. Why would you torture yourself in hells for no reason?"[6]

Resentment over Andy's Asperger's symptoms is a hell of my own devising. It's not going to accomplish anything except to make me miserable. It's not going to mature Andy's amygdala or modulate his tone of voice or accomplish anything productive. Yes, we can work on those things to improve them, but not in the midst of them. Learning to ignore these behaviors and dissipate my own resentment is the way for me to "cultivate perseverance for the sake of wisdom," in the words of Santideva.

Similarly, Jesus recommended that for guidance we "Look at the birds of the air … See how the lilies of the field grow."[7] Luckily, this is something I can do with ease by glancing out the window or walking outside. I don't think flowers feel annoyance, nor do birds take offense. Feelings such as these, as well as elation and contentment, are the purview of the human, both for good and for bad. Sainthood comes from cultivating the good ones and weeding out the bad.

I'll give the final words to Santideva, who seems here to be blessing both Andy in neuron-overload and me in fruitless frustration: "May deities protect the dull, the insane, the deranged, the helpless, the young, and the elderly, and those in danger from sickness, the wilderness, and so on. May all beings unceasingly hear the sound of Dharma from the birds, from every tree, from the rays of light, and from the sky."[8] Amen. So be it!

Loving the Tasmanian Devil

1   For information or to watch episodes from MTV's show *Exiled*, go to http://www.mtv. com/shows/exiled/series.jhtml.

2   In Luke 6: 41-42, Jesus says, "Why do you look at the speck of sawdust in your brother's eye and pay no attention to the plank in your own eye? How can you say to your brother, 'Brother, let me take the speck out of your eye,' when you yourself fail to see the plank in your own eye? You hypocrite, first take the plank out of your eye, and then you will see clearly to remove the speck from your brother's eye." *The Holy Bible. New International Version.* (1997). Grand Rapids, MI: Zondervan Publishing.

3   Hanh, Thich Nhat. (1995). *Living Buddha, Living Christ.* New York, NY: Riverhead.

4   One of my favorite guides to the patronage duties of the Catholic saints is *Saints Alive!: A Book of Patron Saints* (1996) by Enid Broderick Fisher, New York, NY: HarperCollins.

5   Santideva, Vesna A., & Wallace, B. Allan. (1997). *A Guide to the Bodhisattva Way of Life.* Ithaca, NY: Snow Lion Publications. Chapter IV: Attending to the Spirit of Awakening, number 40.

6   Ibid., Chapter IV, Number 31.

7   Matthew 6:26, 27. *The Holy Bible. New International Version.*

8   Santideva, *A Guide to the Bodhisattva Way of Life*, Chapter X.

CHAPTER 14

THE HEAD-TO-HEAD MATCHUP – ASPERGER SYNDROME VS. ANXIETY DISORDER

There is a chapter in Annie Proulx's novel *The Shipping News* where the main character, Quoyle, is helping boatbuilder Alvin Yark finish Quoyle's new boat. The curved timbers leaning against the wall of the shop remind him of the body of Wavey, the strong and quiet woman he has fallen in love with in Newfoundland. If they were to marry, he wonders, would his dead adulterous wife, Petal, and Wavey's drowned philandering husband, Herry, be in the bed with them? "He imagined the demon lovers coupling, biting and growling, while he and Wavey crouched against the footboard with their eyes squeezed shut, fingers in their ears."[1]

This image makes me think of Andy and me, crouched at the foot of our bed, while our respective disorders duke it out, mate, or both.

Loving the Tasmanian Devil

Asperger Syndrome and anxiety disorder, in pitched battle – or union. There were days when I would have loved to claim that Andy caused my anxiety disorder, that his constant state of apprehension, his over-reactions to perceived threats, his loud outbursts at unexpected times, his unwarranted criticisms, were what set into overdrive in my brain the mechanism for releasing high-alert neurochemicals. That my brain became corroded from too much adrenaline, and eventually turned my body into a twitching marionette. But that would be untrue.

I think back over my life and realize that I have always suffered from anxiety, even as early as age eight. In third grade, my arch enemy was Lisa Miller. I really hated her, though I couldn't tell you why.

One day in third grade we were working with rulers and some pink parallelogram-shaped erasers, which I realized in combination would make a tremendous catapult. Mrs. Bergner was writing on the black-board, so I placed the eraser on the end of the ruler, pulled the ruler/eraser back with my right hand, holding the ruler's other end in my left, and TWANG! let it fly. (I *do* have an older brother, after all.) I nailed Lisa right on the side of the head, a direct temple hit. She turned to me, mouth open, stunned, and immediately raised her hand.

"Mrs. Bergner, Maureen just hit me in the head with an eraser!"

"Maureen?" Mrs. Bergner turned from Lisa to me, stunned. I was the class angel. This was unprecedented.

My face turned white. I couldn't speak. My head turned cold, and I could feel my hands start to shake.

"I'll talk to you after class," Mrs. Bergner said to me, clearly mystified.

At 3:30, when everyone else had left, I stammered and stuttered through a complete lie: It was an accident. I was holding my ruler and eraser, and somehow it just happened. Accidentally. The eraser arced across the room, and I was as surprised as anybody. I was sorry. I would be more careful.

One of the benefits of being Class Angel is that the teacher generally believes you. Mrs. Bergner smiled and, knees bent to put her face at my level, said, "I didn't think you could have done something like that on purpose."

I smiled through my tears, clutched my gnome bookbag to my chest, and walked carefully out of the classroom. I walked slowly down the stairs, past the doorway to the basement storage room filled with construction paper and glue where we hid during air raid drills, and out the big front door.

But once outside, I ran. Down the one block of Rogers Avenue, past the dark, narrow driveway where I had fended off Timmy Barrs and his cooties with my umbrella, slowly across East Avenue via Mrs. Meisner, the crossing guard, past the park where I had lost my copy of *Farmer Boy* (found and returned to me by my hero Perry because it had my name on a gnome nameplate on the inside front cover), past Bud's Liquor Store where my father bought gin for Leona, our sick, old lush neighbor, across the street, past the house where our adopted dog, Tuffy, really lived, past Juniper Street where down in the shady depths lived Josie Sowicki, the teenage felon who walked home right on top of my heels to scare me, past my next-door friend Chrissy Caputo's house, and up my driveway. I hurled open the side door, flew up the four stairs into the kitchen, and threw myself on my mother's mercy.

"What's wrong?" she exclaimed, distressed at my tears.

"Can't ... you ... see ... how ... late ... I ... am?" I managed between sobs.

"You're not late, honey."

"That's ... 'cause ... I ... ran ... the ... whole ... way!!" I bawled.

"What happened?" she asked, soothing me.

Of course, I lied to her, too. It was unthinkable that I had done something wrong. Unthinkable. It could not be admitted. I was an angel. So I covered my sin.

Nowadays, our three boys never get this bent out of shape when they get in trouble, so I believe my reactions to the eraser event could count as early symptoms of my anxiety. I don't know where it came from – Catholicism, being the Little Cute One, covering up my parents' problems (which I didn't have a name for at that point), but I knew it would never happen ever again. Ever.

In high school, my anxiety took a more destructive turn, and clinical problems cropped up. My beloved older sister had left for Japan. My silent older brother was home but inaccessible. My father's drinking had gotten worse, and my mother's reactions to it more extreme. I was the perfect invisible daughter with the high grades and the spotless behavior record. The only thing I was not was thin ... well, not thin enough. Gina Everett was gaining eleventh-grade fame prior to the

Junior Miss Pageant by losing lots of weight: Everyone speculated she was using diet pills. That seemed like a good route to the icing on my own cake, so I decided to starve.

The only problem was that when I got home from school, I felt so sorry for myself, and also felt I so deserved a reward for my high grades and perfection, that every day I gave myself a treat – a big treat. A gallon of ice cream. An entire pie. A whole package of Oreos. Once I was blissed out on sugar, an image of Gina would pop into my mind and horror struck. Up I'd go to the second-floor bathroom where I would close the door, drink a glass of water, leave the tap running, and vomit the entire indulgent feast into the toilet.

Again, I think I might call that anxiety. I have since read that bulimia has been linked to abnormalities in serotonin levels in the brain, the neurochemical implicated in anxiety. I do not know if the stress of living in an alcoholic household altered my serotonin levels, if my genetically low serotonin levels caused me to overreact to any perceived threat, or if my eating disorder left a serotonin "scar" that caused anxiety to chase me for years after. I have even speculated that my father drank to self-medicate his own genetic anxiety disorder. Whichever way the sequence went, anxiety got pretty firmly entrenched.

Even through college, I feared new situations, social gatherings, speaking in class, lots of things. Mid-way through my bachelor's, my dad went to rehab, I grew up, met Andy, found my feet, and the anxiety seemed to subside for a while.

Then we moved to the farm. Talk about tense. For years we barely made ends meet. We would throw weeks' worth of mail in the trash because we knew we couldn't pay the bills. I remember sleeping on the floor by the woodstove because we couldn't afford fuel oil and finding the cupboards bare except for a solitary can of kidney beans.

And there was Andy's dad, our financial backer, looking over our shoulders, and me with the high-priced English degree struggling to find a job that paid decently in rural upstate New York, and trying to decide if we could stick it out or if we should give it up and be forever ostracized by the Bartlett family. The work, the worry, the fear.

And also, though not named at that time, there was Asperger Syndrome. While Andy and I, our purest essential selves, cowered at the end of the bed, our two mental difficulties would come out swinging: Asperger Syndrome and anxiety disorder in head-on-head combat. Each would throw its symptom of choice out there to wage war against the other one's symptom of choice. It was like a Pokémon battle.

Asperger's says, "extreme overreaction to perceived threat, I choose you!," and Andy would melt down into a rant and rave over a problem in the barn.

Anxiety fights back with, "feelings of panic, fear and uneasiness," and I would go racing around, quivering, trying to help or deal with the problems or clear the deck ahead of Andy so nothing would cause an outburst.

Asperger's strikes out with "lack of empathy or understanding of another person's perspective," and Andy would call me at 9 AM on my first day of a new job to tell me we were being sued by the neighbor for five million dollars.

Anxiety throws back "abnormal apprehension and fear," and I would spend the day not only worrying about my new job but also practicing my testimony in court about the tractor accident.

Asperger's pulls out "uncontrollable rage" and makes Andy swipe all the items off the top of my dresser.

Anxiety pulls out "sensitivity to criticism" and hurls me out into the cold hay mow where I fume and cry, wishing I had somewhere else to go.

This epic conflict went on for years until it finally came to a head. April truly is the cruelest month. One April I was in a car accident with five of my favorite students, and the next April we had a sociopathic liar holed up in our employee trailer, exploiting a worker's comp injury and threatening to sue us if we fired him. We sent the kids to my mom's for April break and kept the shotgun in our bedroom.

Something about this one-two hit threw me off the deep end. I started developing every physical symptom of anxiety that exists: heart palpitations, hot flashes, dizziness, shortness of breath, tunnel vision, numb fingers and toes, loss of balance. My doctor ruled out all possible physical problems through heart monitors, MRIs, blood work. And still these symptoms persisted.

Finally Andy took the bull by the horns. One really great thing about the Asperger's flight-or-fight response is the fight half. Once Andy turns the corner on a threat, he becomes my knight in shining armor. One morning I was gathering my papers and books for school. I was crying, I couldn't stand up, I felt like I was tipping over, I couldn't breathe, and Andy said, "That's it. We're going to the doctor." He called me in sick and put me in the car.

My GP looked at me and said, "We've ruled out every other possible explanation for this. I believe you have an anxiety disorder, and we're going to have to try medication." And so I entered the wild world of psycho-pharmaceuticals. Celexa gave me a rash, Paxil turned me into a libido-less concrete block, and then we tried Effexor.

As Asperger's and Anxiety were entering the tenth round, in swooped Effexor Woman to halt the fight. This medicine plus weekly counseling for four months had turned me into a person I had never been. Effexor Woman was assertive, she was confident, she was fearless, she used positive dialogue, and she fought off panic attacks with one hand. She had reasonable expectations of herself, she exercised, she tolerated neither guilt nor obsessive scary thoughts.

She was actually quite frightening for everyone in the beginning.

With the use of this very low dose neurotransmitter balancer, I finally feel "normal." I can notice it even now in situations where I used to become anxious, waiting for the stab in the stomach, the sting of adrenaline, the racing thoughts. They just don't happen. Situations that previously would have driven me under the table now elicit only the appropriate amount of apprehension, not debilitating fear.

Finding the "anxiety disorder" name for my behaviors allowed me to find the right antidote to help me out. Now that Effexor Woman is on my team, I can see what is happening with clarity. I took my fingers out of my ears and opened my eyes. In the ring with Asperger's, EW just smiles and steps back from the thrown punches. Let those AS symptoms do as they will. They won't bother me.

According to the *Harvard Women's Health Journal*, "Anxiety is a reaction to stress that has both psychological and physical features. The feeling is thought to arise in the amygdala, a brain region that governs many intense emotional responses."[2] So Andy and I have that in common: We both are affected by atypical amygdala activity. The big difference seems to be that mine is chemical and his is neurological.

Now that we know Andy's issue, I want to have some nice superhero help him out as well. I am completely on the side of the Asperger's Rights Groups that decry people's efforts to "cure" the neurologically different. I have a treatable neurochemical imbalance; Andy has a neurological difference, and that makes him who he is. (I would without hesitation wear a T-shirt that says "I'm with the Aspie.")

But that neurological difference does often distress him and makes him at times anxious and ineffective. It makes him do things he later feels really bad about. Andy guards his hyper-alertness, saying that fear is what allows survival, of an animal or a farm. But excessive fear, as I well know, can cause imprecise thinking and fruitless commotion.

In her book *Thinking in Pictures*, Temple Grandin relates that she began taking anti-depressants when her panic attacks began to seriously affect her ability to function but that she has had to adjust and experiment with the combination that works best. She admits that "Manipulating my biochemistry has not made me a completely different person but it has been somewhat unsettling to my idea of who and what I am to be able to adjust my emotions as if I were tuning up a car."[3]

I admit to the same discomfort. I have read the scientific descriptions of what Effexor does in my brain, and I question whether I am messing with the person I was genetically made to be. However, when I missed a dose lately, and found myself unable to attend to my students or my children, I decided I was OK with being pharmaceutically "normalized."

Every time I talk to my doctor about lowering my dose or going off the medicine, she says, "Has your lifestyle changed?" "No." "Then I would not go off the medicine." She continues, "You might have to accept that this is a lifelong condition, like diabetes." In that light, I would not deprive myself of insulin if I were diabetic. I would not stop taking my allergy medication. Why is manipulation of brain biochemistry any different?

However, Asperger Syndrome and autism are different. The actual neurons – the wiring – is different, not the chemical cocktail that's flowing around them. My drugs alter the amount of serotonin and nor-epinephrine available in my brain. This can be changed. Asperger Syndrome, as far as the biologists can tell, is a condition of the neurons themselves.

This is why Aspies for Freedom oppose the idea of an autism "cure." Their website states, "Part of the problem with the 'autism as tragedy' point of view is that it carries with it the idea that a person is somehow separable from autism, and that there is a 'normal' person trapped 'behind' the autism. Being autistic is something that influences every single element of who a person is – from the interests we have, the ethical systems we use, the way we view the world, and the way we live our lives. As such, autism is a part of who we are. To 'cure' someone of autism would be to take away the person they are, and replace them with someone else … Aspies For Freedom opposes the idea of an autism 'cure', as a real cure would be unethical, and the current myth of the cure is harmful."[4]

However, those with Asperger Syndrome and autism DO acknowledge the benefits of treating the side-effects of Asperger's and autism. Erika Hammerschmidt, who takes five different pills to manage an array of tics and panic attacks, says ... "I'd like to be able to do completely without medications ... I will have to find a time when I have the freedom to risk inconvenient behavior changes and the courage to undergo the emotional trauma that would go with those changes ... I might do it some day, but for now, my pills are too much of a help to be given up."[5]

I don't know if medication is an appropriate option for Andy, but Effexor Woman is ready and willing to fly him down to the doctor to find out. There are days when Andy's stress is minimal and mine is chemically controlled, and we interact like two relatively normal folks instead of puppets handled by battling neurological conditions.

The person I am with unmedicated anxiety disorder is not me, and now that she has been banished from the bed, my real me can take her place. I am not looking to change Andy, but I know that even he dislikes the power that the constant fight-or-flight response has over him and the exhaustion it causes.

This is a territory into which we are treading lightly. Andy was misdiagnosed with ADHD as a kid and was on Ritalin for many years. He still bridles at the stigma of that period of his life. He also fears that quelling his anxiety would make him less able to manage the farm. He says time and again that fear is what propels him to the barn in the middle of the night to save a $500 newborn calf.

But when I am dealing with a Tasmanian attack and stuff is flying, I rage silently, "Sure, it's OK for ME to take anti-anxiety drugs but not for YOU." But this is indeed dangerous territory. Asperger Syndrome, with the grace of biology, provides its own self-medications in stimming and special interests.

I admit this is a tough one, another facet that is going to require further study, talking with experts, discussions, soul-searching, and love. I know that my own capacities for love and compassion are greatly diminished by my untreated anxiety disorder. Maybe in ten years, after retirement, or when some big financial ship comes in, the circumstances of my life will stop triggering so many anxiety responses. But right now, I am needed, and I can't be dysfunctional. As they tell parents on airplanes, affix your own air mask first so that you can then assist your child.

For right now, my disorder is better understood and more easily managed, and I am relatively comfortable with the treatment. Asperger's information is still forth-coming, and it is difficult to find local, well-informed counselors and doctors. So for the time being, I'll wear my air mask and be ready to help Andy if and when that help is indicated. In the meantime, at least we know what we're dealing with on Andy's side of the ring, and we can use the techniques and management tools that are known and have proven effective. It's already making a difference.

Back in *The Shipping News*, Wavey and Quoyle finally do banish the demon lovers from their bed. They find strength in each other and also in the quiet comfort and ease of each other's loyalty. In Newfoundland and in this woman, Quoyle finds that the most profound of miracles – those massive seismic shifts in the human heart – are possible. The book ends like this: "Water may be older than light, diamonds crack in hot goat's blood, mountaintops give off cold fire, forests appear in mid-ocean, it may happen that a crab is caught with the shadow of a hand on its back, that the wind be imprisoned in a bit of knotted string. And it may be that love sometimes occurs without pain or misery."[6]

Yes, I think so, too.

[1] Perhaps my favorite novel of all time. Proulx, E. Annie. (1993). *The Shipping News*. New York, NY: Scribner; page 314.

[2] Anxiety and Physical Illness. (2008, July). *Harvard Women's Health Watch*. http://www.health.harvard.edu/newsletters/Harvard_Womens_Health_Watch/2008/July/Anxiety_and_physical_illness.

[3] Grandin, Temple. (2006). *Thinking in Pictures: My Life With Autism*. New York, NY: Vintage; page 130.

[4] The Aspies for Freedom website may be found at http://www.aspiesforfreedom.com/.

[5] Hammerschmidt, Erika. (2008). *Born on the Wrong Planet*. Shawnee Mission, KS: AAPC Publishing; page 54.

[6] Proulx, *The Shipping News*, pages 336-337.

CHAPTER 15

GRANDMOTHER'S SONG – ASPERGIAN "RUDENESS"

The other night Andy and I got into a discussion about social "lying," and I keep reprocessing it, trying to explain it to myself so I can better explain it to him. Andy is repulsed by the idea that anyone would say, "Call me if you need someone to talk to" and not really mean it. I, on the other hand, say things like that all the time. And on one side of my mind, I do mean it. I mean, "In a perfect world, where I had limitless time and energy, you are most definitely a person who deserves the ear of a thoughtful and caring listener and I would be willing to be that listener in a perfect world." The other side of my words says, "You and I both know that this is not a perfect world, and you know that what I said means that you are a person worthy of my attention but that I don't really mean that you should call because you know I am only a casual acquaintance and you should call someone nearer and dearer."

Hearing myself verbalize this mental negotiation for Andy, I understand why processing all this seems illogical and complicated, and that it would be much easier and more logical if we all said what we meant, as Andy suggests: "I am sorry for your troubles. You need to talk to someone for support, but I am not the one. I don't know you well enough. Here's a quarter, call someone who cares." In his mind, this is the preferable route. The unguents that oil the social machinery appear as so much chicanery to him. And I understand that.

The other day I was sorting through a pile of old family LPs at my mother's house and ran into Steve Martin's 1977 album "Let's Get Small."[1] My older brother was an early Steve Martin fan, and he had bought this album, which features a photo of Steve wearing Groucho glasses, bunny ears, and a blow-up balloon animal around his head. I loved this album even at 11 years of age when I didn't get *all* the jokes, but when I listened to it again recently, "Grandmother's Song," which is meant to be absurdist, suddenly seemed quite close to what I see as the "Asperger Code of Conduct."

It starts off as what most of us NTs would identify as common social mores:

> Be courteous, kind and forgiving,
> Be gentle and peaceful each day,
> Be warm and human and grateful,
> And have a good thing to say.

I think most Aspies would be able to identify and label these behaviors cognitively and attempt to mimic them, knowing it is what we NTs agree to try and do. They also, by nature, live out the first three lines of the next verse, "Be thoughtful and trustful and childlike," as well as "Be honest and love all your neighbors." Aspies are "thoughtful" – very – though their thoughts may take a unique form. And their obsessive special interest may indeed be "considerately" applied to serving their loved ones: gourmet meals, a clean pool, a meticulously planned trip. Taking everything literally, they are "trustful" to the point of gullibility, "childlike" for sure, and witty and wise, honest to a fault, and "loving" of all their neighbors, though often in the form of absolute truthfulness, whether it beneficially "hurts" the neighbor or not.

At a recent informational farm seminar, Andy was explaining how he organizes his time to get out into the fields early and cut the hay when it's at its peak nutritional value. Another farmer responded with, "Yeah, well some of us actually have to milk our cows first." (Andy hired someone to milk as soon as we could afford labor because he realized that this was the simplest task on the farm that he could delegate, leaving himself more time for managing the money-making aspects of the business, such as early first-cutting hay.)

Without sending his thoughts through any filter first, either emotional or social, Andy turned to this farmer and said, "Whose fault is that?"

Not surprisingly, the farmer was offended, though several other excellent farm managers in the audience suppressed laughs. Andy said to me later, "He needed to hear that. I was doing him a favor. Everyone else is too polite to say anything."

I confess to extreme embarrassment if I am with Andy in situations like that. I find myself smiling apologetically at the offended one, commiserating later in a whisper, "Don't take it personally. He does that to me all the time." I know this is disloyal, but my innate instinct to preserve the social fabric usually outweighs my individual loyalty to my husband's discourtesy. After all, what if we need a favor from this guy some day?

Then there is the last line of this verse: "Be obsequious, purple, and clairvoyant." Martin meant this to seem bizarre, but since an Aspie looks at the niceties of social interaction and finds that they clash with his own intense desire to be truthful and logical, is this how we NTs look? That our flattery and kind words are insincere and obsequious? And besides, when we gush positively over something that is clearly distasteful, I am sure our prose does looks pretty purple.

What about our skill at being "polite"? Wouldn't that mean reading someone's mind and knowing what they want? As one Aspergian lamented, what is funny to one person can be insulting to the next. In the "mind-blindness" of the Asperger brain, the NT ability to know the difference, knowing who is likely to laugh at the joke and who is likely to be insulted, must seem like clairvoyance that is beyond attainment.

I have heard Andy say that if he has trouble sorting out someone's emotional intentions or receptivity, he drops that person as a potential friend because it's too much work and worry for him to be second guessing.

There is also the extremely sensitive "bullshit meter" that seems part and parcel of the Asperger brain. Any sign of falsehood, and the Aspie is ready to blow its cover. Aspergian memoirist John Elder Robison tells a hysterically funny story of attending a faculty party given by his parents. As the attendees tout their own sons' acceptances at Harvard and Yale, Robison decides to test their pompous boundaries. He gathers a crowd by telling a fantastic tale of his "job" as a sanitation engineer (i.e., garbage man), finding dead babies in dumpsters and beating off feral children. His justification for this was "Some of [my parents'] friends were okay, but others seemed to me arrogant and conceited, and it was starting to make me angry."[2]

From the NT perspective, looking through our vastly complex and sophisticated social filters, the Aspie and his "honesty" look quite different:

> Be pompous, obese, and eat cactus,
> Be dull, and boring, and omnipresent,
> Criticize things you don't know about.

I can attest to the sometime pomposity of the Aspergian. Aspies do know things and remember things, so Andy can with ease pull facts out of his prodigious memory and correct any error in another's statements.

I'll say, "I think the Fed is going to cut rates again to encourage spending."

"Actually," Andy will respond, "cutting the prime will make Federal funds more attractive to commercial lenders, who will pass on those savings to their borrowers. This might encourage more people to buy durables, for which they likely need to borrow, but it won't directly encourage consumer spending at the perishable or service sector level."

I glare. This, for Andy, is being honest and loving his neighbor, or in this case loving his wife. I was suffering under a mistaken impression, and it was his duty to correct me. He was being helpful. Actually, I know how the prime lending rate works, too. I was just glossing over the technicalities to make a generalization and pass on some news. You know, small talk?

As for eating cactus, Katrin Bentley in her book *Alone Together*, compares her Aspergian husband to a cactus: "a beautiful, strong, resilient cactus."[3] Prickly. Protected. Able to withstand harsh climates. Steadfast. But not so easy to hug, or live with.

"Be dull and boring and omnipresent." One of the common Tazberger traits is to go on at great length, ad infinitum, ad nauseum, about special interests – or really about anything – missing every facial cue emitted by the listener that she would like for the Aspie to stop. I have always noticed that when Andy gets a burr under his saddle, he will work that thing from every possible angle, saying basically the same sentence in twelve different ways.

Exempli gratia: "There's no secret about what's going on. The calves' buckets are not getting cleaned. Bacteria grow in milk. If you don't sanitize those buckets daily, the calves will get sick. There's no silver bullet. No vet is going to come out here and identify some mystery cause for all the scours. They will ask how often we're cleaning the buckets and tell us that's the problem. We've been through this before. Things are fine, and then you get busy and things slip and sanitation deteriorates and the calves pick up a gastrointestinal infection."

By this point, I am giving nonverbal cues to communicate that I've got the message. Point taken. Shut up now. I have tried the smooched-to-the-side lips. I have tried the lowered eyebrows coupled with the grimly set mouth. I have tried the sigh. I have tried the wide-open exasperated eyes, and still he goes on.

"What needs to happen every day like clockwork is that those buckets need to get sanitized. You need to do it. Eldest needs to do it. It's nothing extraordinary. It's just the most ordinary of standard operating procedures. Keep the equipment clean. We don't need special medicines or vaccines or powders. Just cleanliness. Pure and simple."

I have given up on facial gestures and moved on to gross-motor body language. I turn away. I start roughly and loudly doing something else. I try vocalized stage sighs, but he still goes on and on. How many different ways can he say the same thing? Does he never stop talking? OK. Enough said.

"Criticize things you don't know about." See above. Apply to topics outside of actual experience, such as teaching, PMS, migraines, life as a movie star, etc.

Last verse, sung in my mind by the exasperated NT spouse who is about ready to go sleep in the hay mow:

> Be tasteless, rude, and offensive,
> Live in a swamp and be three dimensional,
> Put a live chicken in your underwear,
> Go into a closet and suck eggs.

I could not help but laugh as I reconsidered this verse as an Asperger's description. Does it fit Andy? Perhaps not the tasteless part. From his upbringing, Andy is actually a bit on the silver-spoon tasteful side, but "rude and offensive"? You better believe it. Before I had ever heard of Asperger's, I used to say to myself, "I don't know which is worse, that Andy is so rude or that he doesn't even know he's being rude."

According to Tony Attwood, "Another characteristic associated with Asperger Syndrome is that the person does not know when he or she would be expected to tell a 'white lie,' making a comment to someone that is true but likely to cause offence … Children and adults with Asperger's Syndrome appear to have a greater allegiance to honesty and the truth than to the thoughts and feelings of others."[4]

Or there is the other route to apparent rudeness – the intense need to reach completion and be efficient. The Aspergian sees no need to waste time on social niceties when there is a task to be done, trampling over the small talk and pleasantries the rest of us use to sweeten the air and grease the day's emotional machinery.

In terms of living in a swamp, Andy does in fact smack of Yoda in his swamp on Dagobah on occasion.[5] Luke Skywalker, a novice at moving objects with the Force, is ordered by Yoda to lift his X-wing out of the water in which it is submerged.

Luke says, "I'll give it a try."

"Try, not!" Yoda responds. "Do, or do not. There is no try."

When Luke gives up after a feeble attempt, Yoda steps in to show him how it's done. Extending his little three-pronged hoof, Yoda uses the Force alone to raise the ship out of the water and set it gently on the shore, calling on the fourth-dimension energy that surrounds the "crude matter" of visible three-dimensional objects.

I believe that in Andy's case, this ability to make things happen is pure willpower. When Andy decides what it is he will do, nothing stands in his way. There is never a thought of "try," only do.

I confess to being a try-er. I will set my course, make a plan, and then I will *try* to make it happen. If making it happen means trampling on someone's feelings, disappointing one of the kids, or ignoring a social nicety, I just won't do it, choosing "failure" over offensiveness. I would rather be liked than respected.

Andy, on the other hand, feels obligated to *do*, not just try. He has said this of the hay harvest, moving cows, finishing a project. He will ram it through and devil take the hindmost. He explains that this is what breeds success, this is what makes the farm survive, this is what allows us to have gotten where we've gotten.

Maybe this is more of a male-female difference than an AS-NT difference. On the other hand, my dad was clearly of my ilk, adored by his colleagues and loved by all his neighbors but not always able to pull off his family's dreams on a grand scale. And I have noticed that my sister and I both most deliberately married men who were *not* this way. We are both attracted to men that can "get 'r' done." Of course, it would be nice if the doers could also be polite along the way!

And then there is "Put a live chicken in your underwear." I chuckle over this one because it sounds like a pretty close approximation of Andy's sometime persona that we have taken to calling Mr. Pepper Pants. In exasperation one day I said, "What the hell is wrong with you? It's like someone put pepper in your pants!" Or, in a description of Andy by of one of our former farmhands, "Everything's such a God-damn emergency!"

I know this is the trait that causes the most bewilderment among the uninitiated who walk in on a Tazberger day when too many things are going wrong and Andy truly looks like a live chicken has been put in his underwear. I now understand this better and can commiserate. Having dealt with an anxiety disorder of my own, I know what it feels like to have a stress response to what seems to others to be common daily occurrences. I can be Mrs. Pepper Pants myself on occasion.

In a situation of sensory overload and not enough time to process new information or of diversion from the carefully created plan, I have seen Andy put his hands on the sides of his head to make the bombardment stop, as he stomps off at a frantic pace to get away from it, or at least get to a spot where he can process and adjust.

I confess that "Go into a closet and suck eggs" has been my thought if not my words to Andy on more than one occasion. When the combination of his rudeness and his running rough-shod and his pomposity and his repetitiveness and his criticisms and his agitation have driven me to the brink of psychosis, I am usually the one who ends up in a corner of the hay mow (rather than the closet, which we reserve for passionate trysts), sitting with the silly goose and her nest of rotten eggs, fuming like a small freight train.

It is next to impossible for me to truly empathize with the inability to grasp social rules. To me, it would be like not knowing how to breathe or swallow. But the more I read books by individuals with autism and Asperger's, the better I understand that it is possible to truly not grasp them. Temple Grandin and Sean Barron's book *The Unwritten Rules of Social Relationships*[6] delineates, in very clear and logical terms, the rules NTs seem to know inherently that are boggling and illogical to those on the spectrum. Their ten rules include such seeming no-brainers as "Honesty Is Different Than Diplomacy" and "Being Polite Is Appropriate in Any Situation."

Grandmother's Song – Aspergian "Rudeness"

Addressing social skills is one of those Asperger areas that requires some work on the NT's part. I have always shied away from stepping on Andy's foot under the table when he is interrupting or insulting someone, fearing that he would either overtly startle or else say out loud, "Why are you stomping on my foot?" Instead, I have taken the tack of silently bearing the social inappropriateness and just being extra kind to its victim.

On the other hand, from living with Andy for so long, I have become very aware of truly illogical social codes. I will cut through the endless socializing at teacher work sessions to get us back to the task at hand. I will call the bus garage and ream out the Nazi-esque bus driver who drove right by my kid instead of stopping to pick him up. I will tell the obnoxious telemarketer whom I have asked to stop calling that if he calls again I will take legal action. I have also edged farther from my dad's code of near-doormat-hood and closer to a place where I can say the difficult but uncomfortable things that need to be said, risking others' dislike for the sake of truth or effectiveness.

There must be a way to walk the fine line between honesty and rudeness. Psychologist Paul Ekman, interviewed on NPR's Radio Lab[7] (in a decidedly non-Asperger's-related story), claims that people don't "have to" lie; they do it out of laziness or timidity. After his daughter's birth, he charged himself with the goal of living his life without lying. Invited to a second dinner party by a couple who had bored him and served bad food at the first, he finally said to them that in his middle age and with a busy schedule, he had decided to not pursue any new friendships so that he could instead maintain strong relationships with old friends. True AND polite. This takes time and effort, Ekman acknowledges, but he feels like a Zen master when he pulls it off.

169

Talk about the Force! I have noticed that the Dalai Lama looks a little like Yoda, and that he has that same humility and playfulness and power. That kind of moral stance must be the happy medium between unctuous social graces and unintentionally boorish Aspergian discourtesy. Yoda doesn't pull punches, and neither does the Dalai Lama. Truth is a laudable ideal, but so is compassion, in both of their cases.

The Kabbalist Tree of Life from the Jewish tradition pairs the opposing qualities of Judgment and Mercy (Gevurah and Hesed) by balancing them and joins them through the attribute of Understanding (Daat) as the bridge between intellect and emotion. From my own understanding, the Asperger brain might not physiologically have this neural connection. It might be physically impossible for the intellect to talk to the realm of the emotion. I guess I need to be this connection for Andy, working my way in through his intellect to explain the codes of emotion that guide us in the NT sphere. But Andy, in turn, can help me to summon my intellect when my emotional message system has taken over and is calling all the shots.

There is Darth Vader Power, and then there is Yoda Power: the dark side versus the light side of the Force. Similarly, there is brutal honesty/steamrollering and there is compassionate truth and encouragement. The trick is to merge the opposites.

At his death, Master Yoda says to Luke, "You must confront Vader." Luke does this, and at the end of the last movie (the original last movie), Vader has been redeemed and stands glowing with Yoda and Obi Wan as the Ewoks frolic in the background.[8]

Imagine the moral strength it takes to pull that off. It takes Jedi powers: Judgment, Mercy, Understanding, Willpower, and Compassion. Can we as a species – Aspies and NTs alike – do it? It might require some training time with Yoda. I guess what we need to do is go live in a swamp and be four-dimensional. May the Force be with us!

¹ Steve Martin. (1977). Grandmother's Song. From *Let's Get Small*. Lyrics by Steve Martin. Copyright © 1977 LA Films Music. All rights reserved. Used with permission.

² Robison, John Elder. (2008). *Look Me in the Eye: My Life with Asperger's*. (2008). New York, NY: Three Rivers Press; page 96.

³ Bentley, Katrin. (2007). *Alone Together: Making an Asperger Marriage Work*. Philadelphia, PA: Jessica Kingsley Publishers; pages 13-15.

⁴ Attwood, Tony. (2007). *The Complete Guide to Asperger's Syndrome*. Philadelphia, PA: Jessica Kingsley Publishers; page 117.

⁵ This scene may be found in *The Empire Strikes Back*. (1980). Los Angeles, CA: Twentieth Century Fox.

⁶ Grandin, Temple, & Barron, Sean. (2005). *Unwritten Rules of Social Relationships: Decoding Social Mysteries Through the Unique Perspectives of Autism*. Arlington, TX: Future Horizons, Inc.

⁷ Deception. *RadioLab*. WNYC. February 29, 2008. http://www.wnyc.org/shows/radiolab/episodes/2008/02/29

⁸ This scene is at the end of *Return of the Jedi*. (1983). Los Angeles, CA: Twentieth Century Fox.

CHAPTER 16

ABSTRACT-SEQUENTIAL MARRIES CONCRETE-RANDOM – ASPIE STYLE AND NT STYLE

It must be hard for Andy to be married to me sometimes. I must be one of the most random people in the world, and he is by far one of the most sequential people in the world. I think of those GE appliance ads where the couple with the very opposite preferences stands, arms linked, before the new appliances that suit both of their tastes. "High fashion marries high tech" features a gorgeous brunette in a pink-flowered halter dress and strappy high heels with a nerdy computer geek with glasses, pocket protector, and laptop. "Art marries technology" pairs a wild-haired artiste in embroidered bellbottoms, a belly-button ring, tattoos, and huge hoop earrings with a doctor in white lab coat and grey dress pants.[1]

The old adage "opposites attract" is a fundamental truth. I've seen it in so many marriages. The extremely animated and loving male music teacher married to the restrained and exacting public health coordinator. The straight-laced acerbic lawyer and his red-haired vivacious wife. North and south. Yin and yang. We intuitively seek out in our mate the traits we know we lack. Together we make a complete package.

And so, the Asperger books say, an Asperger male will choose a neurotypical female to fill in his gaps of flexibility and empathy. The most horrifying thing I read was that when an Aspie marries an NT, after several years the Aspie reports better mental health and the NT reports a deterioration in mental health.[2] I can attest to that.

This morning Andy screamed up to me at 5 AM in an angry voice, "Mo! Get up! It's after five!" My first thought was that his left leg had fallen off and he needed to go to the hospital. But no, he was just agitated. Why? Because he had been up for an hour and a half and I had been sleeping? He had left me a note on the kitchen table.

"Mo. Please see me about the following," followed by a numbered list. Something must have occurred to him after he had listed 1 through 4 because he had added an "A" before the 1 through 4. My list for the day read:

A. Scout updates – blue envelope
1. 1¢ stamps & 42¢ stamps
2. Computer paper
3. Blue Seal bill
4. NRCS report – I need to duplicate old format w/some changes

This was signed with a heart and a thank you.

I appreciate the heart and the thank you. I know that took effort and conscious DOS-like thought. What burns me is being treated like a secretary and knowing that these things will be so omnipresent in Andy's mind that the sooner I deal with them the sooner I can proceed with my own day.

I find the blue envelope with the Scout[3] updates and place it on Andy's desk (I knew I should have installed those updates when they came in the mail). This will update the farm management software program that tracks all our cows, lactation records, reproduction data, etc. I lay out the roll of old stamps and the makeup stamps I had already bought. I make a note to self to buy computer paper. I start the virus-infected computer in Safe Mode (finding the Blue Seal bill for the month's grain on Andy's keyboard), save a copy of the comprehensive nutrient management plan spreadsheet onto my flash drive, move it over to the laptop and save it on the desktop.

Then, in my shufflings about in the office, I bump into a birthday card my sister had sent Andy. On the front is a David Jacobson cartoon from *The New Yorker* of "James Joyce's refrigerator"[4] with a numbered to-do list:

1. Call bank
2. Dry cleaner
3. Forge in the smithy of my soul the uncreated conscience of my race
4. Call Mom

My sister had written to Andy inside the card, "This seems like a list you might make. Of course, farm chores, parenting, and dealing with farm labor are missing."

Too true. I have finally come to realize that Andy's lists are a way to keep the neurological chaos at bay. He knows there are certain tasks that will overwhelm his internal processing drives, things like fixing the fax machine or installing software updates, so he calls on my help. I am happy to do it. I am ultra-quick at tasks like that. What I am not so good at are the comprehensive long-term tasks such as moving the business from 100% debt to 100% equity. I look at Andy's desk and notice seven different lists that he is working from. What he expects of me is a small fraction of what he expects of himself.

Left to my own devices, I prefer to live life in a more random manner. I am usually able to hold a full day's agenda in my head, complicated though it is. I am extraordinarily punctual; however, I prefer to let my non-scheduled tasks sort of flow off the mental list as they will. I will put out the fires and take care of necessary business at school first, but then I might drift into five minutes of casual web browsing to clear my mental palate. I am always up for a spontaneous change in plans and can shift gears in a millisecond. I credit growing up in an alcoholic household for this, in my case, very useful skill.

I now know that on-one's-feet processing, multi-tasking, and transitions are hard for the Asperger brain, which pits Andy and me head-on-head on occasion. The best example is leaving for a trip to the Bartlett family camp up in the Berkshires. In my mind, the trip and enjoyment start as we are packing the vehicles to leave. The three boys are arranging their car snacks and electronics and, in years past, stuffed animals. I am filling my bookbag with good reads. The four of us are smiling and already on vacation before we pull out, planning what kind of ice cream we want at the Happy Clown, our mid-trip stop.

Andy, on the other hand, is whirling around like a cyclone, going over his lists, giving directions to our hired man, checking the lights on the camper, and looking at his watch every few minutes. He has obviously set a departure time of X, allowing Y.5 hours for travel and restroom stops, with arrival at destination at time Z. As time X gets closer and closer and I am still puddling around, Andy gets very agitated and loud. And I get extremely annoyed.

I finally explode. "What is wrong with you? Why do you have to turn a beautiful day into a horror show? Don't you realize that the kids are enjoying this half hour every bit as much as being at camp itself?"

"I just want to get up there. I can't relax until we're there and I know everything is set up."

"What are you going to do, make the next four hours horrific so we can get to camp and *then* have fun? Isn't it better to enjoy the trip as well? That's four more hours of happiness."

And so it goes.

On a good day, we make an excellent team. On the financial side, I'm good at micro-managing – bank trips, balancing the checkbook, payroll, paying bills – and Andy is good at macro-managing – commodity market reports, cost-benefit analyses for equipment purchases, negotiating prices. I work the 9AM to 5PM for a boss, get the steady paycheck, and secure the health insurance; Andy works the 4AM to 6PM as his own boss, brings in the big cash, and enlarges our equity.

When working in the barn, we are also a good team. Andy manages the whole day and all the employees, and I run gopher and complete tasks that require brains and quick thinking: drying off cows, giving shots, saving colostrum, marking the synchronized breeding group. With the house and lawn, we have also specialized pretty well. I do the inside, he does the outside. I have personally stripped, re-plastered and painted every wall in the house and coordinate the interior decorating (I was the art major), whereas Andy deals with the gardens, lawn, and exterior repairs.

Cleaning the inside of the house is a task that is left off both of our lists, though theoretically, it's on mine. I raise in my own defense the domestic paradox of the farm household: twice the mess, half the time. We all traipse in covered in manure, blood, milk replacer, hay chaff – you name it, it's on us somewhere. And I have less than half the time available to clean it all up. On a typical school day, I am up at 4 AM, working from 5 AM until 6 PM, eating at 7 and sleeping by 8. Saturdays I fill in for our hired hand, and Sundays I reserve for school stuff, essential laundry, and a nap.

By June, the house looks like a bomb has gone off inside. I usually send the boys to a grandparent and reserve the week after school lets out to find all the floors again. As another farm wife and her husband exclaimed, "We need a wife." Indeed.

I am not bothered by the mess. Ask my sister. She and I were constantly at loggerheads because we shared a huge closet in the hall between our bedrooms. She always hung her things up, and I hurled mine in a pile. I'm still like that, unfortunately. I do prefer the house to be neat and tidy, but given the choice between reading on the hammock or scrubbing the toilets, I'll grab the book. I will step over large piles of discarded clothing on the floor to get to my computer. On a Saturday, I'll go to Youngest's swim meet and leave all the laundry until it hits crisis levels.

I also have times when I am sequential to a fault, especially during PMS week. When the progesterone drops, my mind turns into a snarling and trenchant wheel of razor blades, and I become violently effective. Here is a good example.

We needed to tell the two muchacho farm laborers that we were replacing them. The previous day they had decided to root around in an accident scene across the street, secreting away the case of beer, bottle of rum, police pager, and driver's license they had found. For two guys who were marginally legal, this showed an extraordinary lack of judgment, and we did not want to take our chances with them any longer. Andy was exhausted and still mentally distressed from dealing with the accident the day before. We needed to fire these guys, and Andy just wasn't up to it. Luckily, PMS Woman was available.

I said to Andy, "Step aside. Let me handle this."

We went over to the mobile home together, but I did all the Spanish and stern glances, brooking no baleful looks. I could see the surprised and fearful expressions on the two guys' faces, as if to say, "Don't mess with the patrona, man."

Women's health guru Christiane Northrup explains that "The menstrual cycle itself mirrors how consciousness becomes matter and how thought creates reality."[5] As our eggs grow, develop, and reach peak fertility, so do our thoughts. I'll attest to that. During the happy part of my cycle, I'm bursting with creativity and plans. Ideas are pouring out, or pouring in from the beyond, and I have energy and happiness and more than enough progesterone to care for the boys, my students, my colleagues, my long-distance mom and sister, and Andy.

On the dark side of the moon, however, when the follicle-stimulating hormones and luteinizing hormones take the plunge, my good traits go plummeting with them. I become fixated on all the negatives in my life. I can barely tolerate Andy's Aspier sides, I snap and snarl. As I read in a graffito back in the Happy Valley of Central Mass, "I need my own menstrual hut with a Jacuzzi and no one else." I hear you, sister.

The only benefit to everyone's least favorite week of the month is that I get very, very organized. I start moving around like a banshee: I pay bills and file papers. I send the kids out so I can scour the house. I make the difficult phone calls that require severity. I fire negligent employees. I'm like a little fractal. In the yin-yang of our pairing, with Andy the abstract-sequential side and me the random-concrete, I have a cyclical yin-yang of my own: three weeks R-C and one week A-S.

How's this for horrifying? Christiane Northrup shares an insert that was routinely placed in tampon boxes in the 1960s: "Don't take advantage of your husband. That's an old rule of good marriage behavior that's just as sensible now as it ever was. Of course, you'll not try to take advantage, but sometimes ways of taking advantage aren't obvious. You wouldn't connect it with menstruation, for instance. Yet, if you neglect the simple rules that make menstruation a normal time of month, and retire for a few days each month, as though you were ill, you're taking advantage of your husband's good nature. He married a full-time wife, not a part-time one. So you should be active, peppy, and cheerful every day."[6]

I'll show you active, peppy and cheerful!

Andy, thank goodness, is quite understanding of all this. He has told me the story of sitting in Skinny's Café back in Central Massachusetts when the eponymous Skinny started complaining about his woman's cranky PMS persona. Andy stuck up for her, saying that women are absolutely allowed to be cranky during their period; it's natural due to hormonal shifts. This from the physician's son. In the Happy Valley, a feminist male is usually considered the ideal, but at Skinny's, the truckers and bikers just turned and glared.

Nowadays, I remind Andy of this statement on a regular basis: "Oh sure, it's OK for Skinny's woman to be a harridan but not me." Over the years Andy has learned to wait for me to come back. He simply goes his own way until I have emerged from under the dark cloud of progesterone depletion. I will walk out of the bathroom, announce "The hostages have been released," and there is great rejoicing.

I do try to hold onto the administrative strengths I exhibit during ebb tide, and I have also adopted Andy's finely honed techniques for getting things done even at my most estrogen-sodden. I have picked up from Andy the procedures for not just dreaming a plan, but executing it efficiently. I can think of three very specific techniques I have adopted after living with the World's Most Efficient Man (aka Andy the Aspie).

Technique 1: Backhauling. This is a trucker trick Andy learned driving for Squash, the produce company back in Massachusetts, and uses at all times on the farm. When a trucker makes a run with a full tractor trailer, he picks up another load that needs to go back the other way.

This eliminates the costly and profitless trip back with an empty truck by replacing it with a money-making load. I do this all the time on a small scale. I walk to the dumpster with a bag of trash and walk back with the employees' time cards. I walk down to the barn with the guys' paychecks, feed the calves while I'm there, and walk back up with a full milk pitcher. I walk down the stairs with a full laundry basket, load the washer, and walk back up with the vacuum. Down with all the shoes, back up with the dust rag.

Technique 2: Breaking a large project into small parts. My instincts have always been all or nothing when it comes to big projects – move all the furniture, fix all the holes, paint all the walls. If I didn't have an unappropriated week available for this, I just wouldn't do it. But I have learned from Andy that I can accomplish more by completing small pieces of a large project over a long period of time. It took me five months to repaint the kitchen, one section at a time, but it got done, in the midst of swim season and teaching a new class.

Technique 3: Time management through limiting opportunity cost. I have learned to do a cost-benefit analysis on the use of my own time. Should I spend the next hour driving to Lowe's to get paint or wait until tomorrow when I have to bring the muchachos to Walmart and get it then? Kill two birds with one stone – to a fault.

All of these things add up, remarkably, into more tasks accomplished, less time wasted, more money saved, less money spent. "Of course. What else would you expect?" says the Aspie, in a display of one of the quintessential Asperger traits. At times I feel like I'm married to the founder of scientific time management, Frederick Winslow Taylor.[7] As Ed Pickford said in the "Worker's Song," "with slide rule and stopwatch, our pride they have robbed."[8] However, I do acknowledge that abstract and sequential have their benefits.

The Chinese yin and yang symbolizes the truth that although all concepts can be divided into opposites, it takes both sides to manifest reality in its entirety. Furthermore, the two sides are mutually transforming, so that elements of the one extreme can be found in the other and vice versa. This is the reason for the white dot in the black side and the black dot in the white side. I know that I have adopted aspects of the abstract-sequential mode into my own concrete-randomness, the yang in my yin, but has Andy adopted any of my concrete-random M.O. into his own? Can an Aspergian do that and not self-destruct?

I am truly thankful for Michael John Carley's book *Asperger's From the Inside Out*, in which he challenges his fellow Aspergians to remember that "Happiness for the person with AS, perhaps obtainable, perhaps not, is your *right* just as much as it is for anyone else."[9] It other words, the goal is happiness; not efficiency, not perfection, not competence, not order and organization and absence of chaos, but happiness. Carley says that happiness for an Aspergian may actually *be* these "lesser" qualities of order because they reduce the ever-present stress. But there is also for the Aspergian, under the fear and the vulnerability, a deep desire to experience joy as the rest of the world does.

The yin of Andy's yang is very much there, perhaps in a stronger form than my own, but it gets shaded by the omnipresent anxiety that can only be quelled by order and accomplishment. I see it in Andy when no chaos or problem is encroaching: catching a fish, having a noodle battle with the kids, kissing me spontaneously in the kitchen, delighting in flowers and animals.

My sister sees this more clearly than I do, perhaps because, on her infrequent visits, she gets just a snapshot of Andy's complete mindset instead of seeing and hearing as I do the day-to-day sometimes irritating and endless simulcast of Andy's every passing fear and frustration. Andy very consciously makes time to enjoy his time and his deepest thoughts with her. Thus, her choice of James Joyce's refrigerator and her identification of Joyce's list with Andy's own.

She continues on the birthday card, "You manage to live your days to include such a breadth of life's aspects even if you never leave your land. The physical, mental, spiritual, emotional, and intellectual; the profane and the sacred are inter-leaved and inter-twined in very real ways. You *do* bring the spiritual to the daily work of the farm because of your belief in the good of land, animal, crop, labor. You elevate what too many take for granted. But you also make accessible what too many leave unexamined. Economics, literature, ethics, science, engineering – these tumble around your home easily because you believe in their ability. How rich a life abounds on those acres. Not always easy – but so rich. I have always admired what you aspire to."

My sister is much more spiritually evolved than I am. Also, in my defense, she does not function as live-in secretary and lackey to the agricultural James Joyce. She drops in for a weekend when Andy is on his best behavior, and sees only the wonderful side, not the back side of the mall where all the dumpsters are. In the midst of the trash bins, I have to wrestle long and hard with this. Sometimes I even try to thwart the best laid schemes o' time and man because I feel that otherwise I will succumb to the iron collar of efficiency and order.

Is there a right or wrong way to be? Of course, I claim it's my way. Isn't creation the manifestation of creativity and colors and surprise and not rigid time management? Didn't the creative force of the universe call forth animals in multitudes and fling extravagant galaxies into the heavens? Isn't life and love squelched by "efficiency" and scientific management? Look out! Oops, I just got pinned in a spiritual half Nelson by Robert Pirsig's *Zen and the Art of Motorcycle Maintenance*. In my teaching life, I use this book to introduce the concept of "classical" versus "romantic" to my seniors. The first time I taught it after learning of Asperger's, I had to hush up my little self-righteous random-concrete rant.

Pirsig contrasts the classical understanding of the world – structure, underlying form, clarity, precision (e.g., math, science, grammar, musical theory) – with the romantic understanding of the world – appearance, affect, freedom, colors (e.g., art, poetry) – and says that the place where they intersect is quality.[10] I urge my high school seniors to tell their prospective colleges that they as applicants encompass the best of both sides: They are mighty renaissance students, able to see from both the classical and romantic perspectives AND merge them in their idealistic young-adult selves.

But when I am living right on the razor's edge between these two sides, me fighting for romanticism and Andy fighting for classicalism, I forget this lesson. From what I have read, Aspergians are so "classical" as to practically *be* the illustration of the word in an illustrated dictionary – thus the high number of Aspergians in the fields of engineering, science, and math. Most classically oriented NT husbands have that small black dot of romantic tendency in their middles. But that's hard to find in Andy. And although I am a romantic through and through – thus the English and art double major – Andy expects and needs me to act in a classical way where the business of the farm and household are concerned. He says this is absolutely necessary in order for us to live.

However, in order to live *well*, we also need the romantic. Emotions and pleasure, joy and beauty. These are what we live *for*. So is it the A-S folks or the C-R folks who are following the right path? I know the answer to this and it's tough to swallow. As I teach my students, the answer is *both*: both done really well, both done in exquisite combination, both manifested separately and together, just as light is both wave and particle.

Take a snowflake, for example. Classically speaking, it is perfection. It is precision. It is created in multitudes through a complex mechanism of chemistry and physics. And yet, it is also beautiful. It catches the light and sparkles like diamonds. It joins with others in feathery tails, "covering earth in forgetful snow."[11] It lifts the soul and turns an infinity of colors with the changing day. Quality as manifest in nature: classical and romantic simultaneously.

Jesuit monk Teilhard de Chardin's theory was that we all move closer together as we move toward what he called the Omega Point, or oneness with God:[12] a circle of equi-distant points traveling toward their locus. It looks as though Andy and I ended up next to each other in the circle. Moving together toward the center, we merge to form one complete being with our two sensibilities joined. Through our marriage, perhaps we are meant to form a union that reveals both attributes united as quality.

Our challenge is to become our best selves, both as individuals seeking quality by being the best of our respective sides of the coin, and as one flesh by combining the yin and the yang to create unity. After all, if GE can do it, can't we?

1   I became familiar with these ads in *Country Living Magazine* during the early 1990s.

2   Attwood, Tony. (2007). *The Complete Guide to Asperger's Syndrome*. Philadelphia, PA: Jessica Kingsley Publishers; pages 309-310.

3   Scout dairy management software is available through DairyOne information cooperative.

4   This cartoon, originally published in *The New Yorker* on September 25, 1989, may be seen and purchased at The Cartoon Bank of The New Yorker at http://www.cartoonbank.com/1989/james-joyces-refrigerator/invt/113810/.

5   Northrup, Christiane. (2002). *Women's Bodies, Women's Wisdom*. New York, NY: Bantam; page 105.

6   Ibid., page 115.

7   Frederick Winslow Taylor is known as the father of scientific management, whose efficiency models revolutionized steel manufacturing.

8   To see the history and lyrics of this song and hear it, go to the Labor Notes website at http://labornotes.org/node/1500. This song was recently popularized by the Dropkick Murphy's.

9   Carley, Michael John. (2008). *Asperger's From the Inside Out*. New York, NY: Perigree; page 229.

10 This book is a classic and fascinating. Pirsig, Robert. (1974). *Zen and the Art of Motorcycle Maintenance: An Inquiry Into Values*. New York, NY: Quill/William Morrow. The discussion of classic versus romantic is found on pages 73 and 74, and the discussion of quality is on pages 222-223.

11 With thanks to T. S. Eliot's poem *The Waste Land*. (1980). From *The Complete Poems and Plays 1909-1950*. New York, NY: Harcourt Brace Jovanovich; page 37.

12 de Chardin, Teilhard. (2008). *The Phenomenon of Man*. New York, NY: Harper Perennials.

CHAPTER 17

LIMITING EXERCISES – RESTRICTIONS IN THE ASPERGIAN MARRIAGE

I have been fortunate to twice attend the Colgate Writers Conference[1] at Colgate University in Hamilton, New York. It is an incredible pleasure to be surrounded by a bunch of talented, creative, intelligent folks who want to sit around all day talking about books. The week-long conference includes intensive writing workshops in small groups, public readings, "shop talks" about the publishing process, and "craft talks" about the writing process.

At such events, I am consistently struck by the idea of writing as metaphor for life. Perhaps everything is metaphor for life. Perhaps, as the Kabbalists believe, just as pure white light, passing through a prism, becomes visible as a spectrum, all physical phenomena are essentially divine energy diffused into an infinite myriad of manifestations.[2] Divine energy as farming. Divine energy as dancing. Divine energy as long-distance running. Divine energy as writing. One popular writing challenge in particular has given me plenty to think about in terms of both writing and life as I know it. This is the idea of the Limiting Exercise.

I encountered this idea during college in a wonderful class called Methods and Materials taught by the artist Nathan Margalit.[3] One assignment we were given was to take a famous painting and spend a week? two weeks? (I don't remember) doing nothing but our own original art based on that work. I chose Vermeer's Young Woman with a Water Pitcher and created fifteen variations, each more surprising to me than the last.

Later, in my teaching life, I was once attempting to have my tenth-graders write poetry, and realized that given no parameters, the choices were too vast, and my non-poet students were, for the most part, writing schlock. Remembering my art background, I pulled out my prints of Monet's haystack series and explained to my students that I was going to give them a similar limitation to force their creativity.

I assigned a sestina, a very restrictive seven-stanza poetic form, invented in the twelfth century and still used by poets. I discovered this form in college when I read *The Complete Poems of Elizabeth Bishop*, whose poem titled "Sestina"[4] is one of the most frequently anthologized examples of the form. The summer after my friends and I finished college, we all spent the summer writing these while house-sitting in the Montague hills outside of Amherst (ah, the dilettante life of the English major).

This form restricts the poet to only six end words, rearranged over the course of seven stanzas in a very specific order. As soon as I restricted my students in this way, they began writing much more powerful and beautiful stuff.

Limiting Exercises – Restrictions in the Aspergian Marriage

As we discussed in our Colgate workshop, it is common practice for writers to set certain restrictions for themselves any time they write; point of view, for example. Do I choose first person or third person? If third person, then omniscient or limited? Once the choice is made, that to a large extent imposes restrictions on the text.

However, for the exercise we did, my workshop leader, the wonderful writer Brian Hall,[5] imposed a VERY limiting rule, so limiting that all of us in the workshop were paralyzed for a few moments, and as we worked you could hear grunts and growls of exasperation as we found ourselves roadblocked at every other word. We were to write about a funeral without using the letter "e." Here is a chunk of what I came up with:

> On my way down stairs grimy with dirt, I stop and try my ducts for salt, for liquid, for signs that what awaits within will call from my past's dim rooms any salt or sting. Finding only "dry" and "blank" in locations from which any squall or storm might tug, I walk toward a door I would turn from if I could, but approach anyway, finding it pulls my body through. Within, a hush of lights and aromas surround that I most avoid. Aunts and trailing husbands, boys and girls, dumb with discomfort, old grandma sitting on a dais as at a lost captain's prow, surround a box I avoid at all costs. I hug my mom, my dad. I slowly wind a circuitous path through bumbling cousins who touch or murmur what might sound sad but actually roars, low and ominous. Shalimar and Coty's L'aimant swirl in battling soft clouds. Mascara, lipstick, suits long hung in musty bags, skirts

and shirts in vibrant colors stab at trying on "valor" or
"joy" or any mood that adds a coat of familial gloss to
what lurks in sharp looks or harsh coughs or pointing
hands that sign out a grim truth. I finally draw up to
that obligatory black coffin and scan that craggy chin
and high brow, cold now to my touch as always it was
in mood glaring my way.

When I read this back, I realized that most of what I wrote I would
NEVER have written normally. My ideas had to come out through
some other non-"e" space, like playdough coming out the sides when
the sliding shape-maker is plugged up.

Similarly, my life sometimes feels like it is squeezing out the edges because the shape-maker is askew. Often, if I do reveal to someone that
my husband has Asperger Syndrome, that we have a dairy farm, and
that I am a teacher, people gape and say, "How do you do it?" "How
can you live like that?" and "Doesn't it sometimes just drive you crazy?" On a bad day, my answers to these questions would be "Not with
much grace," "Some days it's really hard," and "Yes."

On my more enlightened and grace-filled days, I am able to see the
whole thing as a grand exercise in creativity. Marriage to an Aspergian:
The Ultimate Limiting Exercise, which could also be the subtitle for
"Life on a Dairy Farm."

Sure, Asperger's imposes certain limitations, but doesn't every marriage? Marry a Ph.D. in history, and you are probably fated to moving
from university to university waiting for tenure. Marry a lumberjack,
and you will be living near forests. Marry someone with diabetes, and

you will be monitoring blood sugar. Look what often happens when people HAVE no limitations: Celebrity athletes worth millions go broke or commit crimes, kids who inherit enormous trust funds become alcoholics or addicts. Limitless money, limitless fawning men or women; people usually do not handle that situation well.

Benedictine monks often talk about the value of their vow of stability. Thomas Merton flopped around like a crazed ne'er-do-well until he committed himself to the most restrictive monastic order there is: The Cistercians, who do not leave the monastery and do not speak. But look at what came out of him then. Perhaps Flannery O'Connor's lupus forced her creative hand. Dorothy Day chose poverty, and her very life became her creation.[6]

The Chinese have a saying that I frequently fall back on: "One disease, long life. No disease, short life."[7] Having some sort of restriction forces us to act wisely within that restriction's confines and to care for ourselves or our marriage or our art in purposeful, thoughtful ways. The absence of restrictions allows us to live in perhaps too daring a way, putting ourselves in dangerous situations. Think of children. In the absence of restrictions, they will touch hot stoves, jump into deep water, wander into traffic. Our oldest son, as he has gotten older and we have allowed him a longer leash, has often run gratefully back into the fold when we have snagged him from some dangerous social precipice, at least until he hankers for another foray toward adulthood.

My theory on this from a scientific standpoint is that our genetic code is hardwired for limitations because that is one of nature's laws: An ecosystem will expand and diversify until some limiting factor stops it at the system's carrying capacity. There is only so much available to the system. As Jane Jacobs so brilliantly pointed out in her book *The Nature of Economies*,[8] our human economies must function under the same laws as nature because they are regulated by the same laws as nature. Our economy is made up of the ecologies on which it is based.

All living beings are forced to survive in conditions of scarcity. Plants and animals do this by instinct or by trial-and-error or stimulus-response: Fly south – NOW. No food here – migrate. Not enough nitrogen – stop growing vegetatively.

We humans employ rational choice in a condition of scarcity. No one has an infinite amount of money, time, or physical resources. You assess what you have, weigh the costs and benefits of each option, and choose accordingly. In the same way, we weigh potential spouses, look at the costs and benefits of each potential mate, and make our choice. (Can you tell the Asperger's has rubbed off on me a bit? Read John Elder Robison's chapter "Units One Through Three" in *Look Me in the Eye*[9] for a thoroughly Aspergian take on mate selection.)

Because we are rational, speaking beings, we have developed rituals that make public some of these rational choices. Marriage is one of the most significant Limiting Exercises we perform. That's what the vows are all about: "forsaking *all others, cleave* thee *only unto* him as long as *you both* shall live." That is a pretty serious Limiting Exercise right there, like writing using ONLY the vowel "e."

Sure, Asperger's imposes more restrictions than the typical marriage, and so does dairy farming. Wendell Berry talks about this in his essay "A Few Words for Motherhood."[10] As he helps a cow give birth, he thinks of Thoreau's farmer-bashing words from *Walden*, decrying the farmers' self-imposed shackling to a farm and animals (Thoreau raises my hackles, too). Berry says that we all commit to *something*, even if it is to the idea of having NO commitments. (And how long did Thoreau actually manage to keep that up? Only two years.) Wendell Berry chose farm animals. There are worse choices.

I chose Andy, and Asperger's came with the package. I could get all frustrated and kick and scream or leave, or I can accept the limitation and use it as an exercise in marital creativity. If you are an artist or a writer, when you impose a restriction on yourself, the creativity moves in other unexpected ways. My Colgate workshop leader Brian Hall encouraged us to "look for unpredictable elegant opportunities" that happen in writing when we don't dictatorially impose our own will on the text, pointing out that these often lead the text in a new direction that is BETTER than the original plan.

This is what I love about reading good literary fiction: You can tell when the writers have allowed the texts to force their hand in a way, and have followed and shaped those sometimes unplanned restrictions into art. For my own tastes, I love when a writer or artist has made beauty out of real and sometimes difficult raw material. I choose to see my marriage that way. The Asperger's has been a "restriction" that forced the writing of my life in a very different direction. Perhaps the creativity this requires of me will make of my life something more creative, and maybe more beautiful, than what it would have been without that restriction.

You can tell when a married couple has had to be creative to live and love around some kind of extreme situation: a handicapped child, an incredibly difficult job, leading a non-violent revolution. What a thing of beauty they create! Like great literary fiction, these marriages, because they *are* true, always *ring* true.

[1]   The Colgate Writers Conference is held annually the last week of June. Their website is http://groups.colgate.edu/cwc/.

[2]   I was introduced to the Kabbalah through Arthur Green's book *Ehyeh: A Kabbalah for Tomorrow.* (2004). Woodstock, VT: Jewish Lights Publishing.

[3]   Nathan Margalit was a three-year visiting artist at Amherst College, from 1986-1989. Oh, how we loved him! He may be found at www.nathanmargalit.com.

[4]   Bishop, Elizabeth. (1983). Sestina. *The Compete Poems 1927-1979.* New York, NY: Farrar, Straus, Giroux; page 123.

[5]   For a brief biography and list of titles by Brian Hall, go to http://groups.colgate.edu/cwc/staff/brian.html

[6]   For a fabulous book on all three of these people plus Walker Percy, I recommend Paul Elie's *The Life You Save Might Be Your Own: An American Pilgrimage.* (2003). New York, NY: Farrar, Straus, Giroux.

[7]   Hoff, Benjamin. (1982). *The Tao of Pooh.* New York, NY: Penguin Books; page 48.

[8]   Jacobs, Jane. (2001). *The Nature of Economies.* New York, NY: Vintage.

[9]   Robison, John Elder. (2008). *Look Me in the Eye: My Life with Asperger's.* (2008). New York, NY: Three Rivers Press; pages 247-251.

[10] Berry, Wendell. (2009). A Few Words for Motherhood. From *The Gift of Good Land: Further Essays Cultural and Agricultural.* Berkeley, CA: Counterpoint; page 196.

CHAPTER 18

ANIMAL HUSBANDRY – ASPERGER'S AND SEXUALITY

The days on the calendar that hangs over Andy's desk are marked in his handwriting with numbers, either circled or boxed, and various notes. *38-K* is circled on August 8, *4804* is boxed on August 22, "Lute CIDR hfrs" is the note on August 7. I know that these mean 38-K needs to be bred on August 8, cow number 4804 will have her calf on August 22, and on August 7 Andy will give hormone shots to start some heifers cycling for breeding.

The calendar itself is printed with daily labels such as "Next Heat 9/19" and "Due 6/4." The gorgeous girlie who graces August is Big Time Kenai Laura, a daughter of 1JE0346 Kenai from River Falls, Wisconsin.[1] She is a luscious thing: tight udder attachment, squarely placed teats, deep crease, strong in the loin, deep in the barrel, level in the rump from hocks to pins – overall hot-babe dairyness.

I look carefully to see if there are any notes on the calendar about me, such as "PMS starts" or one week later "ETA" or a week after that "Full Moon!" because I know Andy tracks my reproductive cycle every bit as carefully as the cycles of our 200+ cows and heifers. The unusual thing about being married to a dairy farmer who also has Asperger's is becoming very, very in touch with my own animal self, because Andy is so animal-like himself.

I mean this as the highest of compliments. Ask any woman if she would run off with her dog and live happily ever after (absent the sex), and I am guessing she would say yes. I know I would. Dogs are awesome. They provide unconditional love, sensitivity to your every emotion, eagerness to do anything you suggest just for the pleasure of your company, oblivion to your face, hair, or clothes, minimal needs, adoring glances, physical affection. If your dog could suddenly become articulate and put all that adoration into words plus maybe some interesting conversation about politics or books, you've got the perfect companion.

With Andy, I get all that "woman's best friend" stuff plus the conversation plus the sex. Again, I say this in the most complimentary of terms. I wanted to live on a farm because, in general, I prefer animals to humans. You don't have to explain yourself to animals, just be with them. And I am sure I was attracted to Andy for the same reason.

Temple Grandin agrees: "An autistic person's feelings are direct and open, just like animal feelings. We don't hide our feelings, and we aren't ambivalent ... "[2] She explains that animals, like many on the spectrum, have four core emotions: rage, prey chase/drive, fear, and curiosity/interest/anticipation, as well as four core social emotions: social attachment, separation distress, play/roughhousing, and sexual attraction/lust.

As an NT, apparently I outgrew these or they became more sophisticated as my frontal lobes grew. However, I did have a renewed experience with my own purely animal-like responses just after each of our boys was born. I would be downtown running an errand, having left little baby Middle home with my mom, and I would know he was hungry from ten miles away. I could feel the oxytocin shooting through my body. My milk would drop, and I would become as agitated as a cow whose newborn calf has stumbled under the fence into the adjacent pasture. I would just about moo in distress the whole way home until my baby was in my arms and attached. That is a powerful feeling.

This helps me understand why some of Andy's behaviors seem extreme and distressing in their intensity. His rage I have seen and despaired of, but just as in an animal, it comes with a fury and then is gone.

His fear response is probably the emotion that makes us all the craziest. I just moved a bunch of calves the other day, and every single step of the process elicited in them a fear response: getting the halter on, coming out of the hutch, crossing from dirt to concrete, entering a dark barn. Similarly, I remember when our farm was chosen as a host site for the Northeast Dairy Challenge.[3] This is a competition in which college teams of dairy management students visit a farm and make observations and suggestions. A panel of professional agricultural consultants judges the student presentations and also offers their own professional ideas to the hosts as a thank you.

I met alone with our farm's judge group to hear their thoughts; this would not have been a good situation for Andy. One of their primary questions, after looking at our equipment inventory, borrowing habits, and management techniques was, "Is your husband always so averse to risk?"

Yes, he's part animal; he is physiologically and genetically and instinctively averse to risk.

On the other hand, if the prey is within sight – if a positive rate of return on investment is one more harvested field or completion of the new addition away – I see the prey chase/drive instinct in as frightening a form as a wolf chasing down a rabbit. Do not get in Andy's way.

And curiosity/interest/anticipation? If Andy gets new hunting gear in the mail or is getting ready for a fishing expedition, he is as irrepressible in his glee as a little kid on Christmas morning, or our dog Riley when I say, "Want to go for a run?"

As far as the animal's primary social emotions are concerned, I know this is why Andy's loyalty to me is so strong, as strong as Riley's. For Riley, *I* am his human; there is no questioning that. Andy would no more have an affair than Riley would choose to run off with a new owner. It's that simple.

It also explains why Andy gets so distressed when I go away for a day or two. I used to ascribe it to the fact that when one of Andy's former girlfriends went to Europe to lead a bike trip, she ended up having an affair with the other leader. But it's much simpler than that. It's separation anxiety, similar to when I left the boys at the sitter the first few times or when Riley sees us getting in the car.

I used to get very angry at this: Here I am trying to get ready to leave for a trip, I'm the one with the tension and difficulties ahead, and Andy is the one stressing out. I am the one who needs reassurance and calm, but Andy is the one who is as agitated as a dog in a thunderstorm.

And then there's sex. Grandin says, "Sex is a very strong drive in any animal, so humans who take care of animals always have to be dealing with their sexuality in one way or another."[4] So do humans married to Aspies. Our somewhat unique case is an Aspie whose business depends on getting his cows rebred on time. Such an Aspie develops a tremendous focus on understanding the sexual needs of his bovine girls.

Grandin shares the story of an extraordinarily successful pig breeder who had discovered the individual "perversions" of each of his boars in order to collect their semen. He also had to learn how to arouse each individual sow so her uterus would maximally pull in the semen; each sow had to be ready to "stand" so that the semen that was inserted would result in the greatest litter. "A good breeder knows when his sows are ready to stand for the man,"[5] Grandin says. Though this breeder blushed in her presence describing the various techniques he had mastered, his business success depended on it.

In our situation, start with an Aspie man who has a simple, direct, and consistent sexual drive, add to that the Aspie's no-holds-barred prey-chase/drive focus on attaining his goal, plus include a dairy farmer's sensitivity to female reproductive peculiarities, make this whole enterprise one of the Aspie's special interests, and you end up with a highly satisfied wife. Enough said.

I do not mean to imply that our sex life is the same as what happens in our barn, because other parts of Andy's brain are fully mature with all the culture, aesthetics, poetry, and passion that mark the apex of cognition in human beings. Maybe being married and living on a farm has just taken us both back to an earlier and earthier form of passionate love. I was recently reminded of a beautiful arrangement by Samuel Barber of the poem "The Coolin'" by James Stephens:[6]

> Come with me, under my coat,
> and we will drink our fill
> of the milk of the white goat,
> or wine if it be thy will.
> And we will talk,
> until talk is a trouble, too,
> out on the side of the hill;
> And nothing is left to do,
> but an eye to look into an eye,
> and a hand in a hand to slip;
> and a sigh to answer a sigh;
> And a lip to find out a lip!

I remember singing this standing next to my Amherst Choir peers, and I can guarantee you none of them had experienced this in real life, but I had ... well, replace the goat with sheep. There is something about having the modern cinematic entrapments of romantic life replaced by the earthy sensuality of farm life that creates a whole different sort of passion.

I truly lucked out, and I am thankful for this every day. My Aspie has developed sex as a special interest, and he has the ability to also provide its emotional complement.

One day when I got home from school, Andy was in the barn but had left me a little poem he had written at some point during the day: "In the last long days of this cold winter, I think of you and continue on.

You are beauty and light."

And that night wasn't even a full moon.

[1] Based on the 2008 CRI (Cooperative Resources International) calendar.

[2] Grandin, Temple. (2005). *Animals in Translation.* New York, NY: Scribner; page 89.

[3] Northeast Regional Dairy Challenge is part of the North American Intercollegiate Dairy Challenge. Their mission is to "To facilitate education, communication and an exchange of ideas among students, agribusiness, dairy producers and universities that enhances the development of the dairy industry and its leaders." Information may be found at http://www.dairychallenge.org/index.php.

[4] Grandin, *Animals in Translation;* page 101.

[5] Ibid., page 104.

[6] Barber, Samuel. (1942). *Reincarnations, No. 3: The Coolin* (The Fair Haired One). Based on James Stephens' poem. Milwaukee, WI: Hal Leonard Corp. Used with permission.

CHAPTER 19

WHAT AN ECCENTRIC PERFORMANCE – THE ASPERGIAN PARENT

X

S
ex is all well and good, but, as we all know, it sometimes leads to children. Andy and I had unprotected intercourse three times. And guess what? We have three children. We used to joke that if Andy simply walked behind me in the kitchen, I would get pregnant. I am so thankful, really. I know this is not the case for all couples. And I do adore my kids.

However, one of the places that Asperger Syndrome causes problems is in the realm of parenting. Let me explain by example.

It is 10 AM on a Saturday morning in mid-January. I have already been to the barn and fed the calves. Eldest is still asleep. Middle and Youngest have recently rolled out of bed. The three of us are crashed in various reclining poses on the living room furniture watching the last half hour of the movie during which we all fell asleep the night before. The accumulated fatigue and information saturation of a long week at school have left us all brain-dead. We are waiting to recharge before attempting to greet the weekend in a house buried under snow in negative-ten weather.

The back door to the mudroom slams. We in the living room exchange glances. Stomp, stomp, stomp. The door into the kitchen slams. We all struggle upright, rub our eyes, and start to rise.

"Boys!? Who left all this food on the counter?!"

"Sorry, I did," I say struggling to my feet and aiming for the kitchen.

Stomp, stomp, stomp, into the office.

"Middle! Get in here now and get these CDs off my desk!"

Middle struggles into the office and starts piling CDs. "OK! OK!"

Stomp, stomp, stomp, into the living room.

"Youngest! Clean up these videotapes! I can't even walk through here!"

"OK, Dad! Jeez!" Youngest rolls off the couch and starts putting videos into sleeves.

"Where's Eldest!?!? Is he still asleep?!? It's TEN!! I've been up since four o'clock!"

How could we not know this, since we are told this fact every day?

Stomp, stomp, stomp, up the stairs.

"Eldest! Get up! It's 10 AM. I need help in the barn!!"

"Arrrr!"

Stomp, stomp, stomp, into our bedroom.

"Are there clean clothes anywhere?!?! Mo?!?! Are there any clean clothes? I am out of underwear. I've been outside in this blizzard for six hours and I'm soaking wet and freezing!!!"

I have crept up the stairs and into our room. "No, sorry. I was just about to put some in the wash."

"I need your help in the barn. I need everyone's help. There's a bad ice storm coming. We need to get the tractor hooked to the generator."

Stomp, stomp, stomp, down the stairs.

"Youngest! Stop messing with those videos and get some warm clothes on. You guys need to feed the heifers, and then I need your help in the barn covering up some gaps in the wall before the ice hits."

Stomp, stomp, stomp, into the office.

"Middle! Stop playing with those CDs and put on your snow clothes. Meet me in the barn. I have something you need to do. Mo!!!! Get Eldest up. He can feed the third-row cows."

The door to the mudroom slams. Stomp, stomp, stomp. The door to the outside slams. Silence.

By this point, all four of us are in the kitchen rubbing our eyes and looking at each other in resigned exasperation.

Parenting, Asperger style: What an eccentric performance.

During a family scene like this, I always think of Tim the Enchanter from *Monty Python and the Holy Grail*. When Arthur and Bedevere and Sir Robin set out on their search to find the enchanter of whom the old man had spoken in scene twenty-four, they round a Scottish mountain and see an explosion on a distant peak. Nearing the spot, they see a strange man standing atop a crag. He points toward another crest and another and another and another and another, each time apparently launching a fire bomb from his finger that explodes in a huge ball of flame. He finally blasts himself down into the presence of King Arthur and the knights and fires another two small blasts nearby for good measure.[1]

What is absurd about this is that these explosions seem to serve no purpose but to demonstrate Tim the Enchanter's powers. In the midst of their greetings, Tim suddenly uses his staff as a flamethrower to singe the immediate area and then launches a rocket from it, setting a nearby tree afire, at which the knights offer polite applause.

Thinking of this, I almost start to laugh when Andy comes striding in and starts pointing out troublesome issues in the house. Point – Pkkkkkooooo! Point – Pkkkkkooooo! Boom. Boom. Boom. I mentally refer to this as the result of Andy's tendency to "look at the world through shit-colored glasses." He walks in, worried and anxious about the coming storm, and all he can see are the problems waiting to happen inside: the milk on the counter going bad, his desk covered with CDs that cover his seven to-do lists, the videos about to get broken, the fifteen-year-old who sleeps until noon. He doesn't see us, our exhaustion, or need for emotional contact, just a long series of problems that need to get solved before anyone should be able to relax.

At best, such a scene can be interpreted as unintentional anger resulting from autistic anxiety. At worst, it can seem like Andy taking out his frustration on whoever's nearest.

In an interview on National Public Radio's Fresh Air, comedian Damon Wayans told of his childhood growing up with nine siblings in a three-bedroom apartment. His father would come home from a long day working at the grocery store, and the children would all run and hide: "You didn't want daddy mad 'cause daddy was like, venting. He would come home looking to spank after a hard day's work. 'All right, who was bad 'cause I need to unwind.'"[2]

Wayans tells this tale laughing and with a voice full of love, admitting that with so many children, order had to be maintained to keep the chaos at bay. He credits the enforced sibling harmony for the sense of humor he and four of his siblings were later able to develop into successful comedic careers.

I am similarly able to credit growing up in an alcoholic household for my ability to read others' emotions, handle rapid change without a hiccup, and completely ignore people's moods when I have determined they were not caused by me. I hope that growing up with an Aspergian will have some positive effects on our boys. Tony Attwood says that "The lack of affection and encouragement, and high expectations [of an Aspergian parent] can result in the child becoming an adult who is a high achiever, as an attempt to eventually experience the parental adulation that was missing throughout childhood."[3] I have heard the same both from Andy's father about his own childhood and from Andy about his.

I had a similar quest, except mine was an attempt to use the McCarthy girls' achievements to cover up the problems at home. (My sister's name and my own are side-by-side on Lockport High School's valedictorian plaque, each of us number one in a class of 400+.)

However, for a parent with Asperger's, the impetus for strictness and control are very personal and understandably self-protective, especially when the Aspergian father is a farmer. When problems arise, the sensations are so overwhelming and fear-provoking that problems have to be avoided and diverted whenever possible. Thus, the eccentric responses even during periods of seeming peacefulness.

To further illustrate, on a typical summer's day, when a given morning's farm problems are finally resolved and we are fully awake, we might start hinting around about our "recreational" plans.

"So, there's a movie the boys want to see at the Colonia Theater."

"Mmmmhmmm?" Andy looks at me questioningly.

"Um, it starts at 1?"

"OK ....?"

"And uh, the boys have been wanting to see it …?"

"Yeah?" Andy still hasn't figured it out. I have forgotten temporarily about not relying on facial and voice cues to relay my message to my Aspie husband.

"So, I was thinking of taking them down there."

Now he's got it.

"Please don't do that! I have hay down. Tim's not here, and I just can't deal with any extra problems or issues! I don't have time to come down there and haul you back up the hill if something happens! Please don't let the boys know you are even thinking about it!"

This is a good example of 0 to 10 in one second – over what? a potential movie excursion.

Back to *Monty Python* – Tim launches into a fearful description of the creature that guards the cave wherein the information about the grail's final resting place is located, "a creature so foul, so cruel that no man yet has fought with it and lived! Bones of full fifty men lie strewn about its lair. So, brave knights, if you do doubt your courage or your strength, come no further, for death awaits you all with nasty, big, pointy teeth," at which point he raises his hand like a mouth full of fangs and bizarrely imitates said nasty beastie. King Arthur turns to his knights and says, "What an eccentric performance."[4]

This is the look the boys and I give each other back in the kitchen after Andy has stomped out: a combination of puzzlement, exasperation, and resignation. We cannot explain his strange performance, but we know we had better join in the horror or there will be hell to pay.

Tony Attwood delineates the issues involving parents with Asperger Syndrome, including "little understanding of the needs and behaviour of typical children and adolescents," the need of the family to "accommodate the imposition of inflexible routines and expectations in behavior, the intolerance of noise, mess, and any intrusion in the parent's solitary activities, perceived 'invasion' of the home by the children's friends, and a black and white analysis of people."[5]

In extreme cases, there can be abuse. This last has never happened in our family, aside from the unintended emotional abuse that results from the children misinterpreting Andy's behavior as lack of affection or tiring of the criticism, public embarrassment, fear of his mood, or feeling like a nuisance. This typically happens when Andy's anxiety is expressed as unintended anger at the boys, besides which it leaves me as "the mediator, negotiator, referee, rule-maker, wiper up of tears, confidante – in other words, all things to all people."[6]

It has been helpful to have the "diagnosis" and explain it to the kids, who were fifteen, thirteen, and eleven when we finally figured it out. Before our discovery, I had already learned as Andy's wife to let these kinds of behaviors roll off me and not take them personally, but the kids have often been unable to understand his actions toward them.

Nowadays, after Andy has stormed from the room, Youngest will sigh, give me a knowing look, and say, "Asperger's?"

I'll smile at him with pride and nod.

All of this has given me a chance to explain adult behaviors to the kids. Having grown up in a dysfunctional household, I remember being mystified and crushed by the behaviors of the adults around me. Finally, knowing about alcoholism and learning about the traits and issues of adult children of alcoholics was enormously helpful.

Too many children spend their childhoods blaming themselves for their parents' behavior: divorce, abuse, exploitation, neglect. I have followed the policy of extreme honesty with the kids, knowing that what children imagine a situation to be is usually much worse than reality.

I wish someone had had the wherewithal to clue me in at a younger age that my particular crowd of adults had issues and personalities that were separate from my ability to influence them. I once heard that Oscar the Grouch was created as a character on Sesame Street to teach children that some people are just grouchy by nature but can still be cherished and not changed.[7]

So in the past few years, I have been able to say, "Dad is very worried. He really doesn't mean to sound mean. He's really anxious and worried about a million details, and he loves you guys. It's just that the Asperger's makes him sound upset. He is upset, but not at you."

"It *sounds* like he's upset at me," says Youngest.

"Why does he have to overreact to everything?" asks Eldest.

Unfortunately, about one time in ten the overreaction is justified. The dire prediction is accurate, and only Andy's massive preparation and marshalling of the troops prevents disaster. In the Asperger world, these odds are good enough. To prevent *any* potential disaster is worth the extreme actions necessary.

Similarly, Tim the Enchanter is right about the scary "beast." Arriving at the Cave of Caerbannog, the knights mock Tim's calamitous warnings when they see that the horrible cruel vicious beast is a little white rabbit that at worst might nibble their bums. At King Arthur's command, Bors plunges ahead without fear to kill the bunny when the fuzzy little thing zooms through the air and latches onto his neck: His headless trunk falls to the ground squirting blood.

Tim the Enchanter rubs it in: "I warned you, but did you listen to me? Oh, no, you knew it all, didn't you? Oh, it's just a harmless little bunny, isn't it? Well, it's always the same. I always tell them …"[8]

Aspergians are the kings of "I told you so." I think this is partly because they are so accustomed to being treated as if their actions are unusual, unmerited, or extreme that when they *are* right, they need to jump up and assert their correctness. Andy must feel relieved and "normal" when his dire actions prove merited.

I am thankful for Temple Grandin and Sean Barron's *Unwritten Rules of Social Relationships.* This has become the new "textbook" for Andy and me. Both authors have a spectrum disorder and have done their readers an enormous service by explaining how the autism spectrum brain operates and how it can be channeled to understand and learn the social skills we NTs take for granted. Rule #2 is "Not Everything That Happens Is Equally Important in the Grand Scheme of Things." I think this rule is what will help bring our Aspergian family into some semblance of a normal family.

In trying to describe the black-and-white thinking of most people on the spectrum, Grandin and Barron say, "Your emotions swing wildly, in an all-or-nothing manner. They're either off or on; nothing in between."[9] In twenty pages, Grandin and Barron give examples of this, explain why it is so, and then offer tools for teaching shades of gray, including the 1-through-5 scale for assessing the importance or danger of a situation.

Rule #2, they say, is so self-evident to NTs "that the idea that it may need to be verbalized and even taught is in itself a revelation." This re-education will fall to me with reinforcement by Andy, who has said that he physically needs to carry with him a small "toolbox" of reminders of these tools and rules that are startlingly new to him.

The boys have adopted their own creative techniques for dealing with Andy's Tasmanian parenting style. Middle (who thought that NT stood for Non-Taz) figured out a few years ago that if Andy is scanning the surroundings looking for problems and his eyes are heading Middle's way, Middle can distract Andy by asking about something Andy is interested in.

For example, Middle was sitting in the midst of a huge Lego mess the other morning when Andy came in. Craftily diverting a huge screaming session he knew would soon erupt over the disarray, Middle told his dad that the Legos he had just received in the mail had been hand-fashioned on a CNC (computer numerical control) machine.

Andy paused, and then said, "I used to work on a CNC machine." Mess forgotten!

Middle caught this entire scene on his digital video camera: a five-minute monologue by Andy on CNC machines and how they work, which Middle played and replayed all day to his own great amusement. Middle has developed an alternate technique to divert his dad's outbursts: to start talking about something he knows will bore Andy. Andy will listen for ten seconds and then wander away.

Youngest has lately developed a wonderfully disarming and effective way of defusing a Tasmanian attack. The other night Middle had gone to a dance at the YMCA, and the rest of us drove downtown to pick him up at 8 PM. Unfortunately, the dance had ended at 7:30. Middle had given up on us at 7:55 and walked off with a friend. We did not know where he was, who he was with, if he planned to return to the Y, etc. I jumped out of the Jeep and did a quick scan of the local pizza places where Middle might have walked for a slice, but soon returned unsuccessful.

I could see Andy was moving quickly toward the red zone: Middle had done a stupid thing, there was no way to find him, Andy needed to get to bed, etc., etc. I was preparing for Andy to completely blow in the middle of downtown Norwich. I knew his reaction was based on fear, but I had given up trying to defuse him in the midst of one of these scenes. I was just intent on finding Middle and removing the negative stimulus.

Andy continued, loudly and irrationally fending off the bad joo joo with screams: "When Middle gets home, he's going straight to bed and no X-Box! Why would he just leave? What a stupid thing to do!" At that point, the ten-year-old sage in the back seat piped up with an adult sigh of self-knowledge, "As if we all don't do stupid things sometimes."

Andy halted, paused, and then laughed. Youngest just turned to me and winked.

The one with the least ability to adjust to Andy's moods is Eldest, who fights back in his own somewhat Aspergian way with logic and determination.

My incensed eldest son will say to Andy, "Why do you have to go on and on? I know I need to do my chores. You don't have to tell me fifteen times. I always do my chores! Have I ever not done my chores? Have I?"

He simply won't let it drop, pushing the point of any hyperbole on Andy's part because the lack of accuracy drives him mad. It still astonishes me how an Aspie can be so alert to everyone else's exaggerations yet so oblivious to his own. Sigh. This is not unusual. Tony Attwood says, "The enforced proximity of two inflexible and dominating characters …. can lead to animosity and arguments."[10]

Except if I send the two Aspergians off to tackle a mechanical issue: pop up the camper, build the Ikea shelves. One day Andy was heading out solo to a nearby lake to test the trolling boat's "check engine light," which had gone on during his previous outing. I suggested that he take Eldest along. I admit that I was irritated that Andy was off to spend two hours alone, leaving me with the three boys. But I also saw a potential bonding experience.

"Why don't you take Eldest?"

"He won't want to go with me."

"Tell him you need his mechanical expertise."

This seemed to do the trick with Eldest: Approbation. Appreciation. Acknowledgment of skill. Predictable dialogue based on problem-solving.

It was a resounding success on all fronts. Andy was able to be with just one son in a situation where the two of them shared an interest, and both got to feel good about solving the mechanical problem. Besides which, once the boat was deemed fully functional, Andy let Eldest cruise up and down the lake, and they both stimmed out on the sparkle of sun on the water.

Meanwhile, I took Middle and Youngest to a bluegrass festival, an event with so much stimulation and so many unpredictable social situations that it would have driven Andy into neurological engine failure.

It was a good day. Everyone stayed calm. Everyone had fun. We had scheduled the day with Asperger's in mind and it worked.

And so, Maureen and Middle and Youngest came back from their quest to see the bluegrass festival of which their schools had apprised them in late spring. At the farm, they met Dad and Eldest, and there was much rejoicing.

And no eccentric performance.

[1]   For the script, Chapman, Gary. (2002). *Monty Python and the Holy Grail Screenplay.* Methuen Publishing, Ltd. For the movie, Sony, 1999.

[2]   Comedian Damon Wayan. *Fresh Air.* Oct 21, 1999. http://www.npr.org/templates/run-downs/rundown.php?prgId=13&prgDate=6-14-1999.

[3]   Attwood, Tony. (2007). *The Complete Guide to Asperger's Syndrome.* Philadelphia, PA: Jessica Kingsley Publishers; page 313.

[4]   *Monty Python and the Holy Grail.* Sony, 1999.

[5]   Attwood, *The Complete Guide to Asperger's Syndrome,* pages 311-312.

[6]   Aston, Maxine. (2002). *The Other Half of Asperger Syndrome: A Guide to Living in an Intimate Relationship With a Partner Who Has Asperger Syndrome.* Shawnee Mission, KS: AAPC Publishing; page 58.

[7]   See the description of Oscar on the Sesame Street website: http://www.sesamestreet.org/onair/characters/oscar.

[8]   *Monty Python.*

[9]   Grandin, Temple, & Barron, Sean. (2005). *Unwritten Rules of Social Relationships: Decoding Social Mysteries Through the Unique Perspectives of Autism.* Arlington, TX: Future Horizons, Inc.; page 145.

[10]   Attwood, *The Complete Guide to Asperger's Syndrome,* page 313.

CHAPTER 20

E-I-E-O WILSON – ASPERGER'S AND EVOLUTION

Living on a farm has given Andy and me lots of opportunities to discuss animal adaptation and evolution, especially since we are both intrigued by sociobiology and evolutionary theory. Why is it easier to chase a cow than to lead a cow? Because cows have no protective adaptations like sharp teeth or claws, so they protect themselves by immersing themselves in a herd. Their defense mechanism is to run back into their group. It is an evolutionary adaptation.

Why do Canada geese fly in a V formation? Because the long distances they fly to migrate south is exhausting and they need to take turns leading and cutting the wind for those behind. When one goose gets tired, he falls back into the V and lets another take over. It is an evolutionary adaptation.

Loving the Tasmanian Devil

Why do cats have so many kittens? Because so many of the kittens get crushed by cows, eaten by coyotes, or walk through a fan. If only half of each litter survives, it's best to have many of them. It's an evolutionary adaptation.

There's a lot of buzz on the Internet over whether Asperger's might be an adaptation that is leading the human species in a new direction. Psychologist and Aspergian Jim Sinclair playfully dubs the emerging subspecies *homo aspergerus*, writing "Progress usually requires one person who can think outside the box, extend concepts into unexpected new realms, and develop new ways of looking at the world. Even in an overcrowded world that increasingly celebrates 'teamwork' as the ultimate human virtue, we have observed in this century remarkable individuals whose novel ideas sparked revolutions in fields ranging from mathematics and physics to music and art."[1] Aspergians excel at this, preferring solitary pursuit of a focused topic to social interaction. The amazing achievements of Einstein and other probable "Aspergian Mutants" have given us remarkable advancements in the sciences and arts.

Sinclair contends that in earlier evolutionary stages, social groupings were essential to human survival. When *homo neanderthalensis* was battling for scarce food resources, tribes and groups were necessary for a successful hunt or to expel a competing group from a habitat with a limited food supply. Nowadays, in a world where managed agricultural ecosystems produce more than enough to feed the human population if distributed equitably, fierce loyalty to national or ethnic or religious groupings leads not to survival but to war and xenophobia. Sinclair writes, "Could it be that this [AS] gene is telling us: focus on development, and stop grouping so tightly that you might war yourselves out to extinction? Could it be that this is the mutation that was there for a while but was discovered in our time, now that we are ready?"

Another Aspergian on the Internet balances the less desirable traits of Asperger's, such as clumsiness, oversensitivity, and rigidity, against the advantageous aspects, such as "honesty (inability to lie and pretend), sense of justice, conscientiousness (including ability to focus on a subject …), and a wide associative horizon (including not being restricted in one's thinking by the conventions of the herd, the dull mass)."[2] Considering the worldwide wreckage some presidential administrations leave in their wakes due to their lack of honesty, sense of justice, conscientiousness, and a wide associative horizon, I think that appointment of at least one Aspergian to any incoming administration's staff might be essential to the species' survival.

On the other hand, much of what we consider the most laudable adaptations in humankind's evolution are the so-called "social skills." Love for another, compassion, self-sacrifice, humility, mercy, these are considered some of mankind's highest callings and necessitate humans coming together and bonding in profound ways. Sociobiologist E. O. Wilson, in one of his at-the-time controversial theories from the 1960s,[3] claimed that even altruism is ultimately attributable to "selfish" evolutionary pressures: Giving to the other in order to barter reciprocation is done ultimately to ensure the group's genetic pool with the ultimate goal of preserving one's own genetic strain, the so-called "kin selection" concept. In other words, social behavior, including religion, familial nurturing, and "love," could all be traced to the individual's biological desire to further his tribe's genetic code.

I find this theory somewhat abhorrent since it precludes and ignores the possibility of a sacred force that might be guiding or drawing species change. I have always been fascinated by the theories of Jesuit monk and geologist Teilhard de Chardin, whose intellectual and spiritual quest was to merge his scientific belief in Darwin's evolutionary theory with his religious belief in a God-driven purpose for creation. His book *The Phenomenon of Man*[4] puts forth a hypothesis that merges the two. He expanded the traditional interpretation of Genesis to see the creative "days" as "eras" long enough to allow the evolution of life from single-celled to human that corresponded to Darwin's evolutionary sequence.

The goal of this process, de Chardin wrote, is what he calls the Omega Point, the draw of God and by God to pull his creation to full consciousness and ultimately Godhood. As life becomes more complex, it becomes more aware, forming a "noosphere" of conscious thought. This would make *homo sapiens* closest in kind to God or "created in God's image." De Chardin posited that the next step in creation's complexification and deification would involve unity, worldwide unity, which would draw living things together and upward into unity of thought and finally unity of spirit, the final destination of the physical universe.

This theory gives me a much better starting point for speculating on a role for Asperger's in an evolutionary context. When I think of the Aspergian advantages as I have experienced them – recognition of complex patterns, awareness of detail, alertness to sensation – these seem to be characteristic of what even the most secular of scientists recognize as an ordering principle in the universe. Call it God, call it science, call it what you will, it can be observed through objective examination.

The snowflake, the starfish, honeycombs, planetary motion, symmetry, or even the more complex concept of "broken symmetry," all of these Christian Wertenbaker offers in *Parabola* magazine as evidence of the complex complexity of creation. "One could say that human beings, the most complex and the most conscious of creatures on earth, are almost the most asymmetric, in a sequence of broken symmetries from the primordial unified force to the asymmetries of the two hemispheres [of the brain]."[5] The Aspergian mind is exquisitely sensitive to these patterns, to the "computer coding" of a divine programmer. Einstein said in 1954, "If something is in me which can be called religious then it is the unbounded admiration for the structure of the world so far as our science can reveal it."[6]

But what about the other abstract essences that people see as irrefutable proof of God, essences such as empathy, love, and altruism? The Aspergian, in the single-minded focus of his quest, can appear to be isolationist, self-centered, or thoughtless. The other day Andy said of this trait, half-joking, "Actually, it can be lonely and grueling to be this way. But it's a sacrifice we're willing to make on behalf of the group."

I can see that: Make the farm thrive on our behalf, figure out relativity so that mankind can advance, create exquisite musical compositions to lift the soul. These are altruistic – helping society, though simultaneously "damaging" oneself through solitude.

So where does this leave Aspergerism in the plan for the universe's emerging complexity? One thing I have studied in order to teach ecology to my students is not the theory of E. O. Wilson, the father of sociobiology, but that of Eugene Odum, the father of ecology, the first to delineate ecosystem theory. In his 1959 text *Fundamentals of Ecology,*[7] Odum explains how all parts of the environment – living and non-living – are necessary to the functioning of the system, from the abiotic elements of soil and water to each level of biota, from single-celled bacteria to third-level consumers. Remove any one of these components, and the entire system can fall apart. Limit phosphorus, for example, and the entire food pyramid collapses for lack of producer species. Remove the wolves, and every trophic level below is impacted by overpopulation of the wolves' prey.

Also, Odum says, ecosystems move from simple to increasingly complex and more life-filled through the process of ecological succession. The more complex the system, the more robust it is, with increased biodiversity and more complicated webs of interdependence and, therefore, stability. If we are looking for God's thumbprint in natural systems, he/she/it clearly prefers complexity, diversity, and interdependence. This means that no one species in the evolutionary process is more important or more advanced than another. One species might be the most complex, but it could be decimated in a week by the simplest of viruses or stopped in its progress by the absence of one nutrient.

So are the Aspies ahead on the evolutionary curve or behind? Is the species moving toward more Aspergerdom or less? Actually, I think this is the wrong question to ask. Taking the rest of physical phenomena as the template, it looks to me like we are moving toward greater diversity of neurological ability, just as the rest of nature tends toward greater biological diversity. Should we all be Aspergians? Should we all be NTs? That's like asking if all bears should be pandas or all insects mosquitoes. Species tend to co-evolve, with change in one species dependent upon change in another.

The Aspergians help the species through focus intensity, truth seeking, and pattern genius. The NTs provide empathy, compassion, and sociability. For this same reason, many decry the genetic screening and possible elimination of "undesirable" conditions such as Down's syndrome, because with it would vanish the unbelievable capacity for unconditional and freely expressed love and joy seen in people with Down's. Also, these differences in neurological and genetic structure call on us all to develop compassion, tolerance, and understanding.

How very like the worst side of humanhood that we vie for position as the "vanguard" of evolutionary progress. If we look at evolution's blueprint, it is not a projectile that rockets forward and leaves everything else behind. After all, the advent of humans did not necessitate the extinction of the amoeba. Each new species moves creation toward complexity not simplicity. Useless or dysfunctional mutations do fall by the wayside eventually, and in the human realm, thank goodness, social conceptions such as slavery and chauvinism are rapidly or more slowly dying away.

Where is it all heading? Who knows? The ape could not have imagined *homo erectus* nor the dinosaur his descendent the eagle. However, sentience does give us the responsibility to observe and be responsible to the pattern of which we are a part. A stable and thriving ecosystem requires each species to inhabit its niche. We need Aspies to do what they do. We need NTs to do what they do. We need people with Down's syndrome to do what they do.

We see this on the farm daily. We need the bacteria to break down the manure. We need the nitrogen-fixing rhizoids to form protein in the red clover. We need the bees to pollinate the clover. We need the timothy and orchard grass to nourish our cows. We need our cows to produce milk for us and for others, and the cows need us to shelter and feed them and protect them from disease.

E. O. Wilson may have explained some of the early evolutionary mechanisms by which group behavior evolved, but de Chardin provides a much more comprehensive picture of why. And since "why?" seems to be a genetically coded question among human beings, it seems a question that evolution wants us to ask and perhaps some day answer. We are born into and live within a pattern of such beauty, such orderly chaos, such intricacy, and richness that even the world's most sophisticated scientists are ultimately left speechless and on their knees in its presence. We humans, whatever our neurological configuration, are but a small part of that enormous mystery. That realization is enough to put all of us in our proper place.

¹ Sinclair, Jim. http://web.syr.edu/~jisincla.

² Paul Cooijmans. (2006-2010). *Straight Talk About Asperger Syndrome.* http://www.paul-cooijmans.com/asperger/straight_talk_about_asperger.html.

³ Wilson, Edmund O. (2000). *Sociobiology: The New Synthesis, Twenty-fifth Anniversary Edition.* Cambridge, MA: Belknap Press of Harvard University Press.

⁴ De Chardin, Pierre Teilhard. (1975). *The Phenomenon of Man.* New York, NY: Harper Perennial.

⁵ Wertenbaker, Christian. (1999, Fall). Nature's Patterns. *Parabola, 24*(1), Nature.

⁶ Kaku, Michio. (2005). *Einstein's Cosmos: How Albert Einstein's Vision Transformed Our Understanding of Space and Time.* New York, NY: W. W. Norton & Company; page 128.

⁷ Odum, Eugene. (1954). *Fundamentals of Ecology.* Philadelphia, PA: W. B. Saunders.

CHAPTER 21

TUCKERED-OUT DUCK – A DAY IN THE LIFE OF AN ASPERGIAN FAMILY

It's true that the unique gifts bestowed on my Aspergian make Andy a darn good farmer. But then there is the dark side of all that perceptiveness. A farm is nothing but a swirling mass of details that must be managed well for the business to survive: 170 mature cows in various stages of reproduction and lactation (cycle of milk production). Almost thirty separate pieces of farm equipment, each of which can break at any time or at least require maintenance. And three employees with their varied strengths and weaknesses, who must be managed effectively and efficiently.

On any given day, none, a few, or all of these interlocking elements can cause a problem, and this is not good for my husband. All of a sudden, too many of these, each with its attendant details, pile up at once and the mayhem – real or perceived – is too much for him. He starts to whirl like an Australian he-devil. And that makes for a bad day for everyone.

Loving the Tasmanian Devil

In one of the classic Tasmanian Devil cartoons, "Ducking the Devil,"[1] Daffy Duck attempts to capture the escaped Taz to get the $5,000 reward. The Taz is doing his thing, spinning like a little cyclone through trees and walls and stopping periodically to flail and slobber. Daffy, hearing on the radio that Tasmanian Devils are soothed by music, starts to lead Taz back toward the zoo using the radio itself, until the cord reaches its limit, comes out of the outlet, and Taz again begins to growl and drool. Daffy quickly orders a trombone through the mail (it arrives in five seconds) and leads Taz along playing the trombone until the slide soars off into a tree. Then, in one of the funniest bagpipe scenes ever created, Daffy plays the pipes until Taz, not considering this "music," grabs the bagpipes, stomps on it, and leaves it wheezing to its death on the grass.

Daffy, "the greedy little coward," realizes his only option is to sing Taz all ten miles back to the zoo. He starts full of energy and bounce, singing "I'm Looking Over a Four-Leaf Clover." With three miles to go, he is tiring through "Nothing Could Be Finer Than to Be in Carolina." One mile to go, parched and hoarse, he is gasping out "When Irish Eyes Are Smiling." At the door of the cage, with Daffy practically whispering "On Moonlight Bay," Taz is one step from capture when Daffy loses his voice completely. Taz immediately starts to snarl and slobber until Daffy spritzes some water into his mouth and croons out the last phrase like Pavarotti. The Taz wanders in with a dreamy look, and Daffy slams the cage shut.

I feel an awful lot like that duck sometimes. Let me give you a typical day.

Andy wakes me at 5 AM screaming "Mo! Get up! The cows are out!" Then he whirls outside, slamming the back door. I get up, throw on some boots, and also rush outside. The sun is making the eastern sky glow over the edge of the hills. It's a beautiful morning. I am happy to be up and executing a heroic cow rescue. Trumpet flourish: Here I come to save the day!

I am happily heading toward my car to go down the road to the pasture, but by that point Andy is flying past me on a tractor at about forty miles per hour, black smoke pouring out of the muffler, and surely waking up all two of our neighbors and every wild animal within five miles with the roar of the engine.

I halt and realize this might not be a scene I want to join. I hear screaming down the road where the cows are in their pasture (or rather out of their pasture). Minutes later Andy whirls back into the driveway on the tractor, flailing out the universal hand signal for "stop," shouting, "We got 'em! We got 'em!"

I am outside anyway, so I grab my five-gallon buckets and head into the barn to mix up milk replacer for the calves. While dumping corn silage into the mixer, Andy opens his tractor door and shouts out, "Can you call Mirabito at eight? We need diesel in the big tank and fuel for the milkhouse."

"Yep."

"Don't forget!"

"Yep."

I mix up twelve servings of milk replacer and stagger out the front door of the barn when Luis stops me with a huge Guatemalan smile.

"*Disculpe.*" ("Excuse me.")

"*Sí?*" ("Yes?")

"*Uh, por favor?*" ("Um, please?")

"*Sí?*" ("Yes?")

"*Escuela hoy a Norwich?*" ("School today in Norwich?")

"*Sí.*" ("Yes.")

"*Por favor, puede enviar dinero a Western Junior?*" ("Please, are you able to send money by Western Union?")

"*Sí. Quanto?*" ("Yes. How much?")

"*Mille.*" ("One thousand.")

"*OK. Yo uso su paga?*" ("OK. I use your pay?")

"*Sí. Por favor. Gracias.*" ("Yes. Please. Thanks.")

"*De nada. No problemo.*" ("It's nothing. No problem.")

I stagger out and feed the twelve calves that are in hutches. It is now 6:30 AM, time to get the boys up.

I jog back up to the house, on the way, checking on the fosterfowl (the four Muscovy ducks and three geese that we took in from the neighbors) to make sure they aren't heading toward the road and almost certain death.

Up in the house, Eldest (so very fifteen) will not get up. Every time I touch his shoulder, he jerks and shouts, "GO AWAY!" Youngest (still precious at ten) follows me around with a constant stream of chatter: "I need a new shirt for my concert tonight, so can I walk to your classroom after school? I'd get it at Salvation Army. We don't need to go to Walmart. Mom? Can we? Can I get a shirt?"

Middle (socially suffering at thirteen) is looking for his clothing of the day. He had put his entire outfit in the washer (shoes, baseball hat, and all), and I had transferred it to the dryer but his Vans kept hitting the door and opening it, turning the dryer off.

"Mom, is my stuff dry? I need those jeans." I wedge the dryer door shut with a ski pole jammed against the opposite wall and start the dryer again.

"Yes, almost dry. Eldest! Get up!"

"NO!"

"YES! Right now! Ten minutes until your bus. I'm not writing you an excuse if you miss it! One more tardy and you have detention, so get up!"

"So Mom, can I walk to your classroom? Or I could take the YMCA bus and then walk over. That would be quicker. Please?"

Middle, wearing a towel, hair wet: "Is my stuff dry? Where's your brush? I've got to do my hair."

"ELDEST! GET UP! FIVE MINUTES 'TIL YOUR BUS!!!!!"

"RRRRRRRR!!!!!!!"

Andy comes whirling in the back door, clomps through the mudroom in his barn boots, and knocks over the ski pole, unwedging it. The Vans hit the dryer door and the dryer stops.

"What the &#!?" He slams through the kitchen door, grabs the bagel I had just made for Youngest, and whirls off into the office, yelling over his shoulder:

"Mo, can you be home at 3:30 for once? Luis can't get the cows in by himself, Tim and I will be chopping, and it's Eduardo's day off." In the office he's dialing the phone.

"Youngest, shoes and socks, now!" I say to Youngest. "YES!" I snarl toward the office.

"Mom, is my stuff done?"

I get the Vans, Levis, black Halo T-shirt, Yankees hat, and Starter socks from the dryer, still slightly damp, and hurl them, fingers crossed, into the bathroom. Fortunately, an overriding crisis trumps the clammy clothes.

"Mom, I'm out of hair gel! Can I go with you guys to Walmart? I also need CDs."

"We're not going to Walmart. ELDEST!!!!!!!"

"WHAT!?!?!?!?"

"GET ON THAT BUS OR NO *WORLD OF WARCRAFT* TO-NIGHT!!!"

"RRRRRRRRRRRRAAAAAAAH!!!!"

Stomp. Stomp. Stomp. Eldest comes down the stairs.

"Great!" he snarls sarcastically. "I don't even have time for breakfast."

"Whose fault is that?!! Next time get up the first time I call you!!!"

"There's my frickin' bus!!"

"GO! GO!"

"I NEED LUNCH MONEY!!"

I follow Eldest to the bus, writing out a check as I go. I shove it into his hand, glare at the Nazi-esque bus driver, and stomp back onto the porch in my barn clothes and gardening clogs. The high-school bus drives off. On the porch, Bluey the cat is meowing and looking at me beseechingly. Her little kittens, the size of finger puppets, wiggle and squirm without her next to them.

"Oh, Bluey." I melt down to her in solidarity. "Do you need some food? You're such a good mommy. Corian! Back off!"

I hurl Corian the tomcat into the lawn, and although he somersaults in mid-air, he lands on his feet and slinks away. What does he care about his kittens? He just wants Bluey's food.

Back inside the house, the saga continues …

"So Mom, can I walk?"

"Mom, I'm missing one sock. Did you see it in the dryer?"

Andy calls from the office, "So, you'll call Mirabito at eight? I'm leaving a note on your desk."

Through gritted teeth. "Yes. Youngest has a concert tonight!"

Loud, exasperated sigh from the office. "I'll try; I'll try to make it. We've got to finish first cutting."

"Oh, really?" I whisper to Youngest's backpack. "I would never have known that."

From the office, "Yes, this is Andrew Bartlett. I've got two cows to breed, 2405 and 14-blue. Use young sires on the heifer and MAP on the cow. Thanks. See ya."

Andy whirls back through the kitchen, grabs the second bagel I have just made for Youngest, and whirls out the back door.

"Two cats got in!!!" he shouts and slams out the back door.

I grab Shadow off the kitchen table and throw him into the mudroom. Flossulous has grabbed a ground beef wrapper and dragged it into the sitting room.

"Mom, I need a note if I'm walking!"

"OK! OK! Take the bus to the Y, walk over to my classroom, and we'll stop quickly at Salvation Army. I told Dad I'd be home to get the cows in."

The phone rings. "Hello?"

"Hi, Mrs. Bartlett, it's Jenny."

"Hi, Jenny." Teacher voice. "What's up?"

"I'm going to be late for class today, but I can stay until five again."

"OK, but I'll have to leave at three."

"OK."

"MOM! My bus is coming! Write me a note!"

Middle flies by with his backpack. "BUS!"

He runs out the front door and leaps off the porch.

I write a note for Youngest as I say in my best teacher voice, "OK, Jenny, I'll see you at ten then. Bye."

I hand Youngest his note as he flies out the door, untied shoes flapping. I see he has put on a shirt that has a huge hole under the left armpit. I am sure Social Services will be calling today. I run after him with his allergy pill, which I notice lying on the table, and shove it into his hand. I glare at the busdriver and return to the porch.

I wave goodbye, give Bluey a handful of dog food (all we have at the moment), and check on the fosterfowl to make sure they aren't heading toward the road. Riley is at the door inside huffing and wagging his tail. I attach him to his leash and let him out.

In the kitchen, I eat everyone's crusts and leftover cereal and start a cup of cappuccino. The phone rings.

"Hello?"

"Hi, Mo. This is Brent."

"Hi, Brent."

"I was just wondering, is Andy using the fertilizer spreader today? I was thinking of fertilizing our field on Peckin Hill."

"I really don't know, Brent. I know they're chopping today."

"Hunh … can you have Andy call me?"

"I'll try. You might have better luck stopping up at the field."

"Where are they chopping?"

"McDonough meadow."

"OK. Thanks, Mo."

"Yep, see you."

I throw on my poop-encrusted jeans and fly out to finish the calves. I have two babies to feed, so I mix up two bottles and go up to the hay mow and feed them. On the way I pass Gigi (actually G.G. for Grey Goose), who is sitting on her unfertilized eggs hissing at me. My head still throbs from the last time I tried to take her eggs and she bashed me with her wing. Her poor webbed feet have gone from orange to a sickly peach due to lack of sunlight. She hasn't been off that nest for three weeks, and her female goose friend sits outside guarding the entrance, getting affection from the calf by the hawmow door.

By this point I'm in a bad and harried mood, and it irks me no end that the stupid goose is staging a hunger strike for no apparent reason.

I grab a plastic shovel and scoop her off her nest, bestowing her outside the barn, and shovel up the nine enormous eggs that are starting to rot and stink. I walk over to the high grass and throw them in. GiGi has returned to her empty nest squawking and flapping her wings. Her guardian is hysterical and flaps in to protect her. I give up my efforts and run to the house. It's 7:30.

I take the stairs two at a time, execute a five-minute shower, throw on the nearest pair of nice pants I can find and a clean shirt. Downstairs, my cappuccino is done. I pour it into a sippy cup and gather my bags. No time for makeup. I shove my makeup bag and blowdryer into a bag and start out the door. Just then Andy is coming back in.

He blows by me.

"I'm leaving," I say.

"OK. Hey! You forgot this note!!!"

He hands me the note that says "Call Mirabito at eight. Fill the large diesel tank, top off the milkhouse."

"Can you do that?" he demands.

"Yes."

"OK. Thanks."

He whirls out the back door. I do a last check on the fosterfowl to make sure they aren't heading toward the road. I get into the Jeep and pull out, singing under my breath, "Nothing could be finer than to be in East Pharsalia in the morning." It's 8 AM.

I go into mind-saver mode for five minutes, letting my thoughts lazily bounce across my brain's LCD until my cell phone picks up service and beeps that I have a message.

Sigh. It will be Jenny.

I finally get to my classroom where one student is already sitting on the floor next to the locked door. All my seniors are preparing a thirty-minute talk using PowerPoint, to be delivered to an invited professional audience, and it's crunch week. They are stressing. I am stressing. I spend the next three hours bouncing from topic to topic and technical issue to technical issue. I help Mike add an MP-3 of the "Jaws" theme to his opening slide on "Shark Poaching and Its Effects." I stop to call Mirabito. I help Jenny write a paragraph on the economic causes of the "emerging adulthood" phenomenon. I help Emily find software to demonstrate speech pathologist use of Smartboards for children with autism. I help Terri find an NPR story on using the Myers-Briggs to analyze presidential candidates. I help Noelle insert a map of school shooting sites onto a slide about school violence. I stop at 9:20 to talk on the cell phone to Brent, who is still wondering if Andy is done with the fertilizer spreader. I tell him that *I* have the cell phone not Andy and that he should call the farm number. Eli stops by to have me look at his paper on separation of church and state. I check my e-mail and see I have received five final drafts from my Writing in Law and Government class: Gang Violence, Darfur, The Insanity Defense, Offshore Outsourcing, and No Child Left Behind. I help Steve find a movie on Youtube of the 1960 Nixon-Kennedy debate. I show Corrinne how to animate a slide listing the benefits of study abroad. I answer Andy's 10:30 call to the cell phone with "Yes, I called Mirabito."

Group one leaves at 11:30.

In my fifteen-minute break, I drive to the bank, cash Luis' check, send the money via Western Union at Walmart, and grab a cold cappuccino at the gas station on the way back.

Afternoon class: Brent writing a paper about Expanding the Meat Goat Market, Jeremy is almost done with his PowerPoint on Agriculture-Based Methane Digesters, Rob is far behind on his presentation about Recombinant Bovine Somatotropin, and Kurt has been MIA for a week and counting, and I have seen nothing of his paper on Sustainable Architecture. In my e-mail are four more papers from the Law class: The War on Drugs, Contingency School Budgets, New York Regional Interconnect Opposition, and Erosion of Civil Liberties in the Patriot Act.

My students leave at 2:15. Youngest arrives, but not Middle. I get Youngest into the car, scoop up Middle along the way from his school, and we stop at the Salvation Army store down the block. Nothing appropriate for the concert. It's 3:15. I am supposed to be home in ten minutes. Youngest is freaking out about his outfit. Middle wants CDs.

"I have to get home!" I shrill.

I can envision Andy, up in the field, chopping hay, and looking at his watch. At 3:30 he will radio down to the house to see if I am home. I darn well better be.

"I'M SORRY!!!" I shout at the boys. "I promised Dad I'd be home to help Luis. We'll have to come down early for the concert and stop at Walmart."

Mid-way home, Middle turns on the cell phone, which beeps with a message. He gives me a look that mirrors my own – of extreme apprehension. He calls the voice mail, listens, and sends me a baleful look.

"Uh, oh."

"What?"

"Eldest missed his bus home. He's at Adam's."

I am seven of the ten miles home. I am not returning to Norwich to get him.

At this point in the day, this news barely blips my radar.

"Well, he's going to have to wait there until six."

As we drive by the McDonough meadow, I see Andy on a tractor with the chopper behind him and a forage wagon behind that. Our helper, Al, is halfway down the hill with a full wagon, and our employee, Hank, is in the opposite lane from me coming from the farm hauling the new double rotary rake that looks like a folded-up amusement park ride in transport mode. Hank gives me a grim wave as we pass. I give him an ironic, forced smile. I've been in the house five seconds when the radio crackles.

"Chopper to base station."

Argh. Base station. Can't he just say "Mo"?

I purposely wait ten seconds while I get a drink of water.

"Chopper to base station. Come in base station."

"Yes?" I say.

"Can you help Luis get the cows in?"

"That's why I'm home," through gritted teeth.

"OK. You better get down there. He's probably looking around trying to figure out what's going on."

"I'm on my way."

I shimmy out of my work pants and into barn pants and barn boots.

Down at the barn, I turn on the ventilation fans and tell Luis, "*Voy a traer las vacas.*" ("I will bring the cows.")

"*Muy bien. Gracias.*" ("Very good. Thanks.")

I hop in the nearest vehicle I see, the green pickup, and pull out into the driveway toward the road to head down to the pasture. I wave at Al as he pulls in with another forage wagon and drive the quarter mile to where the cows are. I pull over, jump out, climb over the fence, and stop my now very hungry body at the pasture's opening to watch for cows in heat. Cow 344 mounts cow 21-Blue and then 21-Blue mounts 344. I start a mental chant of "344, 21-Blue" in my head and open the gate. The cows take off down the lane, and eventually all 140 of them are spread out in a long line from where I am along the cow path toward the barn.

I beat them back to the barn in the pickup and arrive as the first one is coming in the back door. It takes Luis and me twenty minutes to get all the cows in their stalls and snap them in. I am still chanting "344, 21-Blue."

Back up in the house, I write these two cows' names down on a piece of paper on Andy's desk with the words "standing 6/24." In the meantime, Middle and Youngest have attached themselves to various video games. I unplug my children and move them toward cleaning up for a return to town.

"Chopper to base station."

Sigh. "Yes?"

"We've got about five more loads to go."

"I am leaving in ten minutes. Youngest needs a new shirt, and Eldest is at Adam's. Middle wants to come too because his girlfriend is playing in the concert."

"I can't leave right now!!!"

Duh, really? "Yes, I know. I'll go."

"OK, I'll try to get down there, but we've got five acres left and it's about to rain."

"Yep."

"How are the calves getting fed?"

"We'll do them when I get home. I'll get pizzas."

"10-4."

It's 5:45.

I hustle the boys back into the car, buzz back the ten miles to town, buy a blue Oxford cloth shirt and black pants for Youngest, a case of blank CDs and hair gel for Middle, a carton of Slimfast shakes and a Mountain Dew for myself, and off we go. Youngest changes in the car, and I drop him off at school. At Adam's house I knock on the window of the "Guy Cave" down in the basement, and ten seconds later Eldest appears.

"Sorry, Mom, the stupid bus left without me."

"That's OK. I had to go home and put the cows away and then bring Youngest down to get a shirt and pants. We're on our way to his concert."

I flinch and brace myself for the vociferous complaints from Eldest at the prospect of having to attend his brother's concert but am pleasantly surprised when they do not come.

"OK. Can we stop at P&C?"

"Sure."

We run in to the grocery store where Eldest compiles a supply of Monster, SpaghettiOs, Dutch Chocolate cookies, and veggie chicken nuggets. I am too tired to argue. Besides, I want a cookie!

We return to the school, and the three of us find seats in the crowded auditorium.

"Did you call Nina's?" Eldest asks.

"Oops." I pull the cell phone out of my purse, use speed dial to call in the pizza order, and set the phone to vibrate. By this time the curtains are opening and the principal is giving her greeting. The cell phone vibrates in my hand, I look and see that HOME is calling. This will be Andy saying he just got in the house. I turn off the phone without answering.

Loving the Tasmanian Devil

The concert is heart-warming. Youngest looks very handsome and grown-up and quite like my Dad with his saxophone. Middle's girl-friend is cute and, I am relieved to see, not dressed like a twelve-year-old prostitute, unlike many of the other girls. Eldest runs into a buddy with whom he kids around on our way out. I get one hour of reassurance that all is well in the land of child-rearing; the Irish eyes of my children are smiling, as are mine.

We stop at Nina's, grab the pizzas, and head up the hill toward home through the starry skies and fragrance of apple and cherry blossoms and lilacs.

When we pull in at the farm, all is dark in the barn, and the cows are quietly grazing in the pasture. Eldest and Middle run into the house and hop on the Internet to check their I-Ms. I force pizza onto them, and they drift off into other rooms. Youngest asks if he can call his favorite aunt, and I give him permission.

Andy is sitting at the kitchen table with a cold beer. His face is covered with hay chaff and grease, but he has a huge smile on his face.

"We're done. First cutting is complete, exactly on time."

My face needs to smile, but it can't. It's too tired.

"Cool," I manage.

"What's wrong?"

"I'm tired."

"YOU'RE tired?"

244

"It was a long day."

"You think YOUR day was long?"

I don't bother to respond. I just force a smile and grab a slice of pizza.

After the boys have run out and fed the calves, I shoo them to bed, and Andy and I crash.

My eyes are already closing when he throws his arm around me and makes his guttural ram-wanting-to-breed noise, which usually makes me laugh. I can't laugh. I'm too tired. I can't move. I'm too tired. Unfortunately, I'm also fairly seducible, and although I'm half asleep, we proceed to blissful consummation.

When I finally fall back onto my side of the bed again, I sigh, mime spritzing water into my mouth, and croon out "on moonlight bay … !!!!!" We both giggle, snuggle together, and fall asleep.

---

[1] Ducking the Devil was released August 17, 1957, written by Tedd Pierce and directed by Robert McKimson, and available now on *Daffy Duck: Frustrated Fowl* (Looney Tunes Super Stars) by Warner Home Video.

CHAPTER 22

FIELD AND STREAM –
THE SPECIAL INTEREST

For the longest time, I thought *Field and Stream* was a girlie magazine. I must have heard a joke about it when I was eight that clearly implied it was for males and made an incorrect intuitive leap. I avoided looking at it in drugstores, good girl that I was. I grew up in the city, so no one I knew subscribed nor did their parents, which might have corrected my misconception.

Nowadays, we have our own subscription and piles of issues sitting in our downstairs bathroom. We live in one of New York State's top destination counties for whitetail deer hunting, where it's more unusual to *not* hunt than *to* hunt. Shotgun season is such a big deal here that they used to close school on Opening Day because none of the bus drivers would show up. It was labeled on the school calendars as Deer Day, but due to negative P.R., districts started having a staff development day on the opening day of shotgun season. The majority of teachers are female, and even the male teachers tend not to fall into the hunter crowd; you don't need bus drivers and janitors on a staff day.

Lately, in its great wisdom, the state has moved opening day of shotgun season from a Monday to a Saturday because so many employers in other industries complained about absenteeism on Opening Day Monday. Sigh.

I confess openly that deer season drives me crazy. As a teacher, especially as a teacher of environmental science and agriculture, I get really mad when my male students give me a knowing grin on November 1 and say, "Just so you know, I am going to be sick on November 22." I glare back and say, "OK, but I want a two-page typed description of the hunt."

I drive the ten miles to work and see pickup trucks beached along the side of the road like flotsam on the riverbanks, their drivers vanishing into the woods in blaze orange.

"Don't you people have any originality?" I scream through my closed windows to the abandoned trucks. "Oh gee, hunting, what a unique hobby." Are you catching the sarcasm?

I have taken to calling hunting season the Perpetual Male Adolescence Festival. Eighteen-year-old young men revert to age fifteen. Thirty-year-old newlyweds revert to age fifteen. Fifty-year-old fathers of three children revert to age fifteen – for over a month straight! They think, in their buck-induced stupor, "How fortunate am I to be eternally fifteen with no spouse, no children, and no job, and to be able to just spend hours and hours at a time in the woods." Thus, the term "hunting widow." This is not the surviving wife of a man who has been shot in a hunting accident, but the wife of a man who might as well have been shot in a hunting accident for all she sees of him during November and December.

So hunting seems to turn all men slightly Aspergian. One diagnostic criterion for Asperger Syndrome is what is termed the "special interest." It is a major criterion in the diagnostic description of Asperger's in the fourth edition of the *Diagnostic and Statistical Manual of Mental Disorders*, which provides the official diagnostic and classification criteria for all identified mental conditions: "Restricted, repetitive and stereotyped patterns of behaviour, interests, and activities, as manifested by at least one of the following" with number one being "encompassing preoccupation with one or more stereotyped and restricted patterns of interest that is abnormal either in intensity or focus."[1]

At first I found this characteristic to be one of the strangest, like saying that a required symptom of having allergies is an unavoidable urge to walk around with your hand on top of your head. Not all people with AS exhibit the special-interest trait, but might instead demonstrate routines or rituals, motor mannerisms such as rocking, or fascination with small parts like the gears of a clock. "Stimming," as it's called, is relaxing to an overexcited nervous system. Some psychologists link the special interest specifically to a similar need for anxiety relief.

Other psychologists hypothesize that loyalty to a hobby or activity takes the place of social loyalty, which is often confusing and unpredictable for an Aspergian. If you take the loyalty a typical nine-year-old has to his best friend and replace it with loyalty to something like fishing, you can start to understand it. I remember my obsession with my friend Paula at that age. I wanted to spend all my time with her. If being her friend had been beyond my comprehension and abilities, I might instead have pledged my energies to my bicycle, birds, or something more predictable and inert.

Perhaps this is why Andy pledged himself to fishing. I have heard the tales both from his family and from Andy himself that as a kid, whenever possible, he disappeared to fish. Luckily, Andy had the Bartlett family camp on a lake in the Berkshires to go to most of the summer, a creek behind his house, and the Connecticut River once he got a little older.

I have heard his brother's tales about the family's cross-country camping trips and how when they would finally arrive at the campground each evening, everyone else would be setting up camp, but Andy would disappear with his rod. I used to feel angry solidarity with Andy's brother, who still protests – with a laugh – the unfairness of that situation, but in light of the Asperger's, it makes perfect sense. I also realize that Andy's parents probably found it easier to let him go than to deal with the battle of corralling him into helping, not to mention his decreased agitation when he finally returned.

When we moved here, the farm became Andy's special interest, driven by fear of failure and agriculture's own inherent appeal. It wasn't until about ten years into farming that he could loosen his grip on the business enough to start a hobby. He held out for a long time against hunting, repelled by the mania and social obligation surrounding the sport here, but he finally gave in, thanks to our neighbor up the road, nicknamed The Crow for his lack of inhibition in hauling fresh roadkill venison off the side of the road and home to his freezer. Hunting made sense as a hobby that matched our life and location: Andy can walk out our back door and hunt; he can also drive five miles and fish. So Andy has joined the local obsession, except in his own Aspie way.

He started with shotgun hunting and then got into bow hunting, and finally black powder (black powder is a traditional style of firearms hunting using a muzzle loader and a single-shot lead ball and packed gunpowder). And Andy's specific neurological gifts allowed – or forced – him to excel. Successful hunting requires that the hunter can predict the movements, locations, actions, and behaviors of the deer. In Andy's case, it's not that he *can* think like an animal, it's that he *does* think like an animal. Therefore, he mastered hunting very quickly because he saw that the trick was not to out-tech his prey but to out-think it.

Andy is known at the local sporting store as "Hat-Trick Man" for consistently getting a deer with each successive season's weapon: bow, shotgun, muzzle loader. This is next to impossible, and has made him somewhat famous. It's like being married to Pa Ingalls or Nathaniel in *Last of the Mohicans* (well, make that Daniel Day-Lewis).[2]

Of course, also in Aspergian fashion, the hunting can become obsessive and problematic, beyond the normal mania of the season. "Normal mania" was the mornings I used to milk and watch Andy, Hank, and The Crow stand around and talk in the barn. Every half-hour conversation sounded the same to me: "Blah, blah, blah, blah, tree stand. Blah, blah, blah, blah, fifty yards. Blah, blah, blah, blah, sights must have been off."

Loving the Tasmanian Devil

All men who hunt are very focused during the season, but as any wife of an Aspergian will tell you, the special interest can take on a life of its own and cause tremendous problems when it eclipses all else, like the family. Some women love hunting season, seeing it as a vacation from their man. They shop and go out with the girls. For me, it means that besides teaching, caring for the kids, and feeding calves, I often have to take over some of Andy's farm duties and other responsibilities if he is out in the woods – not exactly a vacation.

For example, once when we were honored to be chosen as one of three local host farms for an intercollegiate dairy analysis competition, Andy didn't even appear in the official photo because he was hunting. I remember another year when we temporarily had only one car and I was late to teach my class one day because Andy had gone to the bow shop.

Then there is all the hunting and fishing information to be mastered and so many tangents to explore and gear to play with. If one hunts, there is goose season, turkey season, and deer season. Then there are the hunting weapons: bow, shotgun, and muzzle loader. There are all the types of fishing: trolling, fly-fishing, line casting, ice fishing, shore fishing, boat fishing. I finally had to set up a small bookshelf in our office for the fishing books that flooded in all winter, with such titles as *Walleyes, Bass, Salmon,* and *Trolling the Great Lakes.* Eventually, I had to move into an office of my own because I was crowded out by all the gear. Bye-bye dining room.

The farm is big enough and successful enough now that Andy could buy himself a fishing boat and deck it out with a bimini, trolling rods, GPS receiver. We're talking about stuff. The Spring 2008 Cabela's catalog is 1,507 pages long. Yes, 1,507!

Part of the special interest component of Asperger's is mastery, figuring it out, knowing all the details, getting it right. In his book *The Catch: Families, Fishing, and Faith*, William J. Vande Kopple, whom Andy suspects of Aspie-hood, writes, "What is great about fishing has to do with clarity: Do a certain thing at a certain time in a certain way and a certain place under certain weather conditions and you will catch a certain kind of fish … all this talk about dumb luck or natural caprice or unwavering patience – is the babble of the ignorant."[3] As Andy and Sully from *Nobody's Fool* both like to say, "Luck has nothing to do with it."[4]

Although his adult, sophisticated version of angling focuses on the mastery of expert techniques and access to the appropriate doo-dads, Andy's fascination with fishing comes from a much more childlike place. As a young boy he was entranced by *The Wind in the Willows*, especially the adventures of Rat and Mole alone on the river. He loves to quote the Water Rat: "Believe me, my young friend, there is *nothing* – absolute nothing – half so much worth doing as simply messing about in boats. Simply messing,' he went on dreamily: 'messing – about – in – boats.'"[5]

I have seen the pictures of tiny Andy and his grandfather in boats up at camp, and we have lately acquired quite a collection of boats ourselves. We started with a canoe and a kayak, and have added another kayak and a motorized fishing boat and received an old Hobie catamaran as a gift from our next-door neighbor. The latest purchase was a Starcraft Islander.

In *The Wind in the Willows*, boating is the route to enlightenment. I think Andy would definitely agree. Rat and Mole set out at dusk on the river to look for Otter's missing child, and when the sun rises, they are led by mystical music into the presence of The Piper at the Gates of Dawn. Hunting and fishing both involve accessing the mysteries of dawn and dusk, liminal times of days. Hunting requires being in the woods in the dark before the sun comes up or as the sun goes down. This is when the deer move carefully out of the forest edges into the fields where they graze. As Andy always says, edges are special places: the edges between forest and field, between air and water, between water and shore, between night and day, and between day and night. The edges are where things happen, and Andy's animal instincts are sensitive to them.

There is also the fact that Andy's special interests involve the outdoors and the wild, not anything man-made or mechanical (aside from the thousands of dollars worth of Cabela's shipments, of course). I know that what Andy truly likes is the woods, the water, the wilderness, and he always has. The technology just allows him to justify his time there by letting him almost always come back with food.

As James Taylor, the singer-songwriter and guitarist, has said, "I find comfort in writing about and projecting and thinking about the seasons and the sea, things like that, because I have no control. I find comfort in fatalism and inevitability … I wish I were really part of the environment, part of the land instead of a successful Caucasian."[6]

I know Andy feels that way, too. If Andy had his way, he could let himself go all the way wild and stay that way, but since he is human and Aspergian, he has to make a living, and do it as close to perfectly as possible. The writer Annie Dillard describes a situation when she locked eyes with a weasel, an experience Andy has shared, and she realized how pure are the actions of wild animals, how they grab onto their prey with pure-minded necessity. She says, "We could live under the wild rose wild as weasels, mute and uncomprehending. I could very calmly go wild."[7]

Special interest or not, hunting and fishing – field and stream – these are the places where Andy can relax, where his nerves can vibrate but in a way that is natural, animal-like, harmonious. Harvard-trained scientist and mystic Joan Borysenko maintains that nature is one of seven traditional mystical paths to God. Path one, linked to the first chakra, allows mystic connection to the divine through the natural world. The other six paths include creativity, service, love, discipline, contemplation, and faith.[8] Andy is most definitely a first-chakra mystic.

During November and December, as I sit home with the kids on the weekends while Andy is in the woods, in January when he is out fishing on the ice, or in the summer when he is either waist-deep in a salmon stream or on a boat out in the middle of a huge lake, I acknowledge that such sojourns are both relaxation and spiritual practice for him. They are also his escape from the overwhelming slew of details at home, not to mention a break for all of us from his perpetual state of agitation.

Also, they allow Andy to revert to his most natural, most child-like, most weasel-like self. I see it happen in his face as he pulls out of the driveway with the boat or lopes off toward the woods, and I whisper under my breath, "Just remember to come back home."

Loving the Tasmanian Devil

1   Diagnostic Criteria for 299.80 Asperger's Disorder. From *The Diagnostic and Statistical Manual of Mental Disorders IV*; www.autreat.com/dsm4-aspergers.html.

2   James Fennimore Cooper published the novel *Last of the Mohicans* in 1826, as the second novel in the Leatherstocking Tales series. The 1992 film version was directed by Michael Mann and is distributed on video by Twentieth Century Fox.

3   Vande Kopple, William J. (2004) *The Catch: Families, Fishing, and Faith*. Grand Rapids: William B. Eerdmans; page 23.

4   *Nobody's Fool* is one of our favorite movies. Directed by Robert Benton and released by Paramount in 2003, it is an adaptation of the Richard Russo novel by the same name.

5   Graham, Kenneth. (1967). *The Wind in the Willows*. New York, NY: Magnum; page 11.

6   Music: James Taylor: One Man's Family of Rock. *Time*, Monday, Mar. 01, 1971; may be found at http://www.time.com/time/magazine/article/0,9171,878920,00.html.

7   Dillard, Annie. Ed. Carl H. Klaus et al. (1993). Living Like Weasels. From *In Depth: Essayists for Our Time*, 2nd ed. Florence, KY: Thomson Heinle; pages 186-189.

8   I was introduced to this from the audio version of *The Way of the Mystic: 7 Paths to God* (1997) by Joan Borysenko produced by Hay House Audio Books, Carlsbad, CA.

CHAPTER 23

PARABLES – ASPERGIAN SPIRITUALITY

O nce Youngest was nearing age five and his brothers seven and nine, I started to become concerned about the children's spiritual growth. Andy and I had both been raised as church-goers: Andy in the Congregationalist Church and I in the Catholic Church. When we moved to the farm, church attendance became almost impossible for us. Sunday morning chores lasted until 11 AM, church of either denomination was a ten-mile drive each way, and the last thing I wanted to do was drive to Norwich on the weekend since I spent all week there teaching.

So I made do with my own independent spiritual program. Almost every morning before the kids woke up, I spent the first fifteen minutes reading something that would help me keep my soul on straight. On big holidays, I would get myself to church. I tried taking Eldest a few times, but I spent so much time trying to keep him in one place that I felt much *less* spiritually serene by the end of the service than if I had never gone in the first place.

Earlier in life, Andy had actually considered going into the ministry. But then as a teenager he had some negative experiences in the realm of institutionalized religion, and in the typically black-and-white thinking of an Aspergian, had decided to just say "No" to the entire scene. If he had the opportunity, I think he would have happily worshipped in Native American ceremonies, but he has had to make do with hunting and fishing as spiritual practice.

My mother once confessed that she had secretly baptized each of our boys, sneaking holy water from her church into her suitcase and baptizing each when Andy and I weren't in the house. But I eventually decided that they should have access to organized religion as they grew up, if for no other reason than to have something to rebel against in order to choose their own way. So we arranged a group baptism for all three of them, and the boys attended Sunday School through First Communion at our local Catholic Church.

Nowadays, I am personally so desperate for spiritual edification that I get myself to church all alone whenever I can: just me, no kids, no interruptions. In addition, one marital management technique Andy and I have adopted to counteract the Asperger's is going out to breakfast on Sunday mornings, alone together, after which I usually go to church alone.

One Sunday morning, Andy dropped me off at church and went to do errands on my behalf (cornflour for our employees' tamales and varnish stripper and polyurethane for the sitting room floor). I was sitting there in the pew, wishing Andy were with me, wishing he *wanted* to be with me, but then the readings came along and smacked me upside the head, because they were all about Andy.

Isaiah had this to say:
Just as from the heavens
The rain and snow come down
And do not return there
till they have watered the earth,
making it fertile and fruitful,
giving seed to the one who sows
and bread to the one who eats,
so shall my word be
that goes forth from my mouth;
my word shall not return to me void,
but shall do my will
achieving the ends for which
I sent it.[1]

The psalmist chimed in with "The seed that falls on good ground will yield a fruitful harvest. You have crowned the year with bounty and your paths overflow with a rich harvest; the untilled meadows overflow with it and rejoicing clothes the hills. The fields are garmented with flocks. They shout and sing for joy."[2]

And Jesus had the authoritative word, saying, "A sower went out to sow. And as he sowed some seed fell on the path, and birds came and ate it up. Some fell on rocky ground, where it had little soil. It sprang up at once because the soil was not deep, and when the sun rose it was scorched, and it withered for lack of roots. Some seed fell among thorns, and the thorns grew up and choked it. But some seed fell on rich soil, and produced fruit, a hundred or sixty or thirtyfold."[3]

The deacon who delivered the sermon did not read the subsequent verses in which Jesus explained the analogy, saying that, being in a rural county, we certainly all either gardened or knew a gardener and could visualize and understand what the parable meant. He went on to say that we all tend a garden of some kind: the students we teach in education, the children we raise as parents, the product or service we provide in commerce, the funds we make available in finance, etc.

I was thinking about Andy preparing the literal gardens on our farm. He currently maintains four large gardens, in addition to flowers on the porch and in window boxes. This is not counting the 200 acres of pasture and hayland he uses to feed 300 head of cattle.

I focused on the gospel by imagining Andy preparing the vegetable gardens, which he starts on as soon as the ground warms up in April. He breaks up the soil clods and compost he had spread the previous fall. He hoes and digs and removes every rock, weed, and weed seed. He rakes, smooths, and breaks up clumps until the soil looks like brown velveteen. He purchases lettuce seeds first, and, making narrow shallow furrows, drops in the seed and then lightly sprinkles soil over top and showers the seeds with water. Later he transplants the broccoli and cabbage plants from our neighbor lady to whom he brings compost. Then he prepares the pumpkin and squash garden, enlisting us to break up soil and pull up dandelions. Then he carefully drops seeds in each carefully spaced hole. When the plants sprout, he watches for weeds and cultivates any out. When the late frosts come, he covers the baby plants. When the rains do not come, he waters. He sets aside time every morning to see what needs to be done and to do it.

And in mid-July we have broccoli, cabbage, lettuce, baby summer squash, and beans. We have tiger lilies and fuchsias and window boxes of petunias and snapdragons and phlox. We have raspberries and strawberries. In the fall we have winter squash and pumpkins and onions. I manage to create one small garden of herbs: parsley, oregano, basil, rosemary, sage. But the bulk of the fresh foods we enjoy are because of Andy: his diligence, his care, his competence, his love for plants.

More than once, Andy has said to me, pointing to these small plots, "This is my prayer." Or he has turned, kneeling in the soil, and said, "Here is my prayer rug," a tapestry of verdant plants and deep red tomatoes and bright orange pumpkins.

I was thinking of the extreme literalness of Aspergian thought and wondered how Jesus would handle an Aspie. Jesus taught in parables to illustrate the abstract secrets of the Kingdom in concrete terms. But can this go in reverse? What if a person takes Jesus literally and manifests the *concrete* components of the parable? What if, instead of living the analogy through "hearing the word and understanding it," a person were to concentrate on *literally* preparing rich soil, tending plants, and producing fruit a hundredfold? Would a person manifest the Word by literally living the parable?

After all, in the physical realm, the sower has control over the conditions of planting. What if, due to his hard work, there were no path from which the birds could pluck the seed? What if there were no rocky soil because the rocks had been removed? What if no thorns could choke the plants because the brambles had been pulled out? What if everywhere the seed fell was rich, tilled, weed-free, watered, and sheltered? Would that gardener be embodying the traits of the Kingdom by caring for his plants? After all, Christ was the sower of the seeds, who desired for his words to fall on only fruitful soil. Is Andy then literally manifesting Christ when he grows plentiful food?

What if a person, an Aspergian, were to say this: "The concepts of the Kingdom of God are too abstract for me, but I completely understand the literal part of the parable. If I live the parable, I manifest the Kingdom. I effect the hundredfold harvest that is possible with diligence and proper tending. These characteristics of a good disciple are also necessary in order to feed others, so I will live them and literally feed others."

I asked Andy about this, and he said I had hit the nail right on the head, that he favors a literal interpretation of the Gospel parables. He explained, "If I do my job as a farmer right, I won't have to worry about loving my neighbor. I will have fed him."

I was taken aback by this as with many of his Aspie comments. What Andy said sounded rude and unempathetic, but I can see the logic for a person who does not have the wiring for instinctive empathy. For example, I think of Jesus feeding the thousands after the apostles were going to send the crowds away. Jesus had compassion because the people were hungry. He did not deliver a sermon but did what the people needed him to do: he fed them, literally.

The other night I heard Andy responding to his brother's questions about Joel Salatin, a holistic farmer who promotes pasture-based, grass-based foods.[4] Andy explained it to his brother like this: "That's what we do just on a very large scale. What Joel Salatin proposes is all well and good, but it's only going to feed a small number of people. That's not going to help some poor guy in inner-city Detroit who's trying to put food on his table. We produce over 700 gallons of milk a day, enough for 700 families for several days."

I struggle with this, I truly do. Andy's words denoted a criticism of the very kindhearted and well-meaning Joel Salatin and also a criticism of a market that provides publicity to niche growers who cater to the food-conscious wealthy. Isn't this judgmental? However, it also sounds like the same type of diatribe Jesus delivered to the scribes and Pharisees. "Woe to you, niche marketers. You peddle your expensive wares to the wealthy gourmet connoisseurs and neglect the thousands crying for basic food."

So how am I to regard this type of spirituality: a person who struggles with empathy but who manifests actions like feeding the hungry in a literal way?

Temple Grandin shares the same sentiment as Andy has shared. She says that her first slaughterhouse engineering job at the Swift cattle plant in Arizona brought her face to face with the direction her life would take. She had intended to make a significant contribution to the world. Having thought the life of a scientist would lead her toward this significant contribution, she instead moved into applying her scientific skills to humane slaughter.

She says in her diary, "The Swift plant was a place where beliefs were tested in reality. It was not just intellectual talk." At a recent talk at Cornell, she railed against what she called "abstractification," the tendency to theorize and pontificate with no hands-on experience of the issue. She said of her work at a kosher slaughtering plant, "When the animal remained completely calm I felt an overwhelming feeling of peacefulness, as if God had touched me. Operating the chute has to be done as an act of total kindness … It was then that I realized that there can be a conflict between feeling and doing. Zen meditators may be able to achieve the perfect state of oneness with the universe, but they do not bring about reform and change in the world around them."[5]

If what I attempt to do is embody the *feeling* part of a parable, Andy embodies the *doing* part. Like me, he was also raised hearing the parables in church every Sunday, but he took from them the literal charge, saying to himself, "I will make sure my family's house is built on solid bedrock and not on shifting soil, a house that is well-maintained and safe and straight. I will invest my literal 'talents' wisely, analyzing every farm purchase for its rate of return. I will seek out and find that lost sheep or calf or cow that has wandered out of her pasture. I will prepare fertile soil for the vegetables that feed my family and the flowers that lift their spirits. I will bake bread for them and the yeast will be evenly distributed. I will feed four thousand people with affordably produced milk. I will forgive my employees their debts to me, even when they buy expensive vehicular toys they don't need. I will be the farmer who works in the field when other farmers dissipate their time. I will invite my lonely neighbor to dinner and take him out fishing. I will always have my lamps and my diesel tanks full of oil so that my family is not left in the cold. I will be the always girded servant ready to leap from my bed and into action every morning at 4 AM. I will be the persistent manager who will call and call until I get my tractor repaired or my cow treated. I will be the shepherd whose voice the sheep know, the cowherd whose voice the cows know."

So now, once again, I am the one who is humbled. I have once again been pushed back into the student's desk, I, who can recite the parables but not always live them. Perhaps Andy is our living parable. His neurological differences make it physiologically difficult for him to express the abstract fruits of the Spirit: love, joy, peace, patience, kindness, goodness, faithfulness, gentleness and self-control.[6] But they make him remarkably proficient at living out the physical symbols of these qualities. He is the embodiment of the traits the parables teach: dedication, planning, wise building, consistency, quality, endurance, dedication, preparation, investment.

So I'll go to my church and hope that my be-kind-to-others feelings are relit, and Andy will work in his garden and live those feelings out in front of us.

1 Isaiah 55: 10, 11. *New American Bible.* (1992). New York, NY: Catholic Book Publishing; page 881, OT.

2 Psalm 65: 11, 12, 13, 14 (1992). New York, NY: Catholic Book Publishing; page 643, OT.

3 Matthew 13: 1-9. *New American Bible.* (1992). New York, NY: Catholic Book Publishing; page 31, NT.

4 Information about Joel Salatin's farm may be found at http://www.polyfacefarms.com/default.aspx.

5 Grandin, Temple. (2006). *Thinking in Pictures.* New York, NY: Vintage Books; page 238.

6 Galatians 5: 22, 23. (1992). *New American Bible.* New York, NY: Catholic Book Publishing; page 291, NT.

CHAPTER 24

APOLOGY –
THE SAD SIDE OF
ASPERGER'S

X

Some days, when I am not feeling sad for myself, I feel really, really sad for Andy. If I look back over his life, his struggles, his issues because of the Asperger's, I realize how hard it has been for him, harder than things have ever been for me. And I feel I need to write him a letter and apologize for anything that has happened due to society, to the educational system, to my lack of understanding. Here is what I would say.

I am sorry.

I am sorry that when you were young you were labeled ADHD, or retarded or strange. I am sorry the neighborhood bully harassed you and cut out your shirt tags. I am proud of you for finally punching that kid and getting some relief, respect, and space.

I am sorry that for the first ten years of our marriage I retreated behind the castle walls and kept you out. My own defense mechanism has always been retreat, and I have always been good at being impenetrable. I am sorry I made you guess and ask what was bothering me instead of briefly telling you. I grew up thinking that fights were bad and caused irreparable damage, so I avoided them at all costs. I am sorry that I didn't get mad sooner but instead stewed. Thank God you Aspies are so relentless.

I am sorry for all the times you asked for my help with the computer or the banking and I thought you were being obtuse when, in reality, you were having trouble with speed of processing. I am sorry I felt superior and exasperated.

I am sorry that when you handed me lists I took offense and resented being treated like your secretary. I am sorry for the times I didn't just do the things to relieve your stress. Most of them were simple and not time-consuming. I am sorry my raging little internal feminist rebelled and labeled you a misogynist when all you were doing was trying to get things accomplished for our benefit and to limit your anxiety.

I am sorry for being embarrassed by your rudeness in public and for siding with your victims and for disparaging you. I am sorry that my social mortification trumped my spousal loyalty.

I am sorry that I thought that little notebook I found in our bedroom could have belonged to that cute little dairy nutritionist instead of the crusty old Ag-bag salesman. I am sorry I spent a day fuming, imagining an affair, imagining that you could be disloyal. That is a route that you cut off with lopping shears when we met and will never pursue. And it's absolute. The great thing about black-and-white thinking is that infidelity for you was labeled black and discarded, never to be considered.

I am sorry that I followed you upstairs and into our bedroom, pressuring you to spend time with us instead of go hunting, making you feel trapped. I am sorry that when you slammed the door and grabbed me, showing me you were overwhelmed, I continued to yell and then threw tomato soup bowls at you and bruised your arm. I thought you could control all that, and I wanted to prove it by boxing you in. But instead I made it worse. Your nerves must have been zinging and your emotions exploding, and instead of letting you go away and calm down, I just kept pushing. Now I know better than to do that, to wait until you are in a space to talk first.

I am sorry about the many times I let the kids know how angry I was at you, sharing their frustration and hurt feelings and pitting them against you. I am sorry if I damaged their relationship with you. I am hoping that I can now be your advocate and also a teacher to the kids about Asperger's so they can get to a place of compassion and understanding.

I am sorry for the times I intentionally tried to thwart your plan for the day by delaying or stalling or not doing what you asked. I did not understand that your strict schedule was meant to prevent or at least limit overload and stress but thought instead that I was being controlled for the sake of control. I am sorry for all the times I imagined myself asking you, "Can I breathe in? Can I breathe out? Can I stand with my weight on my left foot? My right?" I am sorry for the many times I cursed being a mere cog in your wheel, being ignored, being seen as a gear in a machine. I thought you were objectifying me when really your intent was to get through the day as efficiently as possible so that we could relax at the end.

I am sorry that I get so mad during hunting season and call it the "Perpetual Male Adolescence Festival." I understand about special interests now and can use it as a little vacation from wifehood.

I am sorry that my PMS symptoms are so severe. I am usually pretty go-with-the-flow, but during those seven days each month everything annoys me. I am sorry that when my progesterone dives, my ability to be compassionate and understanding dives with it. I am sorry that I seem like Dr. Jekyll and Mrs. Hyde.

I am sorry for all the times I said things knowing you would take them literally and then laughed when you did. I am sorry I tested your gullibility. That was not kind.

I am sorry for all the times I was vague or used hints, suggestions, or body language to communicate my needs instead of being clear and overt. I am sorry that I expected you to read my most subtle of cues and then got mad when you didn't.

I am sorry for the times I withheld sex, especially after a Tazberger day, because I fumed that you could drive me crazy for sixteen hours and then expect comfort. I didn't get it. You had been scared and upset all day and needed consolation. It's just that "scared and upset" comes out as angry and asshole-ish. On nights like that, I felt exploited. I had learned at a young age that sex was a powerful weapon, especially in its withdrawal. I knew sex would calm you down and bring us back together, but I withheld instead and I'm sorry.

I am sorry I am so irregular with the finances when you are so regular. I am sorry for the late fees because of my lack of promptness, and I am sorry that I don't deal with the bills every day and just pay them.

I am sorry for getting upset at your loud voice and your "criticisms." You do not intend to come across as you do. And you are always dismayed by the effects.

I am sorry it took me twenty years to figure this out. I am sorry I labeled you as ADHD or obsessive-compulsive or an asshole.

I am sorry for all the times I was sorry I had married you.

CHAPTER 25

THE BAND – ASPERGIAN GENIUS

When the boys were still in elementary school – meaning still young enough to want to hang out with Mom and Dad at night – we used to have what we called "dance party." Once it got dark, we would put bright scarves over all the lights in the living room, dress up in silly outfits, turn on the stereo full blast, and dance like crazy fools. This is a true benefit of living in the country with no visible neighbors.

Since the kids were too young to know any better, Andy and I always chose music that we liked, mostly classic rock. Andy came of age in the late 60s and early 70s, as did my older brother. Most of the music Andy liked was also the music my adored older brother listened to, so I knew it, too. Creedence Clearwater Revival, the Rolling Stones, Van Morrison, The Doors, and very often The Band.

I hadn't even heard of The Band until I met Andy. I was more familiar with Aretha Franklin's version of "The Weight" than with Levon Helm's, but while we were still in Massachusetts, Andy's buddy mixed a cassette that I played non-stop during our courtship. The first song was The Band playing "The Weight."[1] I used to play it in the car on my way to the Dead Mall where Hampshire Bank had its processing offices. I went there after my classes to encode checks, earning money for our planned move to our own farm. I usually arrived a little early, and if The Band was still playing on the tape, I would sit in the parking lot and let the song finish.

That tape got lost, and after we moved to the farm, I forgot all about The Band until one Christmas when my sister gave us Martin Scorcese's film of The Band's last concert called *The Last Waltz*.[2] When Andy opened the present, he said to her, "The Band!? Did you know they're my favorite?" I didn't even know they were his favorite.

So we watched *The Last Waltz*. I heard "Cripple Creek" and "King Harvest" and saw Rick Danko and Robbie Robertson and was hooked. I got myself "The Band's Greatest Hits" and in a month had all eighteen songs memorized. I read the liner notes like they were the key to Andy's soul. One morning I asked him why he liked them so much. He thought for a minute and then said, "Because their sound is funky and rural and creative, bordering on genius."

Well now, that's interesting: "Funky. Rural. Creative, bordering on genius." Quite an accurate description of Andy himself.

But as I read the liner notes, I also realized that although I sang at college and can play passable piano and about seven chords on the guitar, I am not really "musical," not like these guys. Listen to this from "The Band: Greatest Hits" liner notes. This is Robbie Robertson describing the song "Chest Fever": "This music, for us, started as something that felt good and sounded good. Chest Fever was like, here's the groove, come in a little late. Let's do the whole thing so it's like pulling back and then gives in and kicks in and goes with the groove a little bit."[3] What?! My linguistic gifts allow me to comprehend this, but I sure don't get it. It's like he's describing some other brain waves that I don't either generate or receive.

Even more mind-boggling is watching him and Rick Danko and Richard Manuel talk about this or do it in footage from their studio at Woodstock. They say all this musically, from their gut, on instruments. It happens some place in the body that is not frontal lobe, maybe it's the amygdala. Listen to this description of Robbie Robertson's guitar solo in "King Harvest," or better, watch him play it in their Woodstock studio on YouTube: "This was a new way of dealing with the guitar. This was very subtle playing, leaving out a lot of stuff and just waiting until the last second and then playing the thing just in the nick of time ... This was the kind of thing that was slippery. It was like you have to hold your breath while playing these kind of solos. You can't breathe or you'll throw yourself off."

I suppose we all have something, some gift, like this. If someone asked me why I cringe when I hear "Thank you for shopping your local Walmart," my true answer would make them look at me oddly. I would say, "Because 'shop' is an intransitive verb. You can't make 'Walmart' its direct object. You have to make 'Walmart' the object of a prepositional phrase, such as 'Thank you for shopping *at* your local Walmart' or add both an adverb and a prepositional phrase and say, 'Thank you for shopping *here at* your local Walmart.' You can't just make 'shop' transitive to suit your needs, letting Walmart of all entities steer our language into some change of syntax. Like 'The new way to office.' Sorry.

No. 'Office' is a noun. Period. Don't go altering the language is some major way to generate profit. As Calvin would say to Hobbes, 'it got verbed.'[4] No way, José. A legitimate need to change a part of speech? OK. But changing the language to suit Madison Avenue's capitalistic greed? Not with my language, buddy."

At this point, everyone has walked away, and the lonely girl burdened with the linguistic intelligence looks around wistfully for her fellow English majors to commiserate with her. I actually felt this stuff as a kid even before I had the grammatical terminology to describe it, I guess from reading so much and practically imbibing language by osmosis. Sentence structure has always hit the strings of my linguistically attuned brain and resonated.

When Andy starts describing his vision of a day, I realize I am in the presence of something like this. A type of intelligence I cannot partake of, a language that is foreign to me or, rather, since a language can be learned, a connection in the brain I do not have. When I take the Multiple Intelligence survey based on Howard Gardner's work,[5] my obvious high score is Linguistic. Were Andy to take the test, my guess would be high scores for Linguistic, Logical/Mathematical, Visual/Spatial, Bodily/Kinesthetic, and Naturalist. Ah, those talented Aspies!

Andy has, in his astral body somewhere, this interlocking mechanism of finance, plant biochemistry, materials processing schedules, grass maturation processes, and weather systems. It's like in those films when the director creates a montage of psychic message reception or genius calculations. The music gets all dreamy or techno and diagrams and numbers swim across the screen. In Andy's mind, I imagine the Krebs cycle engaging gears with amortization schedules and cold front thermal systems overlaying this, with a hefty dose of time management curves.

I asked Andy to describe for me how he does this, what it feels like, what it looks like in his mind. Like Matt Damon in *Good Will Hunting*, he finally said something to the effect of, "When it came to stuff like this, I could always just play."[6] Pressed, he said that it takes an hour every morning to first write down all the disparate pieces of a three-day period – all of them, because otherwise the risk is that, just as in science, the researcher will only see what he is *looking* for, what he *wants* to see, not what he *needs* to see. To make a breakthrough, he must be open to what he is *not* expecting.

Howard Gardne,r in his book *Creating Minds,* wrote that what Einstein was able to do, perhaps because his almost certainly autistic brain retained some nodes of immaturity, was to return "to the conceptual world of a child … unhampered by conventional delineations of a question."[7] Yes, I know that Einstein was explaining the mysteries of the universe while Andy is organizing the schedule for a dairy farm. However, many people have commented on the somewhat unconventional means Andy has used to take an enormous pile of debt and a defunct dairy and in fifteen years create wealth in a milk market that is far from rewarding or even predictable.

Step two, Andy says, after listing the various factors, is to not force upon them a plan but to allow the mix of pieces and the rotating events in his mind to "tell their own story" and crystallize naturally into the optimal pattern. Embarrassed to refer to such mundane work as a combination of science and art, he says that at this point it becomes choreography: interlocking movements of various people, machines, and nature.

According to Andy, a farm, any farm, can be seen as a unique combination of resources: land, labor, and capital. And that success in farming – which is close to impossible, especially for a first-generation operation starting with near 100% debt – is to use management to optimize the interactions of the specific set of resources the farmer has to work with: "Rational choice in a condition of scarcity." I get this, but only because I teach one economics course outside of my English certification area. But I get it in the same way I can play simplified Chopin after months of practice and twelve years of lessons. By contrast, Andy could "always just play" on the keyboard of economic and biological patterns.

There is something remarkably charismatic about a man using his best gifts. It is why Yo-Yo Ma playing the cello is as sexy as Andre Agassi playing tennis. The Ego-Man dissolves into the Gifted-Man, and all that is visible is the pure act. As Yeats asked, "How can we know the dancer from the dance?"[8]

On *The Last Waltz* DVD, I can't help but be magnetized to Robbie Robertson. He is so clearly the inspirational leader of The Band. If I had been a real Band groupie, I'd have fallen all over him for the same reasons I fell all over Andy. Robertson is obviously a musician and lyricist of enormous gifts, "funky, rural, creative, bordering on genius." In very much the same way, Andy has assembled the modern "instrumentation" necessary to tap into the best of rural American life, using his giftedness in economic resource choreography to create a modern farm that grooves with the best of them.

The Band – Aspergian Genius

[1] If you are unfamiliar with The Band, I recommend *The Band: Greatest Hits*, remastered in 2000, available from the Capitol label.

[2] This fabulous movie, *The Last Waltz,* was produced in 1978 and rereleased in 2002 by MGM, Los Angeles, CA.

[3] Liner notes. *The Band: Greatest Hits.* (2000). Hollywood, CA: Capitol.

[4] Bill Watterson, *Calvin and Hobbes.* This strip, originally published January 25, 1993, is available in the collection *Homicidal Psycho Jungle Cat: A Calvin and Hobbes Collection.* Riverside, NJ: Andrews McMeel Publishing; Original edition, 1994; page 53.

[5] For information about Howard Gardner and his theory of multiple intelligence, see his website at http://www.howardgardner.com/.

[6] The entire screenplay for *Good Will Hunting* may be found at http://www.dailyscript.com/scripts/goodwillhunting.html, and the movie itself is available through Miramax, 1998.

[7] Gardner, Howard. (1994). Creating *Minds: An Anatomy of Creativity as Seen Through the Lives of Freud, Einstein, Picasso, Stravinsky, Eliot, Graham, and Gandhi.* New York, NY: Basic Books; page 10.

[8] From "Among School Children" by William Butler Yeats. From *The Collected Poems of W. B. Yeats.* (1996). New York, NY: Scribner Paperbacks; pages 215-217.

CHAPTER 26

RUMPELSTILTSKIN IS YOUR NAME – THE POWER OF THE DIAGNOSIS

I just reread *Rumpelstiltskin* and was reminded that it is quite grim, as seems to be the case with most stories by the Brothers Grimm. When the queen finally finds out the little manikin's real name, he screams, drives his right foot into the ground, grabs his left foot, and tears himself in two. The End.

The story reminded me of finally figuring out about Asperger's. I had been held captive for years, with that which is precious to me – my family, Andy, our life – held captive by something whose name I did not know. I had searched the kingdom for its name, and when I finally had it – Asperger's – I was as overjoyed as the queen knowing she would keep her son.

I hear myself, in my castle, and some disturbing behavior stamps its little foot.

"Now, my lady Queen, what's my name?"

Slyly, I ask first: "Is your name attention deficit-hyperactivity disorder?"

"No."

"Is your name obsessive-compulsive disorder?"

"No."

"Is your name perhaps, Asperger Syndrome!?"

"Some demon has told you that! Some demon has told you that!" screams the little man, and in his rage he drives his right foot so far into the ground that he sinks in up to his waist; then in a fit of passion, he seizes his left foot with both hands and tears himself in two.

Wow. Quite the scene.

But now that Andy and I have a "diagnosis," we seem to have that kind of power to put the little man in his place.

The other morning in the barn, I could sense Andy starting to spin. He was at his shelf in the barn's command central with his row of clipboards on the wall (Cows to Dry Off Soon, Cows Eligible for Insemination, Whole Herd Data, Vet Check List), and I could feel a whirl coming on. I walked over, put my hand on his upper arm, and he looked at me.

I could see him forcing the spin to a stop. Andy looked at me, knowing that I was notifying him of imminent tazzing, and he stopped himself.

In past years he would have frowned and spun off, and then said to me later, "You don't know what it's like to run this farm! If you had to do what I have to do every day, you'd be as wound up as I am!!"

But now, with a name for the spinning tendency, he knows what it is. He recognizes that the imminent whirl is *not* how anyone else would react, he recognizes that the behavior is out of proportion to the stimulus, and he stops himself. Little man tears himself in half and disappears into the earth.

It also helps on my end. I pull in the driveway from school at 5:30 PM ready for a run with the dog and a dip in the pool, and Andy is freaking out a mile away chopping hay. I hear him on the radio.

"Is anyone at base station!!"

In former years I would have read the annoyed voice as "Mo's finally home from a day of lolly-gagging at school sorting paperclips, and is finally available to do some actual work! I have needed her all day, and I am pissed that she had an easy day while I spent the whole day in the tractor!"

But now, I hear this on the radio, say "Asperger's is your name," and realize that not only is Andy *not* comparing his own day to mine, he is not even thinking about me or remembering I exist. He is just very overstimmed. Some part of the interconnecting cogs of the day's mechanism is going awry, and he just needs it back in gear. The cogs are not meshing but grinding and making in his head a terrible noise, and they just need to get back in line. Nothing to do with me and my "frivolous" job. Nothing.

"Yes, what do you need?"

"Please tell Eduardo that the fence has not been changed and that they cannot let the cows out until I have come back and changed it."

This was a completely value-neutral statement. Mechanical. The cow-milking-and-releasing system must slow and wait for the mowing-chopping-hauling mechanism to catch up, and someone needs to slow down that gear.

"10-4," I say and immediately go to the barn.

"Eduardo, el campo no est listo. Por favor espere por Andy a cambiar." ("Eduardo, the field does not you are ready. Please wait for Andy to change.")

"Muy bien." ("Very good." Thank God he understands my Spanglish.)

Gear re-engaged.

When I get back to the house, Andy is on the radio again.

"Did you tell Eduardo?"

Less than one minute has elapsed since he issued the order. But in Asperger time hours have passed.

"Yes, all set."

"Thank you!"

It was nothing about me. For twenty years, I thought incidents like that were about me: I was lazy. I didn't work as hard as Andy. I should be home at 3:15 every day to help out. But no. Really no. Asperger's no. In Taz mode, the apparatus of the day dominates Andy's head space. The grass and its state of maturation, the tractors and their use of diesel, the cows and their need to eat pasture, the money riding on the timing of the hay harvest, the risk calculated on the purchase of the new rake, the cold front bringing possible thunderstorms, the cost of the two guys hauling the wagons, the work agendas for the next week – these complex systems are more than enough to overload Andy's neurological system. They would overload mine if I had the neurological ability to comprehend them.

So, I dealt with this cow-release message, and then changed my clothes and took the dog for a five-mile run. In past years, I would have hung by the radio, guilt-ridden, afraid Andy was out there cursing my name because I was not hauling wagons, and I would have been simultaneously pissed off for being treated like merely a little mechanism in his mighty wheel, fuming because I had also worked a day and deserved to go running if I wanted to.

But no. I re-engaged the correct gear, put on my running shoes, and went for a long run, while Andy was still out in the field! Why? Because I realized what his request was. It involved no value judgment; it was simply an Asperger overstim issue, and I had resolved it.

When I got back, there he was, sitting on the deck with a beer and smiling. He was overjoyed to see me. There was no lingering anger, no spinning, nothing. Three of four mental gears had shut down for the day – Andy was down to only the dinner-calf-chores mechanism, and that would not engage for half an hour.

"Hey! How was your run?"

"Great! Riley stayed right near me the whole way."

"That's progress. Are you taking a swim?"

"You better believe it! I need to go rinse off the sweat first."

"Great. I'll see you back out here."

That's progress.

However, knowing the name of the controlling little imp also has a down side. The other day, she (me) with the syndrome's name on the tip of her tongue turned into the evil little man himself.

I was having a bad day. I was tired and sore from stacking hay the day before. Andy had been fishing all morning and was finally home. At 4 PM Youngest's best buddy called and invited him for an overnight, and Youngest became so excited he was practically jumping out of his skin. I was just back from a trip to Walmart and was really not up for another twenty-mile round-trip drive.

"Could you take Youngest downtown?" I asked Andy.

"Sure. I'd be happy to," Andy answered.

Five minutes later, Youngest came out of the house with his sleeping bag and Andy followed him to the truck.

"I can just drop him off at the corner where Friend's house is, right?"

I looked up from my book and glared. "You really should park and bring him to the door and check in with Friend's mom."

Andy looked a bit rattled at this news, but said "OK," and off he went.

I settled back into my book.

Thirty minutes later Andy pulled back in the driveway, went in the front door of the house, stayed in there for a few minutes, and came out the back door with a beer to join me on the deck.

He said, "Youngest called and left a message. He wants to know if it's OK to go to the movie with Friend's family. What's that all about?"

"I am sure Friend's mom just wants to check with us before taking him to something PG and wants us to know that Youngest won't be at their house but at the theater in case of an emergency. She's being a conscientious hostess."

"Oh. Could you call her back, please?"

Andy was still standing, and I was very much sitting. Loud exasperated sigh from me. How many hundreds of these phone calls have I had to make? How many hundreds of times have I dropped off the kids and checked in with the moms? Could Andy not just handle this one play date in its totality?

"No. You do it!"

This tipped him over the edge. Andy hurled his unopened beer at the garage where it hit and exploded.

"I already drove him downtown! I took him to the door, which you know I was nervous about! I am sorry! I know it's pathetic, but I am scared to make this phone call! I don't know their number! I don't know the parents' names! I don't really understand the purpose of this call! I don't get the rules of this game! I am just asking you to do this one thing for me! I know it's pathetic! I know! But I'm scared, OK? It's the Asperger's," and he stomped off to his truck, got in, slammed the door, and drove away.

I was fuming. Why am I so tired all the time? Because I usually deal with every one of these issues: play dates, school open houses, swim team practice. Normally I don't even try to ask Andy to handle them, but I thought we were making progress. I thought I could ask him to deal with one entire kid issue alone, but no.

I found myself storming up from my deck chair and stomping toward the house. I started flapping both my hands in front of my face, something that Andy has never ever done.

I muttered to myself, "Oooooo, oooooooo, I'm autistic. Don't make me make a phone call, Mo. It's too scary! I can't do it! Help me! Help me! I can run a half-million-dollar business but I can't call Friend's mommy!"

The evil gremlin himself had appeared, and he looked just like me.

Any words of great power can be used for either good or for evil. The power of knowing the name "Asperger's" can be a tool of compassion in my hands or a tool of great cruelty. I can use it to drive that nasty little controlling Rumpelstiltskin back into the ground where he belongs, but I can also use it to imprison Andy in a dungeon of my own creation.

I made the phone call, and then called my spirit back inside me where it belonged. By the time Andy came back, I had calmed down and was contrite. Andy had calmed down and was embarrassed.

Most people know that *Grimm's Fairy Tales* have been toned down through the ages from their original gruesome and terrifying editions into versions that are more prim and moral and suitable for children. However, I find it good to remember the awful reality that the Germanic originals were meant to portray: There is true evil in the Black Forest just as there is true evil in the human heart.

If we use our cognitive power for evil – to imprison, to label, to intimidate, and mock – we are no better than Rumpelstiltskin and deserve to rip ourselves in half and sink into the earth. To use that same power for good – to protect the vulnerable, to stop understandable behaviors from terrorizing a family – we must have the strength of character to choose the right path through the woods, because that is the way that leads to happily ever after.

CHAPTER 27

KNOCKING 'ROUND THE ZOO – LOVING THE ASPERGIAN HOUSEHOLD

When my older sister got James Taylor's "Greatest Hits"[1] album for Christmas in 1976, I was ten. I was not hip to the music scene at the time, but I was hip to the photo of the dreamy guy on the jacket of the LP. The album cover itself was classy: white with an elegant list of the songs on the front, but inside was his photo, those soulful eyes and dark eyebrows, something in the expression that said, "I am a sensitive guy and I'm singing just to you." And then there was his voice: gentle, warm, quiet but strong. I listened to that album over and over and still know all the lyrics by heart. And I gazed at that photo thinking, in a ten-year-old kind of way: that is my ideal man.

Be careful what you wish for.

As any James Taylor fan can tell you, JT spent a great portion of his early life battling depression and drug addiction. There seemed to have been a genetic strand of mental illness in the Taylor clan, with not only James but also his siblings Livingston and Sister Kate spending periods of time during adolescence at McLean Psychiatric Hospital in Belmont, Massachusetts. As Alex Beam explained in his book *Gracefully Insane: Life and Death Inside America's Premier Mental Hospital*, [2] all three Taylors benefited from the hospital's Arlington School, and especially the music therapy program, which began with the hire of Paul Roberts, a rock musician who played the sitar and helped organize four different bands during his tenure at McLean.

Taylor describes his time at Arlington as a "reprieve" from a "life [he] couldn't seem to lead,"[3] far better than the stultifying atmosphere of the extremely traditional Milton Academy where he had failed miserably. As many connected with McLean in that era attest, including Susanna Kaysen, author of the memoir *Girl, Interrupted*,[4] McLean was only accessible to the well-to-do. During the 60s and 70s, it was a place for the wealthy to send their drug-experimenting and free-loving teenage children who were rebelling against the grand wishes of their Great Generation parents.

Some former Arlington students even claim their "diagnoses" were a sham, a way for McLean to get money from insurance companies that were more liberal then with their mental treatment payments, as well as a way for the wealthy to ease their mind that their children's wayward lives were not their own fault but resulted from an "illness" in need of the best possible scientific care. As one of Kaysen's doctors said of her "diagnosed" borderline personality disorder, "That's what they call people whose lifestyles they don't like."[5]

I am not suggesting that Andy is mentally ill. As any good source on Asperger Syndrome immediately asserts, AS is not an "illness" that can be treated and potentially cured. I have recently hit some websites alleging that James Taylor has Asperger's, though this is one of the fringier sites that also lists Michael Jackson and Keanu Reeves.[6]

I find it more interesting that JT's father was a doctor who thought his son would be a doctor as well, similar to Andy's situation. In 1965 Taylor signed himself into McLean and found there a sanctuary and place where his musical talents could thrive. Similarly, how fortunate that Andy's parents had the money and wherewithal to recognize that the Simsbury Public Schools were doing their son nothing but harm and to have close at hand Westledge School.

Westledge was a progressive high school started in 1968 by Lou Friedman as an experimental multiracial private school that eventually went broke and closed in 1978.[7] My mother-in-law has told me the story of Andy's first day in eighth grade there. Tucking him in that night she asked, "So how was your first day?" to which Andy responded in all seriousness, "Do you know what it's like to go from hell to heaven in a single day?" Telling this story still brings tears to her eyes, as it would to any mother who finally feels she has found for her misunderstood son what he needs.

I have seen the pictures of Andy's Westledge graduation, class of 1977. He made new friends who were black and Hispanic and accepted his differences much better than the WASPy crowd at Simsbury High. He had teachers who desired to teach in an experimental way, having their students read Thomas Kuhn's *The Structure of Scientific Revolution*[8] and allowing Andy to conduct experiments of his own design. This led Andy to first-place medals at the Connecticut State Science Fair and his first experiences with academic success and acknowledgment.

Since I also rail against schools and teachers that teach their *content* not their *students*, my teacher heart rejoices that Andy was able to find this place and it, in turn, was able to find Andy. James Taylor said of Arlington, "We didn't have that jive nothingness that pushes most kids through high school."[9] I am sure Andy would agree that, similarly, Westledge for him was a lifesaver, rescuing him from a 1970s public school system that had never heard of Asperger's much less was tolerant of a student who had it.

Knowing the milieu of Arlington during Taylor's residence there gives new meaning to his song "Knocking 'Round the Zoo,"[10] which he released in 1968 at age twenty-six, describing life at McLean:

Just knocking around the zoo on a Thursday afternoon
There's bars on all the windows and they're counting up the
spoons
And if I'm feeling edgy there's a chick who's paid to be my slave
But she'll hit me with a needle if she thinks I'm trying to misbe-
have

I like to imagine this Thursday afternoon, JT and his music therapy buddies hanging around playing guitar in a space that looks like any upperclass living room except for the bars on the windows. The kids ignore the bars or, if anything, welcome them because they are protective and keep them in this place, which is a place they like to be.

Like James at Arlington, Andy was happy at Westledge, though the move to a private school was proposed by the principal at Simsbury Junior High as the only alternative to expulsion: "Mrs. Bartlett, I have devoted my life to public education, so it grieves me to say this, but get this kid out of the public school system. There's nothing for him here."

I think back to my own high school days. There was a period of time when I begged to go to a private school, specifically the Calasanctius School[11] in Buffalo, New York, a school for gifted students where a childhood friend of mine went. I felt so out of synch with my peers at Lockport High School. Luckily, my childhood friend invited me as his date to the Calasanctius prom, where I got to hang out with his friends, yes, all whiz kids, all more comfortable in an alternative setting, and all tremendous fun.

I don't know if it's better for the gifted, the Aspergian, or the depressed to learn to live in the real world by attending public schools, or to have their own separate place where their peculiarities and unique gifts are welcomed and embraced. I struggle with this both as a teacher and as a mother. I suppose the best solution is a combination of the two: some time in a "normal" setting where kids can learn to play the game, fit in when necessary, master the skills of expected social life, but also some place, be it a club, counseling, friends, or family, where they can let their hair down, be themselves, show their hidden quirky sides.

I have been a somewhat gifted rebel since elementary school, and was fortunate to find friends with whom I could be strange inside of my very normal high school, which was big enough to include all kinds of kids if you looked hard enough. Andy had Westledge; Taylor had Arlington. I like to think I provide this kind of setting for the students I teach, even if in a public school.

I also like to think that our household is a place where Andy and I and our boys can let it all hang out. One of the most surprising things about moving to very rural America was how much freedom we found here. One would think that small towns and rural areas would be straight-laced and traditional, but that is far from true. Compared to the Five-College Area of the Connecticut River Valley, where it was *de rigueur* to be earthy-crunchy, where it seemed you had to practice yoga, eat organic and see foreign films, Chenango County is a place of true originality. Strange people move here to hide out, where no one can see them and criticize them for not fitting any of society's standard molds. They move to back roads and are exactly who they are, with no apologies. If you want to be a nudist, live in a bunker, and repair cars, no one's going to stop you. African-American artificial insemina- tor who plays the banjo? Cool. Long-haired welder, motor-cyclist, and guitar player? All welcome here!

When we first moved here and started creating a life, I remember so often thinking, "We are just *so* making this up as we go along." If we wanted to do a thing, we did it. If we wanted to throw scarves over all the lights and wear funny costumes and have a Dance Party with the boys, we did and we didn't even have any neighbors who could see us or hear us. If we wanted to sleep on the living room floor and eat Chi- nese food and watch weird movies, we did. If Middle wanted to take ballet lessons, we let him, not to prove how sophisticated and Baryshnikov our kid was, but because he wanted to. If Youngest wanted to create a cave in the circle of trees in the west pasture, fine. If Eldest wanted to read *Utopia* at age fourteen, more power to him.

During summer vacation when we are all home and the chores are all done and we're kicking around the place doing what we please, I sing that refrain: "Just knockin' around the zoo on a Thursday afternoon." Andy is winding lead core onto his salmon rods, I'm reading obscure books about Cistercians, Eldest is creating a movie montage of every cow in the barn to the tune of "La Bamba," Middle is recreating a scene from *Lord of the Rings* in Lego, Youngest is off on an otter adventure in the woods, the brain-damaged cat is weaving crazily across the driveway, Riley, our strange dog, is hacking saliva balls onto the lawn, Gigi is sitting on more sterile eggs. It's a great place to be. Everyone is accepted.

Sure, we all have our "diagnoses." I have an anxiety disorder, Andy has Asperger's, Eldest is turning into a "foodie," Middle is going though testoster-slosh, Youngest has more energy than most teachers can deal with, the cat has a traumatic brain injury, Riley damaged his throat as a pup, and Gigi is instinct-addled.

But I am sure if you go into anybody's house when no one's around, you would find that the whole family is letting their strange hang out. We've all got our issues, our illnesses, our gifts, and if we are lucky, we all find a place where they are embraced, where we are quite comfortable just "knocking 'round the zoo."

1 *James Taylor's Greatest Hits.* [CD]. (1990). Burbank, CA: Warner Brothers.

2 Beam, Alex. (2001). *Gracefully Insane: Life and Death Inside America's Premier Mental Hospital.* New York, NY: Public Affairs.

3 Beam, *Gracefully Insane,* pages 192-193.

4 Kaysen, Susanna. (1994). *Girl, Interrupted.* New York, NY: Vintage.

5 Beam, *Gracefully Insane,* page 200.

6 *What famous people have Asperger's Syndrome?* WikiAnswers. http://wiki.answers.com/Q/What_famous_people_have_Asperger%27s_Syndrome.

7 Andi Rierden. In Pursuit of Peace and Ecological Balance. *New York Times.* http://www.nytimes.com/1992/09/13/nyregion/in-pursuit-of-peace-and-ecological-balance.html?pagewanted=all September 13, 1992.

8 Kuhn, Thomas. (1970). *The Structure of Scientific Revolutions.* Chicago, IL: University of Chicago Press.

9 Beam, *Gracefully Insane,* page 192.

10 *James Taylor.* December 1968. Produced by Paul McCartney; remastered & re-released on CD and cassette by EMI Records, 1991.

11 A website for the now defunct Calasanctius School may be found at http://www.villasubrosa.com/Cal/.

CHAPTER 28

FIFTIETH WEDDING ANNIVERSARY – REFLECTIONS ON AN ASPERGIAN MARRIAGE

On our fiftieth wedding anniversary, I will be seventy-four and Andy will be eighty-one. What will we look like then? Andy will still have all his hair, but shocking white, like his Morfar's. I will have gotten even shorter, well below five feet. When we stand together, Andy will be twice as tall as I am, literally; he could hold me, standing, on his outstretched palm like a trinket. Andy still won't need glasses, his eyes having flattened down from eagle sight to mere 20-20, and my eyes will have flattened out enough so that I won't need glasses for nearsightedness any more and will be enjoying my three years of perfect vision before I need bifocals.

Will our boys, married with families of their own, have a party for us? What will we say about each other? Will I say, "I am lucky to have been married for so long to the most amazing person I know?" Will Andy say the same of me?

I have noticed that people always say this about someone they have known well and known long. How can every person about whom these words are said be so amazing? Because, I feel sure about this, we humans are all that amazing. If you are fortunate enough to have long years with someone, and you get to know them in the intense way that a marriage or deep friendship or mentorship or colleagueship allows, you eventually get an actual view: You are allowed to taste the sweet meat from deep in that precious coconut that to most people remains merely a hard shell.

We are all endowed with riches and graces that are perfectly unique and perfectly astounding. Just look around. That man over there, for example, can fix any car and feels the workings of an engine like the workings of his own heart. That woman there can take the most complex educational situation and see it spread out in her mind as a beautiful and thriving configuration that would rival the Rose Window at Chartres. That man cannot read that well but possesses the native chivalry of a medieval knight. That woman feels her native land inside her every day, and in her heart warm breezes blow over the fields of canola onto a small thatched cottage on the edge of the sea, even while she stands in line at the bank. That woman, if you knew her well, would show you a heart that opens like a chest of molten gold and pours over anyone she sees. That man, if you had fifty years with him, could show you how jazz makes his very lungs vibrate in wondrous harmonics.

And even this young girl, this student you have known for ten months, will display for you, if you really get to know her, how passionate she is about teaching kids to speak. And this young man, the one with the impish grin, will surely set the world on fire some day with his passion for history. And this young man, the one recently diagnosed with diabetes, will no doubt become an MD and might even discover the cure for his own disease.

In case Andy or I, or both of us, don't make it to the fiftieth anniversary, here is my speech:

I am honored to have been given the great good fortune to spend the past fifty years with the most amazing man I know. He is a man who has given me the deepest wishes of my heart and brought me back in time to the life I knew I was born for. He is childlike and wise, complicated and simple, maddening and gladdening. His soul grooves to nature's beat, his hands heal animals and plants, he can operate equipment like his own limbs. He has an impish grin and an awful temper. His loyalty is beyond question. His dedication to me is complete. He sees like an eagle, hears like a wolf, yells like a foghorn, touches like a feather, cooks like a gourmet, dances like nobody's watching, and smells like incense. He can track a wounded deer, pull enormous salmon from the depths of a lake, analyze foreign policy situations, and diagnose a sick cow at 100 paces.

He can drive me wild with frustration and crazy with pleasure. He tolerates my weaknesses and teaches me to overcome them. He chases me down when I have locked myself in my castle, and he always comes back even when he has fled from his frustrations. We all have our asshole qualities – there's no escaping that. My own personal theory on marriage is that when you meet the person whose asshole qualities you can tolerate, marry him or her immediately!

Loving the Tasmanian Devil

I'll admit it took me a while to fully tolerate Andy's less-than-ideal sides, but it's taken me equally as long to tolerate my own. Also, the point of marriage – the point of the unavoidable friction – is that we wear each other smooth. Like two rocks rubbing together, each rubs off the other one's rough spots. So at this point, we are both about as smooth and bland as two cue balls! Andy hates it when I try to assign some celestial meaning to our lives – beyond the celestial meaning of having been placed in a beautiful universe beyond comprehension that we are to honor and conserve – but I do feel that if worldly existence is indeed a school preparing us for our own future divinity, I could not have chosen a better lab partner.

As Father Laurence at New Skete Monastery once said to a married couple, "Beyond what you feel, beyond what you know, beyond everything, is what you're *willing to do* for one another. Each of you controls that. Once you realize that you can *will* to love – *to act for the good of the other for its own sake and not simply for what you might get out of it* – then your love will mature and ripen. Then your love will really mean something. Before that, it's not really worth talking about."[1]

What if after the whirlwind of infatuation and intense courtship, honeymoon, and romance, the marriage settles down to its day-to-day grind? What if furthermore a monkey wrench is thrown into the cogs? Asperger's, cancer, poverty, a dead-end job, MS? That's when the going gets tough. That's when both people have to say, Here's where the rubber hits the road. We can change, we can learn, we can let this thing smooth off our bumps and knobs and sharp injurious points, or we can rigidly resist, unwilling to do for the good of the other because we are unsure it will benefit ourselves.

Andrew Tyler Bartlett, I am so grateful that I was paired with you and that you were paired with me. You helped me through my anxiety, and you let me help you with the Asperger's. I worked downtown to help get the farm established, and you slaved like a peasant to keep it afloat. Our courtship was magical, blinding, and giddy, but now that fifty years have tumbled us down the river, our love really and truly means something: something genuine.

I don't know how many years are left to us, but it's been quite an adventure so far. Thanks for letting me in. Thanks for battering down my walls. Thanks for sharing the journey. Thanks for your willingness to change and grow. Thanks for allowing me the grand experience of loving the Tasmanian Devil and of having the Tasmanian Devil love me back.

---

[1] The Monks of New Skete. (1999). *In the Spirit of Happiness.* New York, NY: Little Brown and Company; page 238.

AFTERWORD –
THE TAZ SPEAKS

X

I was asked to write a short section for this book that might enable the reader to see a few ways in which the writing of the book has affected me and our marriage. Rather than attempt to arrange this as if it were my own idea, I thought it would be more direct to structure this "afterword" as if it were a series of questions from readers followed by my responses.

Q. Can you describe what it was like when your wife told you she thought you had Asperger Syndrome and how involved you were with investigating the possibility that AS has had a major influence in your marriage and life together?

A. Mo (my wife Maureen) was very purposefully transparent in her early ramblings about AS, so it wasn't like a bombshell dropping when we more or less "agreed" that she had discovered a useful way of looking at certain behavioral patterns in my life and how they affect our marriage. As a child, I had difficulties fitting into and meeting certain expectations in school, and my parents put a good deal of time and energy into getting me in for testing and counseling, so the idea that I didn't exactly fit into life's puzzle like most of the other pieces around me was not new to me.

Q.   Has the knowledge that you have AS changed the way that you think, feel, or act?

A.   Reading about the generalized thinking and awareness patterns present in the lives of people who are affected by the broad spectrum of autism has helped me to make sense of many seemingly disconnected events in my life, from how I weathered adolescence to my ability to catch a full glass of soda that one of our kids elbowed off a restaurant table without spilling a drop. I have personally come to believe that my most instinctive AS/autistic traits involve an inordinate awareness of how the parts of any dynamic situation within my sensory zone are connected to one another. There is no on/off switch for this anywhere in my body, so it's hard for me to change how I act with respect to the fact that as my wife is trying to involve me in a discussion, a very significant part of my brain is warning me that the angle of one of my kids' arms has reached critical mass with respect to the previously observed precarious location of the soda glass. However, the knowledge that this extremely intense awareness of the interconnectedness of things around me is always switched "on" has enabled me to understand why I appear to be distracted or uninterested in what someone is saying to me. This is but a small example of what I have learned about the way AS behavior affects me and the people around me.

Q.   What do you think NT spouses need to understand about their AS mates?

A.   I think that perhaps the most challenging thing for NTs to understand about AS is the intensity and pervasiveness of the emotion of fear. For those of us who experience a primitive sense of fear on a regular basis, it is no easy feat to behave "normally." My fear response is an instinctive, instantaneous reaction that I have come to feel represents the most fundamental challenge for my wife to deal with. I don't know for sure how important this is overall, but I'm guessing this difference between NT and AS behavioral patterns constitutes a profoundly difficult chasm to bridge.

Q.   Doesn't it make you feel uncomfortable that your wife has made a public story out of your personality and the way it has affected your relationship with her?

A.   This is the first thing most of my wife's family and circle of close friends ask me, and the answer is no! First of all, practically speaking, the people I associate with on a daily basis are not likely to read a book about love and autism. The matters that concern most of the guys I have associated with for the past twenty-two years involve diesel engines, hydraulic pumps, the reproductive cycle of dairy cows, and, most importantly, the pursuit of fish and game.

In addition to the simple fact that hardly anybody I come into contact with will read this book, I also have the perhaps uniquely autistic tendency to not really be able to care what other people think of me most of the time. To be "worried" about what people think of me instead of moving forward would, from my perspective, be a worthless and inefficient expenditure of energy. While this trait is often a hindrance, in this particular instance, it is an advantage. I only see this book as the result of my wife's love for me and a desire to find ways we can work and live better together.

Andrew T. Bartlett
December 2010

ACKNOWLEDGMENTS

There are many people I need to thank for this book coming into existence.

First, of course, my husband Andy, aka Chowder, who read every "letter" with grace and humor and has picked this all up and moved on with it and taught me to do the same.

Second, thank you to my sister Kathleen, usually my first reader, in this case my second – after Andy – of each chapter as I wrote it. Always my cheerleader, always my sister.

Third, thanks to the Blog Babies. You know who you are. You were the first non-family to like my writing and help me find my voice. Especially in this regard, thanks to Sher Fick (also the artist who created the sculpture on the cover), Amanda, BH, Amy, Linda, Carrie, Jim, KitKat, MollyBug, KatieCakes, Carol, George, Gigi, MaryLou, Sarah, Amber, and all the other graduates of that cosmic nursery school in the sky that made us all so similar. And also to my friend Liz, whom I kept in a separate special spot all to myself.

Thanks to all the other wives of Aspies who either commented on my blog or e-mailed me. It has been enormously strengthening and reassuring to chat with you and share our odd existence and to support each other.

Thank you to the very gracious John Elder Robison for lunch and advice, and for all he does for the ASD community.

Thank you to Kevin, my friend and writing buddy of twenty-six years, for reading several chapters, giving me the image of polishing them like pearls on a string, and suggesting several excellent editing ideas.

Thank you to Tristan, my ace editorial assistant.

Thank you to my friend Joanne for hearing all of these stories and emotions in their raw and angry form before the diagnosis and being so supportive of my writing, and to Mike and Mary and Becky and Melissa for taking over in the listening role.

Thanks, finally, to Kirsten McBride at AAPC for cheerleading publication of the book and loving it and offering wonderful editing ideas, and to everyone else at AAPC for bringing this book into print.

REFERENCES

Asperger Syndrome and Autism

American Psychiatric Association. (2000). *Diagnostic and statistical manual of mental disorders* (4th ed., text rev.). Washington, DC: Author.

Aston, M. (2002). *The other half of Asperger Syndrome: A guide to living in an intimate relationship with a partner who has Asperger Syndrome.* Shawnee Mission, KS: AAPC Publishing.

Attwood, T. (2008). *The complete guide to Asperger's Syndrome.* Philadelphia, PA: Jessica Kingsley Publishers.

Bentley, K. (2007). *Alone together: Making an Asperger marriage work.* Philadelphia, PA: Jessica Kingsley Publishers.

Carley, M. J. (2008). *Asperger's from the inside out: A supportive and practical guide for anyone with Asperger's Syndrome.* New York, NY: Perigee.

Grandin, T., & Jones, C. (2006). *Animals in translation: Using the mysteries of autism to decode animal behavior.* New York, NY: Mariner.

Grandin, T. (2006). *Thinking in pictures, expanded edition: My life with autism.* New York, NY: Vintage.

Grandin, T., & Barron, S. (2005). *Unwritten rules of social relationships: Decoding social mysteries through the unique perspective of autism* (Veronica Zysk, Ed.). Arlington, TX: Future Horizons.

Kanner, L. (1943). Autistic disturbances of affective contact. *Nervous Child, 2,* 217-250.

Robison, J. E. (2008). *Look me in the eye: My life with Asperger's.* New York, NY: Three Rivers Press.

Other Books on Thinking, Learning, and Psychology

Copland, A. & Slatkin, L. (2011). *What to listen for in music.* New York, NY: Signet Classics.

Covey, S. (2004). *The 7 habits of highly effective people.* New York, NY: Free Press.

Gardner, H. (1994). *Creating minds: An anatomy of creativity as seen through the lives of Freud, Einstein, Picasso, Stravinsky, Eliot, Graham, and Gandhi.* New York, NY: Basic Books.

Jacobs, J. (2001). *The nature of economies.* New York, NY: Vintage Books.

Kuhn, T. (1996). *The structure of scientific revolutions.* Chicago, IL: University of Chicago Press.

Odum, E., & Barrett, G. W. (2004). *Fundamentals of ecology.* Florence, KY: Brooks Cole.

Pirsig, R. (2008). *Zen and the art of motorcycle maintenance: An inquiry into values.* New York, NY: Harper Perennial Modern Classics.

Sacks, O. (1998). *The man who mistook his wife for a hat and other clinical tales.* New York, NY: Touchstone.

Spirituality

Borysenko, J. (1999). *7 paths to God: The ways of the mystic.* Carlsbad, CA: Hay House.

de Chardin, T. (2008). *The phenomenon of man.* New York, NY: Harper Perennial Modern Classics.

Elie, P. (2004). *The life you save might be your own: An American pilgrimage.* New York, NY: Farrar, Straus, Giroux.

Fisher, E. B. (1996). *Saints alive! A book of patron saints.* New York, NY: HarperCollins.

Green, A. (2004). *Ehyeh: A Kabbalah for tomorrow.* Woodstock, VT: Jewish Lights Publishing.

Hanh, T. N. (1995). *Living Buddha, living Christ.* New York, NY: Riverhead.

Hoff, B. (1994). *The Tao of Pooh and Te of Piglet boxed set.* New York, NY: Penguin Books.

The Monks of New Skete. (2001). *In the spirit of happiness.* New York, NY: Back Bay Books.

Northup, C. (2002). *Women's bodies, women's wisdom.* New York, NY: Bantam Books.

Peck, M. S. (2003). *The road less traveled, 25th anniversary edition: A new psychology of love, traditional values and spiritual growth.* Austin, TX: Touchstone.

Santideva, A. (2003). *A guide to the bodhisattva's way of life: A Buddhist poem for today* (Translated by G. K. Gyatso and N. Elliott). Glen Spey, NY: Tharpa Publications.

References

Vande Kopple, W. J. (2004). *The catch: Families, fishing, and faith.* Grand Rapids, MI: William B. Eerdmans.

Fiction, Essays, Memoirs, and Poetry

Berry, W. (2009). A few words for motherhood. From *The gift of good land: Further essays cultural and agricultural.* Berkeley, CA: Counterpoint.

Berry, W. (1999). A vision. From *The selected poems of Wendell Berry.* Berkeley, CA: Counterpoint.

Bishop, E. (1984). *The complete poems 1927-1979.* New York, NY: Farrar, Straus, Giroux.

Carroll, L. (2010). John Tenniel, illustrator. Ed. Hugh Haughton. *Alice's adventures in wonderland and through the looking glass.* New York, NY: Penguin Classics.

Chapman, G. (2002). *Monty Python and the holy grail screenplay.* London: Methuen Publishing.

Damon, M., & Affleck, B. (1998). *Good Will Hunting: A screenplay.* New York, NY: Miramax.

Grahame, K. (2006). *The wind in the willows.* New York, NY: Signet Classics.

Hannah, S. (2004). *Longing distance.* North Adams, MA: Tupelo Press.

Kaysen, S. (1994). *Girl, interrupted.* New York, NY: Vintage.

Lee, H. (2006). *To kill a mockingbird.* New York, NY: Harper Perennial Modern Classics.

L'Engle, M. (2007). *A wrinkle in time.* New York, NY: Square Fish.

O'Connor, F. (1998). Everything that rises must converge. In *Three by Flannery O'Connor.* New York, NY: Signet Classics.

Proulx, A. (1994). *The shipping news.* New York, NY: Simon & Schuster.

Wiese, K. (1931). *Joe buys nails.* Eau Claire, WI: E. M. Hale Publishers.

Wilder, L. I. (1994). *The complete little house nine-book set.* New York, NY: HarperCollins.

Wilder, L. I. (1991). *Little house in the Ozarks: A Laura Ingalls Wilder sampler. The rediscovered writings* (S. Hines-Stephens, Ed.). Nashville, TN: Thomas Nelson.

Wright, D. (1998). *The lonely doll.* New York, NY: Houghton Mifflin Books for Children.

P.O. Box 23173
Shawnee Mission, Kansas 66283-0173
877-277-8254
www.aapcpublishing.net